The National Element in the Development of Fiscal Theory

The National Element in the Development of Fiscal Theory

Orhan Kayaalp
Lehman College
The City University of New York
USA

palgrave
macmillan

First published 2004 by
PALGRAVE MACMILLAN
Houndmills, Basingstoke, Hampshire RG21 6XS and
175 Fifth Avenue, New York, N.Y. 10010
Companies and representatives throughout the world

PALGRAVE MACMILLAN is the global academic imprint of the Palgrave Macmillan division of St. Martin's Press, LLC and of Palgrave Macmillan Ltd. Macmillan® is a registered trademark in the United States, United Kingdom and other countries. Palgrave is a registered trademark in the European Union and other countries.

ISBN 1–4039–2077–X

This book is printed on paper suitable for recycling and made from fully managed and sustained forest sources.

A catalogue record for this book is available from the British Library.

Library of Congress Cataloging-in-Publication Data
Kayaalp, Orhan, 1943–
The national element in the development of fiscal theory/Orhan Kayaalp.
p.cm.
Includes bibliographical references and index.
ISBN 1–4039–2077–X (cloth)
1. Finance, Public – Europe – History. 2. Fiscal policy – Europe – History. 3. Taxation – Europe – History. 4. Economics – Europe – History. I. Title.

HJ1000.K39-2004
339.5′2′094—dc22 2003059621

10 9 8 7 6 5 4 3 2 1
13 12 11 10 09 08 07 06 05 04

Printed and bound in Great Britain by
Antony Rowe Ltd, Chippenham and Eastbourne

For Emmy

Contents

List of Figures

Acknowledgements

I thank Professors Emilio Gerelli and Alberto Majocchi of University of Pavia and Giancarlo Pola of University of Ferrara for letting me acquire a lasting taste for Continental fiscal thought. Their support for my obtaining an Italian government travel grant in 1986 and a Fulbright research award in 1988 was instrumental in my initiation. The help of Professor Harold Hochman and Herbert Geyer of The City University of New York was also essential in this regard. I also thank Dr Marco Greggi of University of Ferrara for his help with references and my editor, Amanda Watkins, who could mix professionalism with grace.

I owe a great debt of gratitude to my daughter, the historian, who guided me through the major turning points of British and Continental political thought, and my son, physician *cum* philosopher, who provided excellent commentary and critical analysis. My largest appreciation is reserved for my wife and colleague Emmy, to whom this book is cordially dedicated. Her belief that the book one day would come to completion was my greatest encouragement.

1
Introduction

Contrary to the ecumenical flavor that has long emanated from price theory, an unmistakable aura of provincialism pervades fiscal theory. The local color is, in fact, so thick in the latter sphere of economic scholarship that an analysis of the development of fiscal thought along national parameters is in order. A few relevant surveys do exist, but each focuses on the evolution of a selected national body of fiscal thought. An illustrious example is that of James Buchanan, in which the Italian tradition in fiscal theory was presented in detail.[1] In more recent times, David Lindenfeld has surveyed the nineteenth-century German university curricula geared to train officials in different areas of public service, including public finance.[2] The only work that alluded to a national taxonomy of fiscal doctrines was that of Richard Musgrave and Alan Peacock, in which were collected representative excerpts from the works of pivotal British, Austrian, Italian, German, Dutch, French, and Swedish writers in the theory of the public economy.[3] Musgrave and Peacock did not intend to trace the evolution of various national fiscal doctrines: their aim was rather to impart a sense of the many dimensions endemic to the theory of the public economy from the mouths of the selected authors.[4] Such an intention is discernible in a later work of Musgrave's, in which he traces the development of five central themes in the theory of public finance.[5] Yet, nearly half a century since the appearance of the *Classics* and Buchanan's 1960 essay, there is still the need for a full-fledged study of the development of national fiscal doctrines, which the present work attempts to meet. It is hoped that this work, while helping students of the public economy discern certain dimensions specific to various national fiscal doctrines, will encourage them to reconcile these differences within a more general theory of the public economy.

Price theory has been embraced by academics, researchers, and practitioners of all national and cultural backgrounds, all ideological and ethical persuasions. In the past century and a half, the fundamental notions of this theory have been implemented uniformly to find solutions to myriad problems affecting modern society. Even some adherents to the Marxist framework have incorporated the price mechanism in their particular characterization of economic relationships.[6] Thus, as was remarked by Mises, price theory, though conspicuously based on aprioristic assumptions rather than actual experiences, has provided a singularly effective framework of analysis, one that has greatly contributed to the attainment of human goals by affording the choice-maker, not absolute thought, but the forethought directed toward projected acts and the afterthought to reflect upon acts accomplished.[7] More impressive still, price theory has provided this guidance without invoking any precepts beyond those encapsulated in the standard economic postulate, namely that individuals act rationally to promote selfish motives.

Fiscal theory, all the while, has remained closely attentive to the political, historical, sociological, and other circumstances that evidently bear upon the fiscal act. The effect of this methodological duality upon the development of fiscal theory has been a mixed blessing. On the positive side, the inclusion of non-economic considerations in the attainment of fiscal equilibrium helped to greatly expand the horizon of the theory of the public economy. Public economists no longer adhere to the premise that the private sector is a self-regulating decisional environment and that any government action beyond maintenance of law and order is interference with it.[8] Fiscal theory now encompasses the study of the entire breadth of government economic activity – that is, not just public expenditure and taxation, but also borrowing, debt management, distribution, and stabilization – with a particular emphasis on the effects of this activity upon the welfare of individual citizens in the given political setting. As such, fiscal thinking has become an intrinsic part of political decision-making, one that leads to and measures the effectiveness of any government action. On the negative side, the inclusion of non-economic considerations in fiscal theorizing has turned the resulting text into an overly empirical, if not often polemical, discourse. It was precisely for this reason that Vilfredo Pareto called the emerging "science" of public finance in Italy a mere "art," one that employed scientific language only to persuade the readers to swallow some flagrantly normative premises championed by their proponents.[9] Italian fiscal scientists immediately rose to this criticism by pointing out that, in their analyses of the public economy, fiscal activity was subordinated to a patently positive-economic precept, marginal valuation, which ensured the maximization of social welfare regardless of the political convictions of the person doing the analysis. The counterargument did not sway Paretian critics, who responded that even if all fiscal activity were indeed directed toward this singular end, the *process* through which maximization of social welfare would be obtained would unfold differently in different political contexts.

This line of reasoning was picked up six decades later by Anthony Downs, who, after establishing that a fiscal theory was necessarily both economic and political in nature, concluded that "a different fiscal theory must be formulated for each different type of [political] constitution."[10] The direct extrapolation of this conclusion is that a fiscal theory will necessarily draw upon the political culture espoused by its author, normally the one prevailing at home. This is a widely observed phenomenon in the history of fiscal thought. A glance at the works of classical British, German, Italian, Austrian, or Swedish fiscal theorists would reveal that the spectacle of the public economy beheld by each of these authors was indeed influenced by the particular array of historically determined considerations traceable to the author's own national heritage. These influences continue to color much of today's fiscal-theoretic discourse, notwithstanding the positive backdrop against which the theorizing is usually cast. It is in this context that there emerges the need for an analysis of the development of fiscal thought along national traditions.

There is evidently an inverse relationship between the breadth of price theory and fiscal theory and the degree of behavioral complexity each theory accords to its respective protagonist – the consumer and the taxpayer. Price theory has achieved a veritable feat in this regard by delivering a formidable body of universally applicable rules of optimal choice and action from the singularly narrow set of behavioral attributes it ascribed to its main character. Occam's razor, sharpened by the sparest of postulates that individuals act rationally to attain self-interested goals has cut once and for all through many a complicated problem that would deter even the most appropriately endowed economic agent. Sowell supplies a vivid example of how scientific parsimony in price theory would yield efficient solutions in the face of otherwise impossibly complex problems of optimal choice:

> The physical and psychic costs of digging a ditch are subjective to whoever digs one. However, the compensating inducement necessary to get A to dig a ditch is objective data to B. If B simply wants a ditch

> dug, and does not care who digs it, then the lowest of the various subjective costs of ditch digging – among A, C, D, E, etc. – becomes [B's] necessary objective cost. Conversely, how much someone wants a ditch dug is subjective to him, but is objective data to anyone else considering such work.[11]

The devilishly simple behavioral model underlying the above illustration of human action has auspiciously transcended the confines of the marketplace. Auspiciously, because price theory has thus been successfully applied to many problems – lying, cheating, fraud, divorce, alcohol abuse, and so on – whose solutions were sought, to no better avail, in other social sciences.[12] To be sure, the emergence of price theory as a general problem-solving tool has materialized only after substantive modifications. Specifically, in the 1930's two other axioms, perfect knowledge and voluntary exchange, were added to the basic economic postulate. For, it occurred to price theorists that Economic Man, notwithstanding his[13] resplendent rationality and unflinching egoism, could not choose effectively from among scarce alternative resources those that produced the maximum utility under the conditions of incomplete information and market rigidities.[14] The operational framework has progressed further in the succeeding decades by the acquisition of the axioms of comparability and transitivity of individual preferences.[15] Bolstered by these new dimensions, price theory greatly expanded its descriptive prowess. Economic Man has since come to be envisioned not as a hedonistic automaton, but as a human being endowed with the necessary intelligence, purpose, and computational ability that allow him to employ his means in the most effective manner possible in the attainment of predetermined ends. Thanks to these enriched axiomatic expansions, price theory now offers an operational framework that enables its user to determine optimal human action under decisional contexts previously unimaginable.[16]

This conclusion does not square with the views of some detractors who find the price-theoretic decisional environment irrelevant in addressing a host of problems afflicting contemporary human society.[17] The skeptics detect in the "massive bulk of technical baggage" characterizing mainstream microeconomic theory serious flaws, such as an excessive preoccupation with the concept of equilibrium, an unfortunate perspective on the nature and role of competition and self-interest, and grossly inadequate attention to the role of knowledge, expectations, and learning.[18] Hidebound price theorists remain unfazed by these and related criticisms. As for the stock argument made by the critics that most human decisions defy the presumption of rational egoism, conventional price theorists invoke Friedman's assertion that the choice-maker need not to be assumed *in fact* rational and self-interested: economic theorizing is to be judged solely by its predictive power for the class of phenomena which it is intended to explain.[19] Conventional economists similarly remind their critics of Machlup's admonition that Economic Man is just a necessary analytic tool, constructed in order for the economist to interpret the effects of human action, a tool not unlike the concept of "role" used in social psychology or the model of "ideal type" used in Weberian sociology.[20] From this line of reasoning emerges the conclusion that Economic Man is only the role attributed to individuals in certain situations, a mere generalization in our attempt to understand our world and the system of causes under given circumstances.[21]

The conclusion leads to the inevitable question: If the Economic Man construct is just an operational generalization, then how well has it served its purpose? Detractors of conventional price theory relish in pointing out that the economic postulate, even when applied to minimally complicated market situations, displays an embarrassing record as an instrument of generalization.[22] Dennis Mueller points out that the postulate suffers even greater embarrassment when applied to *non*-market settings: in a particularly telling presidential election, situationally deterministic predictions were off by millions of votes.[23] These critics especially focus on the widely observed lapse conventional price theorists routinely fall into, namely that they confound what they must *assume* about Economic Man with what they *expect* of him.[24] In other words, economic analysis, in the hands of its practitioners, is used as a test to ascertain whether an individual's action is identical to that of the ideal choice-maker. As a result, economic analysis has become but a judgmental endeavor, an investigation intending to determine what the precepts of rationality and self-interest dictate that Economic Man *should* do as elicited from his preferences, perception, and computational skills.[25]

Mathematical characterization of individual choice in the last quarter of the nineteenth century, while providing the emergent price theory with tremendous predictive power in the applicable decisional environment, brought about a deep rift between economics and the other social sciences. The latter disciplines have maintained their model of Man as a maker as well as a product of his domain. To wit, sociologists have continued to hold that only a small part of the role played by Social Man is prescribed by a script: the larger part is left to his interpretation.

Similarly Political Man is assumed to be only partly subordinate to the ideological and hierarchical relationships prevailing in the polity. Economic Man's preferences, conversely, are entirely subordinated to some prescribed decision rules. It appears, accordingly, that the recognition of the price-theoretic framework as a general problem-solving tool came only at the expense of stripping Economic Man of autonomous action.

The apprehension that scientific parsimony in economic theorizing would lead to overly restricted decisional behavior was felt right from the beginning.[26] Even Edgeworth was wary of the conception of man as a self-seeking egoist, and admitted an element of altruism in actual human conduct.[27] The discontentment with the basic economic postulate is felt only more intensely among some members of today's community of economic scientists. These critics remark that conventional economic logic, after over a century of intimacy with marginal utility analysis and over half a century with the ordinalist teaching, is still hopelessly ineffectual in explaining and predicting commonplace economic behavior.[28]

Remedies to rehabilitate conventional economic logic abound. One group favors dropping the second component of the economic postulate, egoism, emphasizing that *all* human goals, when taken in a functional sense, are self-serving.[29] Another group, focusing on the motivational aspects of human behavior, suggests that economists preserve but tone down this component, remarking that even the most selfish individuals engage in mutually helpful acts when they discern appropriate rewards.[30] The controversy concerning the first part of the postulate, rationality, is even more animated. It reflects the long-standing argument against standard economic logic that it is inadequate in the analysis of individual choice since it discounts the obviously relevant social,[31] political,[32] and psychological[33] considerations.

In the public-economic sphere, the observed individual behavior appears only more irreconcilable with the standard economic postulate. The application of rational choice models in this decisional environment leads to conclusions that are entirely out of line with ordinary human experiences. Margolis, for one, considering the lamentable record of the prime vehicle of the process of rational choice, voting, wonders:

> Why should a rational citizen bother to vote in an election with millions of other voters? ... [E]ven in a very close election, the chance that his particular vote would make a difference in the outcome is ... trivial ... Yet most people do vote, and in general the propensity

> to vote increases with education. Thus the voters more likely to be aware of the argument that voting is not rational are in fact particularly likely to vote.[34]

The lapse of economic logic becomes only more pronounced when economic agents act collectively. There was certainly no provision in Smith's conception of the invisible hand to generate a collectively optimal equilibrium and no such link has been offered until the second half of the twentieth century. Only afterwards have economists been engaged in such discussions as whether competing agents would not be better off if they acted in a "socially-minded" manner rather than adhering to conventional profit maximizing behavior[35] or whether competitors facing negative externalities of production would not end up compromising their respective profits if they insisted in unmitigated rationality and self-interest.[36]

How do conventional price theorists react to all these developments? J. Hirshleifer detects a palpable willingness among a majority of these scholars to render their discipline coextensive with other social sciences, even if this would entail dealing with Man as he really is – self-interested or not, rational or not.[37] This line of reasoning largely complies with the warning evoked three decades earlier by a young economist in the recapitulation of his doctoral dissertation:

> the assumption of rationality in the sense of one-dimensional ordering of all possible alternatives is [not] absolutely essential for economic theorizing. [We] could just as well build up economic theory on other assumptions as to the structure of choice functions, if the facts seemed to call for it.[38]

Hirshleifer's and Arrow's statements are hardly announcements of the demise of the basic economic postulate as we know it. If anything, they are a reaffirmation of it, since the main impetus behind their argument remains that many choices individuals make presumably autonomously in the family, the community, as well as the marketplace would simultaneously pass the muster of economic logic. In other words, economic logic remains operative as long as human action represents a plausible approach to achieve predetermined goals. In Tullock's and McKenzie's words:

> human beings are [not] cold, calculating machines who always pursue selfish interest with perfect precision ... [However,] most of the

> time most human beings are making at least some calculations and ... are attempting to achieve whatever goals they deem sensible.[39]

This remark opens up a propitious interface in which sociologists, political scientists, anthropologists, and psychologists may find a powerful operational framework to solve their own brand of problems, while economists, by drawing upon the contributions made by their cognate social scientists, may get the opportunity to enhance the descriptive and explanatory capability of their science. Such collaboration may eventually culminate in a final stage in which all social scientists, economists included, finally comply with Popper's well known exhortation. Namely that, after having prognosed falsifiable generalizations from some initial conditions, and having subjected these hypotheses to empirical corroboration and verification, they can finally elucidate the universal laws that underlie actual human behavior.[40]

There is a most welcome movement toward that direction. Most social scientists outside the domain of economics already have demonstrated their willingness to adopt price theory as the analytical foundation of their disciplines. Hahn and Hollis remark:

> Rational economic man has already entered sociology [and political science]. In social exchange theory social life is seen very much as a market in varying states of co-operation and competition. The giving of gifts, for instance, can be increasingly explored on the assumption that recipients always reciprocate somehow to the same amount. The forming of friendships, the working of charities, the conduct of elections, the basis of coalitions, the stockpiling of weapons, the diplomacy of nations have all been treated as [economic] transactions. The medium of exchange varies from one realm to another, but the constant aim of each agent is to enact his highest preference at lowest cost with regard to risk and uncertainty.[41]

The problem with the above argument is, naturally, that it falls short of conveying the indispensability that in order for the economic approach to constitute the foundation of a Comtean grand structure it first must be rendered sufficiently descriptive of the human condition. A unified Social Science would necessitate the interpenetration of all social disciplines rather than a mere reorganization of them under the dominance of one. Sixty-five years after Talcott Parsons demonstrated that a fusion of sociology, anthropology, political science, and social psychology was at hand,[42] it behooves modern economic scientists must also demonstrate willingness to induct their discipline into this union.

Such a fusion is apt to prove especially useful in the study of the public economy where the economic agents' responses to the applicable decision-making process are particularly complex. Comparing the fiscal theories that accord centrality to collective choice (Swedish, Italian, and Austrian) against those that explain the fiscal process either within the parameters of the conventional theory of voluntary exchange (Anglo-Saxon) or by the fiat of the officials of the State (German), one would see that the first group of theories has fared much better than the last two in providing insight into the process of attaining equilibrium in the public economy. Italian and Austrian fiscal theories, and to some extent the Swedish theory, have welcomed and readily assimilated the contributions of scholars grounded in cognate disciplines. In fact, an examination of these theories would show that many a pivotal insight into the attainment of fiscal equilibrium came from authors whose roots lied not in economics, but in sociology, law, and history.[43] Similarly, many contributions have sprung from the fields of politics, psychology, and ethics.[44]

This eclectic approach has served the characteristic features of the public economy remarkably well. For, the fiscal exchange – unlike the private-economic exchange, which entails only the assessment of relative prices between the consumer and the entrepreneur – evokes a rich repertoire of variables (attitudes, ideologies, alliances) that evidently affects the decisional behaviors of the payer and the collector of taxes. Thus, the student of the public economy espousing the fiscal framework that accords centrality to collective choice is presented with an opportunity not available to the conventional price theorist sticking to his axiomatic wares. Accordingly, the student of the public economy, who is attuned to examining the fiscal act along with its political, social, historical, and ethical causes and consequences, proceeds as a matter of course to explore not only the deductive, but also the inductive path. Economic Man evidently treads in the public-economic territory toward his intended destination.

There is no compelling reason why the broad analytical approach habitually adopted in fiscal theory should not have permeated price theory. Schmölders remarked four decades ago that the analysis of any economic act, regardless of whether it takes place in the private or in the public sector, requires a model compatible not only with the aprioristic assumptions underlying economic methodology but also with the empirical findings demonstrating the actual response of Economic Man to his immediate surroundings.[45] Simon and Stedry similarly argued that, if the aim of economic science is to explain the economic act as much as to predict its outcome, then no economic scientist, regardless of whether he or she is focusing on the private or the public sector, should shy away from reconciling the deterministic behavior accorded to Economic Man with the actual perceptions, beliefs, attitudes, and preferences that this creature clearly brings forth in the attainment of economic equilibrium.[46]

Fiscal theorists fared better in abating the axiomatic intensity of their discipline, whose horizon has greatly widened thanks to the paradigmatic contributions of Arrow, Musgrave, and Buchanan.[47] Public economists today are in full agreement with Buchanan's observation that their field is fully interdisciplinary, straddling at least two fields, economics and political science, with a bridge provided between the two by collective choice.[48] Compared with their counterparts grounded in price theory, fiscal economists are decidedly more conversant in both the positive and the normative mode of economic analysis. They employ positive analysis to demonstrate the observable and measurable consequences of the fiscal act. But once this is done, they readily switch back to normative analysis to ascertain whether these consequences comply with some pivotal ethical or political precept, say, individual liberty or parliamentary democracy. Normative analysis thus assumes an important role in fiscal theorizing to elucidate the means–ends relationships between observed fiscal phenomena and some pivotal criteria of evaluation – say, equitable taxation – regardless of whether the origins of these criteria lie outside the boundaries of economic science. By navigating through both modes of analysis, the public economist brings to light the individual decisional process adopted not only by the taxpayer, but also by the bureaucrat and politician who, as assigned agents of the former, as well must comply with the collective decision-making process put forth by the superordinate political or ethical schema.[49] The inclusion of the preferences of bureaucrats and politicians in the determination of fiscal equilibrium, along with the relevant historico-institutional framework, gives rise to a *political* market, an exchange milieu enriched by the normative parameters applied by the fiscal theorist. Yet, the analysis proceeds in strict compliance with the positive-economic method. Benefiting from the synergy generated by the two spiraling analytical approaches, normative and positive, the fiscal economist stands the chance of tackling not only the individual rationality underlying the fiscal act, but also the causal relationships underlying public policy. The analysis is followed by a discussion of the appropriate policy rules and instruments that seem likely to produce improvements in individual welfare under the auspices of the prevailing constitutional framework, normally that of representative democracy.

A serious problem facing fiscal economists in this endeavor is that they may get carried away with the normative trappings of their operational protocol. In fact, fiscal theorizing typically starts off with some pivotal political, historical, legal, or ethical precept, say, equitable taxation. The theorist then formulates this precept into a fiscal premise and subsequently builds upon it a seemingly positive construct. Admittedly, most of these tenets have a convincing ring. Who can disagree, for instance, with an ethical precept commonly used in fiscal theorizing that "No one should be forced to contribute toward the costs of a given government economic activity which does not further that individual's own interests?"[50] The problem, naturally, is that a "positive" fiscal model constructed on some "proper" ethical foundation is an oxymoron. For, such tenets originate not from economic logic, conventional or revised, but directly from the political and ethical culture with which the model-builder has some affinity.[51]

Conventional price theorists are liable to dismiss these hybrid constructs as anomalies. Downs warns that such a summary reaction is tantamount to throwing the baby away with the bath water. He remarks that there is nothing wrong for fiscal economists to start off with a normatively sound rule along the lines of "the 'proper' function of government is to maximize social welfare," provided that they place strong restrictions on the preference orderings of both the governed and the governors, so that the problem is formulated in positive terms whereby both groups of economic agents are allowed to act in accordance with their selfish motives.[52]

The crux of the foregoing discussion is that even the purest fiscal models are influenced not only by the obvious institutional constraints, but also by the perceptions, attitudes, and information processing abilities of the payers and collectors of taxes. The literature of applied public economics is full of insights in this respect. Empirical studies have long detected a definite array of national tax mentalities attributable to the prevailing community-mindedness of the peoples of different western European countries.[53] These studies demonstrate that the political philosophy prevailing in a given society has permeated the very concept of collectivity, thus giving a local character to the fiscal model that is built upon that platform. Other studies focus on the link between attitudes and other concepts and their role in taxpayer behavior.[54] The common theme of all these studies is that public economists can improve the accuracy of their predictions of the consequences of fiscal policies if they incorporate into their analyses such variables as the age, occupational status, level of education, and degree of fiscal awareness of taxpayers, the motivations of the tax collectors, and the prevailing political, historical, and institutional considerations.[55] What emerges from this line of research is a view of the public economy in which the attitudes, values, ideologies, expectations, and motivational considerations of taxpayers as well as tax collectors converge with the economic and organizational constraints long used in the determination of fiscal equilibrium. This operational framework is more likely to elicit the true relationships that exist between the taxpayer and the fiscal authority, hence to prove more instrumental than conventional public economics in predicting as well as explaining the public-economic act.

Contemporary fiscal theory has yet to comply with this paradigm. Two alternative views continue to govern fiscal-theoretic discourse. Writers subscribing to the first view portray the public sector as an autonomous entity withholding any explanation of the observed behavior of the fiscal authority. The opening paragraph in Pigou's well-known work fully reflects this orientation:

> In every developed society there is some form of government organisation, which may or may not represent the members of the society collectively, but certainly has coercive authority over them individually ... The governing authority, whether central or local, is endowed with functions and duties, the detailed nature of which varies in different places. These duties involve the expenditure and, consequently, require also the raising of revenue.[56]

The analysis that follows in this strand of fiscal economics focuses on the most appropriate method available to the governing authority to secure an efficient provision of public goods, an equitable distributive scheme, and an effective policy of stability. In this tradition, the expenditure side of the public budget is treated only tangentially. The main thrust of the fiscal discourse largely concentrates on a search for a tax base that rests not on society's aim to override or suppress individual preferences, but on helping to implement these preferences in an equitable manner.[57]

Public economists subscribing to the competing view consider the actions of the fiscal authority as largely determined by such factors as the various influences of social classes and pressure groups, the social mechanism of selecting the leaders of central and local government, and individuals' knowledge or lack of knowledge when making fiscal decisions.[58] In this tradition, collective goods are deemed to have been supplied by the fiscal authority for the satisfaction of the demands not of individual citizens, but of the community as a whole. This orientation requires a much greater measure of historical, political, and sociological analyses than the first, since the applicable valuational criteria are thought to have derived from the community's political culture rather than individuals' subjective utility calculus. This view, finding its best representation among German fiscal theorists, is based on the organic view of State whereby in the public sector the interests of the individual are subsumed by the collective will. The difference between the two views is stark. The first approach, referred to as the sacrifice theory of taxation, is characterized by its emphasis on finding a way to minimize the burden that the financing of public services evidently inflicts on individual taxpayers. It is for this reason that the literature of this school of fiscal thought is rife with partial equilibrium models, each one reflecting the inferred effect of an alternative tax policy. The second approach, the organic, deals with the effect of government economic activity upon the electorate as a whole. What is similar between the two views, conversely, is the fact that in both approaches the applicable method is one of positive economic theory, though not necessarily marginal valuation, which becomes moot under the organic concept of State.

We now turn to the ensuing chapters to explore how various national doctrines attempt to explain the fiscal foundation of human society. The explanations range from entirely organic (German) to wholly individualistic (Austrian), with Italian, British, and Swedish theories falling in between. According to the first extreme, the fiscal authority sets public-economic objectives without referring to the preferences of individual taxpayers. These individuals nevertheless contribute to the attainment of these objectives out of their historical affinity with their cohorts. On the opposite end of the spectrum reigns the view of society as a mere collection of individual citizens who, either directly or with the help of duly elected representatives of the State, determine the quantity as well as the price of public goods. Fiscal coercion emerges as an intrinsic feature in both views of society, though the individualistic school strives to minimize this eventuality. Fiscal theorists subscribing to the organic concept find this effort superfluous, since, according to their view, the State is by definition a compulsory association:

> Thanks to its sovereignty, the State is free to define its own tasks, the manner of their discharge and thus the amount and kind of services to be provided for the people, without reference to their demand for these services. The State can carry out these tasks thanks to its fiscal supremacy ... [It] can acquire the necessary income by compulsory means, without having to produce any specific benefit in return.[59]

To the fiscal theorist nurturing individualistic ideals, this explanation represents a grossly aberrant view of political organization, one that fails to construe the State as a contrivance created by individuals to better achieve their individual goals.[60] In the eyes of this group of public economists,

> the State is seen as the community of all citizens [and] public needs ... as the needs of that community. This is tantamount to admitting that the satisfaction of these public needs ultimately benefits the individuals who together make up the State. The premise is quite sufficient for the individualistic tax theory ... Once the fiction of the State as a supra-individual is abandoned, it is no longer permissible to speak of the "general advantages" of public activity as of good fairies hovering aloft, but it must be acknowledged that these advantages consist in some sort of promotion of the interests of the physical persons composing the State.[61]

Between the two extreme groups of fiscal theorists are grounded those who analyze government economic activity within a historically determined framework of tasks rather than sheer demand and supply of collective goods as determined by individual valuation. These authors attribute the problem of coercion to the special nature of such goods. For example, Pigou remarks:

> If battleships were goods that people need for individual personal use, that would not, indeed, matter. There could still be the same sort of balancing at the margin between clothes purchased individually and battleships purchased through the government as there is between clothes purchased individually and coal purchased through a co-operative buying agency. But battleships are a collective good, to be used in the general interest by the government. Consequently, any taxpayer's desire to contribute towards buying them is dependent, not only on his desire that the country shall possess them, but also on the number of them which are being made available by the contributions of other people. The government is not, therefore, simply an agent for carrying out on behalf of its citizens their several separate instructions; it cannot simply balance at the margin each man's desire to buy battleships against his desire to buy clothes, in the way that an individual balances his desire for clothes against his desire for coal. As the agent of its citizens act collectively, it must exercise coercion upon them individually, securing the funds it needs either

> by a contemporary tax or by a loan associated with a subsequent tax to provide for interest and sinking fund.[62]

The controversy is far from resolved. To make matters even more unsettling, opinions diverge within each tradition. To illustrate, within the community of fiscal theorists adhering to Pigou's view, there are libertarians who argue that governments should play no economic role in society while there are those whom we may call social democrats who believe that a substantial amount of government intervention is required for the good of individuals.[63] The question is moot only in the context of the historico-organic view of government where the State is considered as supra-individual organism whose economic needs must be covered by the citizens' tax payments.[64]

These arguments highlight an important aspect of fiscal theorizing that government economic activity takes place not in the rarefied venue reserved for Economic Man, but in an arena bustling with political, social, ethical, historical, legal as well as psychological considerations influencing the taxpayer's and tax collector's conduct. These factors give rise to a particular fiscal mentality, which is greatly influenced by the tax system existing in a country. Fiscal theorists naturally draw upon these variables and fashion their theory of the public economy along these proclivities. It is on this note that, after a necessary detour, we turn to examine each of these different theories.

2
A National Taxonomy of Fiscal Doctrines

Coinciding with the rise of marginal utility analysis in the early 1880s, many European political economists turned their attention to fiscal theory. In less than 20 years, a vast literature was generated, which manifested the different emphases British, German, Austrian, Italian, and Swedish authors placed on the fiscal process. Writers in the British tradition, having long considered the taxation side of the public account independently from the expenditure side, and having deemed the services provided by the State inherently unproductive, concentrated their energy to minimize the burden that public expenditures would inflict upon taxpayers' budgets. With this objective in mind, British writers experimented with different concepts of equal sacrifice – equal absolute, equal proportional, equal marginal – to ascertain which would produce most effective outcomes. Seen from another perspective, these writers were striving to transform a fiscal precept they inherited from their classical predecessors, ability to pay, into a workable paradigm of tax policy. Italian fiscal scientists, meanwhile, were dwelling on the benefit principle of taxation, which had originated in their country as a principle of social justice by Tommaso Campanella,[1] if not even earlier by Thomas of Aquinas,[2] and which, in the 1850s, had been reformulated as a principle of taxation by Francesco Ferrara.[3] Maffeo Pantaleoni, Antonio De Viti de Marco, and Ugo Mazzola, all pupils of Ferrara's, agreed with and elaborated on their mentor's pivotal premise that public expenditures were patently productive and taxes were nothing else but the prices of the productive services provided by the fiscal authority. The three writers were, at the same time, champions of the representative-democratic system that had been instituted in Italy in 1870. Combining two relevant fiscal precepts, one grounded in economics and the other in politics – respectively, the productive nature of public goods and the appropriateness of the representative-democratic framework as the basis of an equitable fiscal choice process – these authors developed a theory of political markets whereby fiscal equilibrium would be achieved in conformity with taxpayers' demand as implemented by their elected representatives through a bilateral process of choice.

The Swedish political economist Knut Wicksell, joining the debate a decade later, criticized the views of both British and Italian fiscal theorists. He proceeded from a purely normative precept that in contemporary society no taxation scheme, regardless of how efficient it appeared to be, could be acceptable if it inflicts fiscal injustice on even a single individual, that is, if it coerces any citizen to contribute to the cost of a public expenditure that he or she has deemed overpriced.[4] Wicksell found the fiscal-theoretical construct expounded by British authors manifestly unjust since they had no qualms about distributing the total burden of admittedly unproductive public expenditures among the citizenry through sheer coercion. As for the Italian theory of demand and supply of public goods epitomized in Mazzola's 1890 work, it was inefficient on top of being unjust. Unjust, since this process readily equipped the providers of public services with the power of compulsion, which they would readily inflict upon those citizens deeming a public good overpriced. Wicksell considered the fiscal equilibrium process depicted by Mazzola also inefficient, for it was based on the conventional theory of individual exchange, which would break down in a multi-partite system of choice due to a peculiar characteristic of public goods, non-excludability. Wicksell was intent on developing a collective choice process that, while efficient, that is, was based on individual preferences for public goods, was at the same time just for *all* members of the community. Only a fiscal policy approved by 100 percent of the electorate would solve the free-rider problem that resulted from the non-excludable nature of public goods.

Austrian and German writers, all the while, were stressing, respectively, the psychological and historical aspects of determination of collective wants. According to Austrian political economists Emil Sax[5] and Friedrich von Wieser,[6] the psychological foundation of want determination was basically the same in both private and public economic spheres. In the latter sector, individuals demanded a public expenditure line either because it served a personal want or it contributed to some collectively meaningful end. In either case, taxpayers determined the utility stemming from the public expenditure entirely subjectively. The natural corollary of this premise was that the tax shares individual citizens would be required to pay for the goods apt to satisfy these wants must also be determined by those individual valuation. Neither the bilateral choice process adopted by Mazzola nor the collective choice process elaborated by Wicksell offered an appropriate mechanism to lead to an efficient and equitable fiscal equilibrium. Mazzola and Wicksell were right in one aspect, however, namely that marginal calculus was the only instrument conducive to optimal outcomes. Individuals always equated the marginal utility of a good to its price within the standard framework of individual hedonism, regardless of whether that good was available in the private or in the public economy. This fact was easily observable in the analysis of the productivity of a public good deemed by an individual to satisfy a personal want, say, having access to health-care. The prices of this category of public goods would be determined by the simple rules of marginal calculus applicable to private markets. The interesting finding was that the same process of valuation would be applicable to those public expenditures directed to satisfy a purely collective need as well, such as when an individual proceeded to determine the extent of national defense and his respective tax share in the financing of this public good. Despite the obvious problem of non-measurability, individual citizens achieved this computational feat by the same process of subjective valuation. The psychological attribute responsible for this result was none other than ordinary human empathy and collegiality. Endowed with these attributes, and in continuous interaction with his cohorts, the individual taxpayer would naturally ascertain the importance his fellow citizens ascribed to a particular public good, and would go along with the majority's will with respect to the total as well as personal tax burden associated with the provision of a particular public good.

The German fiscal theory, in contrast, revolved around the central notion that the goals pursued by the fiscal authority were categorically different from those of individual citizens. Most German fiscal theorists agreed with their Austrian, Italian, and Swedish counterparts that collective utility and private utility were closely related and that citizens demand goods apt to satisfy both kinds of wants. But this was not to say that collective and individual wants shared equal footing. Actually there existed a hierarchical relation between the two kinds of wants in the public-economic sphere whereby collective utility subsumed individual utility. Collective utility was paramount for the perpetuation of the community within which individuals strove to serve their private needs. This hierarchical construct did not preclude subjective valuation: it was just that ordinary citizens were not cognitively endowed to ascertain and value collective utility accurately. This task fell on the functionaries of the fiscal authority, who possessed the required expertise and had at their disposal all the necessary decisional resources. In other words, the classical principle of division of work rather than the principle of subjective valuation reigned in the public economy. In this decisional environment, both the extent of public expenditure lines and the shares of the corresponding tax burden were determined by public servants who shaped fiscal policy in accordance with the relevant economic, political, social, historical, and cultural variables, but not necessarily the preferences of individual members of the community.

By the turn of the century, the different emphases European fiscal theorists placed on their models of the public economy already had been solidified along distinct national strands of fiscal thought, each with peculiar concepts, principles, operational conventions, and problems. These models were by no means marked by impregnable boundaries. If anything, their originators exhibited a keen interest in the fiscal constructs of their foreign counterparts. Wicksell's 1896 work, for instance, demonstrates a thorough knowledge of the theories of Mazzola, Sax, Wagner, and J. S. Mill. English-speaking authors, by contrast, pretty much kept to themselves. To illustrate, the index of A. C. Pigou's definitive 1928 work[7] lists 32 English-speaking writers – Barbour to Sidgwick – but only three continental authors – Einaudi, Rignano, and Viviani. That this inward look stunted the development of the Anglo-Saxon theory of public finance was remarked some time ago.[8] Unfortunately, most continental writers were inflicted with a different sort of malady. Namely, the problem-solving approach based on partial equilibrium analysis, a hallmark of the Anglo-Saxon public finance, did not find a sound reflection in Continental theories of the public economy. These theories, particularly the Italian theory of public goods, suffered from an excess of "system" at the expense of "problem solving," which led to sterile arguments and fuzzy normative discourses.[9]

A taxonomy of fiscal doctrines along national lines stands to benefit the contemporary student of public economy, more than some two-way demarcations perpetuated in the curriculum. One dichotomy of long standing, alluded to in the previous section, revolves around the basic problem of how to distribute the cost of public expenditures among taxpayers. A fiscal theory envisaging a distribution method whereby taxpayers contribute to the financing of public services commensurate with their perceived benefits is said to comply with *benefit principle* of taxation. Alternatively, a fiscal theory is said to comply with *ability-to-pay principle* if it envisioned a distribution pattern whereby taxpayers' shares are determined according to their capacity to contribute, as usually measured by their income. The benefit approach is thought to lend itself better to the analysis of the fiscal process since it affords a simultaneous treatment of the two sides of the public account to reach an efficient solution. The difficulty for fiscal theorists subscribing to this approach is that in order for it to be operational, the perceived benefits must be elicited, quantified, and recorded. Unfortunately, taxpayers acting in conformity with the economic postulate would understate their preferences to dodge the corresponding taxation. As for ability-to-pay principle, its peculiar weakness stems from its treatment of the tax side independently of public expenditures, hence its glossing over the role of the latter side of the public budget in the attainment of fiscal equilibrium. Musgrave and Musgrave summarize the shortcomings of each of the two approaches in following terms:

> The benefit approach ... cannot handle taxes needed to finance transfer payments and serve redistributional objectives. For benefit taxation to be equitable, it must be assumed that a "proper" state of distribution exists to begin with. This is a serious shortcoming since, in practice, there is no separation between the taxes used to finance public services and the taxes used to redistribute income. The ability-to-pay approach better meets the distribution problem, but it leaves the provision for public services undetermined ... These are formidable difficulties and neither approach wins on practicality grounds. Moreover, neither approach can be said to deal with the entire function of tax policy.[10]

The second well known dichotomy, also briefly discussed in the previous chapter and referred to again in this chapter, ascribes a fiscal theory either to the *organic school*, according to which public expenditures are determined by the functionaries of State in line with special considerations, or to the *individualistic school*, whereby fiscal equilibrium is determined by means of individual taxpayers' subjective valuations. The distinguishing feature of the organic approach, comprising mostly German scientists of State of the late nineteenth century, is its adherence to the overarching fiscal principle that the valuation of collective utility transcends the cognitive limits of individual members of the community. Conscious of their inability, individual citizens delegate the task of making fiscal decisions to the appropriately trained functionaries of the State. The essential characteristics of the organic approach are expounded in Adolf Wagner's 1883 work, *Finanzwissenschaft*:[11]

> The nature and the extent of State activities must be directed towards the fulfillment of objectives which are recognized as proper and

determined in accordance with the interests of the people. In this respect, the State and hence also its fiscal economy are outside the competitive market.[12]

Authors grounded in the individualistic camp are appalled by this line of reasoning. R. B. Ekelund and R. F. Hébert remark in this connection:

> If economics is a science of choice, then one must look to the *chooser* to understand economic relations, ... [even if] some choices ... are made by a body of people (e.g., a committee) rather than by a single individual. There are two things to consider in response to this question. One is that any collective decision-making body is composed of persons whose individual decisions make up the collective judgment. The other concerns the nature of aggregates ... [but] aggregates only matter where individual considerations don't matter; yet for [proponents of methodological individualism] individual decisions *always* matter.[13]

The controversy is far from resolution, as each fiscal approach suffers serious shortcomings. The first, the organic school, poses a major obstacle in the determination of fiscal equilibrium in that, by taking into consideration an array of non-economic objectives, it effectively precludes the application of marginal calculus to this process. As for the second approach, the individualistic, its main problem stems from its unsubstantiated premise that fiscal preferences arrived at by individuals in accordance with the general framework of voluntary exchange can directly lead to efficient outcomes. Wicksell commented on this impossible scenario over a century ago:

> [T]he actual scope of the public service is not determined by the evaluation of the single individual, but by that of *all* (or at least of all voting) members of the group. Equality between the marginal utility of public goods and their price cannot, therefore, be established by the single individual, but must be secured by consultation between him and all other individuals or their delegates. How is such consultation to be arranged so that the goal may be realized? On this point [the individualistic school] does not say a word, but, as I see it, this is precisely the question which ought to be decided.[14]

Thus, according to Wicksell, it is the task of the fiscal theorist to spell out what kind of collective evaluation framework he assumes to be operative in the attainment of fiscal equilibrium. He warns the fiscal economist not to take majority voting as a close estimate of the price of public goods and to never disobey the dictum that Pareto optimality would not be attained unless a fiscal decision is made with 100 percent approval. The presence of even a single negative vote would mean forcing the caster of that vote to pay for an unproductive, hence overpriced economic good.

Not all fiscal theorists have heeded Wicksell's warning and many have eschewed a collective choice scheme, much less one based on unanimity. These scholars have constructed their models of the public economy within the parameters of the conventional framework of *voluntary exchange*. Their approach is based on the premise that two members of a community, unable to satisfy their needs for a collective good in the private market, will pool their resources to purchase that good in the public economy. More specifically, two taxpayers will decide upon the extent and variety of public expenditures and will distribute the corresponding tax burden through voluntary contributions.[15] The inevitable problem with this approach, naturally, is that the cooperative mechanism will break down when the number of participants is increased. In that case, some participants, having construed that the public expenditure may be offered anyway, will hide their actual preferences for the public good under consideration, thus will not contribute to its financing. The alternative orientation, that of *collective choice*, whereby the extent of the public expenditures and the distribution of tax shares among individuals are determined in line with the rules established by a direct-democratic constitution, provides a solution to the problem of free-riding, but only under the condition of unanimous voting. Otherwise the dissenting voters will again be compelled to contribute to the cost of public services.

One reason a taxonomy based on national doctrines of fiscal thought seems more useful than the three dichotomies explained earlier is that fiscal models often challenge bipolar demarcations. Take Erik Lindahl's model of fiscal cooperation, for example, which depicts the determination of the extent and the pricing of a public good between two groups of citizens, one well-to-do and the other not.[16] What unfolds between the two parties resembles neither that which evolves between the seller and buyer in the marketplace nor between the politician and the voter on an election day. Lindahl calls the fiscal process that he is describing "isolated" exchange, in which the two parties settle their differences by a "particular kind" of collective choice akin to direct democracy, in which the two parties "vote simultaneously on all the expenditures" while applying the ordinary rules of economic exchange, that is, offering "different prices ... for the units successively exchanged."[17] As such, the fiscal decision-making process envisaged by Lindahl falls somewhere *between* voluntary exchange and collective choice. The fuzzy nature of the political market mechanism inherent in Lindahl's model threw off many a public economist used to dichotomous categorizations. To wit, Musgrave and Musgrave have placed Lindahl's construct under the rubric of voluntary exchange while Rosen has viewed it as a model of public choice.[18] The problem does not end there. For, the roots of Lindahl's model can be traced back both to the benefit principle (since each party pays a price that equals the marginal benefit at the efficient output of the public good) and the ability-to-pay (since the equilibrium reflects the given distribution of income accommodating the demands of the two parties). This occurs because the Lindahl solution:

> meet[s] the requirements of both the ability-to-pay and the benefit doctrines. The requirement of ability to pay is complied with because different taxpayers contribute different amounts, depending on their incomes; and that of taxation according to benefits received is met because each contributes an amount based on his personal evaluation of public services.[19]

Finally, in what part of the dichotomy with regard to individualistic versus organic valuation would we place the theories of Italian fiscal scientists? Pantaleoni's, De Viti's, and Mazzola's theories should be considered within the purview of the individualistic school since they entail a fiscal equilibrium process based upon the demand and supply of public goods stemming from individual preferences. On closer analysis, however, it is not taxpayers, but their elected representatives (in fact, the public servants appointed by these agents) who do the actual valuation. Shouldn't this feature of Italian fiscal theory relegate it to the organic camp?

A five-way taxonomy organized along national doctrines would avoid such problems. Each theory would stand on its own feet and would be judged on its own merit in terms of the effectiveness with which it explains the nature and predicts the consequences of the fiscal act. But there are some practical problems. First, national fiscal doctrines do not have ironclad boundaries. Even the strictest representatives of a national fiscal theory have appropriated many a contribution from their colleagues from across the borders. Some authors have done so to sufficiently differentiate their product from those emanating from other traditions. To illustrate, the Swedish Wicksell undertook a detailed critical review of the fiscal theories of Sax (an Austrian), Wagner (a German), and Mazzola (an Italian) before expounding his own in his 1896 work. Similarly, the British Edgeworth[20] referred to the works of Italian fiscal scientists De Viti de Marco and Graziani to explain how his theory differed from theirs. Some authors made references to other traditions to add consistency and support to their own theories. For example, Italian fiscal scientists made ample references to Jevons, and later to Marshall, to make it obvious that their theories were fully entrenched in the marginalist framework. Other writers eschewed the doctrine of their land and espoused that of another. For instance, the Italian G. Ricca-Salerno,[21] rejecting both the German school of fiscal thought crystallized in the work his mentor, Ritschl, and the Italian tradition elucidated in the works of three fellow colleagues of his, Pantaleoni, De Viti de Marco, and Mazzola, embraced the fiscal construct expounded by an Austrian, Emil Sax. Still other authors rejected not just their respective national tradition, but the entire political-economic framework currently raging in British and Continental academic circles. To illustrate, Pareto, Mosca, and Goldscheid, convinced that the sociological rather than the economic method would be conducive to the maximization of collective utility, developed an alternative approach to fiscal equilibrium. Finally there are those who subscribed to an essentially collectivist process of fiscal decision-making, such as the Italian Enrico Barone and German Lorenz von Stein.

The taxonomical exposition followed in this work does not include all the important representatives of a given national fiscal doctrine. Many economists are omitted because their roles in the development of their respective national school of fiscal thought were less than central. To give an example, Einaudi, Cosciani, and Borgatta are left out not because they were not prominent contributors in their field, but because they helped to refine rather than define the Italian fiscal tradition. These omissions serve to present each doctrine in its purest form, as expounded by the pivotal representatives of the particular corpus. Some other important national figures are left out because their work would be better studied within the confines of another fiscal tradition. Ricca-Salerno's allegiance to the Austrian theory was already stressed earlier. Similarly, the contributions of the French Leroy-Beaulieu and Dutch Cohen Stuart should be better examined within the framework of the British doctrine and those of the Italian Nitti and Cusumano within the German. Finally, as alluded to earlier, such eminent political economists as Barone, Fasiani, and Masci, in addition to Pareto, Mosca, and Goldscheid, are omitted because their non-market oriented models of the public economy explain fiscal processes exclusively by the behavior of socially and politically dominant elites.[22]

No survey, taxonomic or otherwise, can profess originality. Such projects necessarily deal with previously produced work. What is more, there already exist a few previously produced surveys on selected national bodies of fiscal thought. The present work displays a wider horizon. It intends to bring to the attention of English-speaking students of public economics the important aspects of the *entire* body of classical European fiscal thought and assesses in the last chapter whether and how these different traditions could be integrated into a satisfying synthesis.

Taxonomical approaches are prone to peculiar problems. Some of these were already discussed in the above sections. A further problem is that the criteria used to distinguish one national theory from another (e.g., public goods, subjective valuation, the expenditure side, fiscal coercion) are selected entirely arbitrarily, and, more seriously, do not always entail substantial differences among various doctrines. For example, Italian, Austrian, German, and Swedish fiscal theories all subscribe to some notion of public goods. Still another problem is that a taxonomy based on "national" parameters may give rise to unwarranted stereotyping. To illustrate, one may construe German fiscal theory as one that summarily rejects subjective valuation. Actually, this theory acknowledges subjective valuation; however it restricts it to the use of properly trained functionaries of the State. As such, it merges with Italian fiscal theory, in which the demand and supply of public goods result from the individual valuations of taxpayers' representatives. Additional problems will undoubtedly surface as the proposed taxonomy is applied in analysis and teaching. As for the latter case, it is hoped that such problems will be alleviated by appropriate inputs from the teacher and effective feedback from the learner.

3

British Fiscal Doctrine: The Sacrifice View

The realm of public economics is vast. It far transcends the public finance proper, which comprises the principles and procedures concerning public spending and collection of taxes. Public economics is the study of *all* government economic activity and the effects of that activity upon the individual citizen. These effects can assume huge proportions. For one thing, the livelihood of many individuals directly depends on government, which is often the largest employer in the economy. Second, governments provide a wide range of services that many individuals deem essential for their existence. Finally, considering that the costs of these services must be sustained by taxes, a large part of individuals' income is given up to the fiscal authority. This occurs even in those societies in which self-interested behavior is valued and promoted. Then why is it that a substantial part of the economy has always been left to the hands of the government rather than that of the market mechanism?[1]

As was touched upon in the preceding chapter and will be elaborated in Chapter 5, the adherents of the organic view of society answered this question by invoking two standard arguments. The first concerned the principle of division of labor, according to which the task of making fiscal decisions rested with the functionaries of the State rather than private citizens, since only the former were though to have been trained appropriately for the task and to have access to the necessary information to make adequate fiscal choices. The second argument was that the State, a product of historical process itself, should be respectful of a society's traditional values and be committed to preserve the resulting social cohesion. A famous proponent of organic view reminds his readers in no uncertain terms that they "are all alike born into the community of [their] nation ... and have in common the great figures of [their] past, the same hatred and suspicion of the hereditary enemy; have in common joy of victory, the sacrifice of [their] sons, maternal sorrow, the grief of defeat and the bitterness of bondage."[2] Consequently, according to fiscal theorists subscribing to this approach, the appropriateness of a fiscal measure must be determined vis-à-vis the current political, social, legal, and cultural contingencies affecting the community as a whole. These contingencies are different from those taken into account by individual economic agents operating in the private market. In other words, there are two separate economic organizations in a society – communal and private. In the private market, self-interest reigns supreme and price theory remains the ultimate operational tool in the analysis of human conduct. In the communal market, alternatively, the aim is to promote *collective* interest. This task falls on the fiscal authority, which, acting as an independent decisional unit, determines, first, the extent and variety of public expenditures, and second, the total and relative shares of corresponding taxation. A fiscal decision that is simultaneously in line with the personal preferences of individual citizens is a welcome eventuality, but there is no such requirement as referring to taxpayers' individual valuations in the attainment of fiscal equilibrium. What is being maximized is not the sum of the interests of each individual citizen, an outcome that is attained in the private economy, but total collective interest, that is, the social utility felt by the community as a whole. The organic theory of State thusly answers the question why people need fiscal authority at all.

The organic beginnings of British fiscal theory

In a historico-political culture in which the community is viewed as just a sum of individual members, and collective utility the sum of the individual interests of these members, the question cannot be answered so summarily. The archetypal proponent of this second view of community is Rousseau, who considers human society an association geared to "defend and protect with the whole common force the person and goods of each associate [who], ... while uniting himself with all, may still obey himself alone, and remain as free as before."[3] This objective is accomplished by means of a social contract whereby "each of us puts his person and all his power in common under the supreme direction of the general will, and, in our corporate capacity, we receive each member as an indivisible part of the whole."[4]

Rousseau's conception of State differed considerably from those of two earlier British contract theorists, Hobbes and Locke. Hobbes had postulated that individuals, in need of peace and security, relinquished their liberty by subjecting themselves by means of a covenant to the will of a ruler. The covenant authorizes the ruler to take any measures he chooses to establish and maintain peace and security. The ruler, while not responsible to his subjects for any of his actions, cannot treat them unjustly. For, the initial consent given by the subjects entails a clause that precludes the ruler to do them any harm.

Hobbes's model of State beleaguered both monarchists and parliamentarians. The first were offended by Hobbes's rejection of the monarch's divine rights and the second resented his adherence to the concept of absolute ruler. Locke detected a fatal mistake in Hobbes's political construct: a ruler equipped with both the legislative and the executive power inevitably would emerge as a corrupt tyrant. Locke interpreted social contract as a fiduciary agreement whereby the people armed the sovereign only with executive power, delegating the legislative power to an elected assembly.

Rousseau believed both Hobbes and Locke missed the essential premise that sovereignty of the people is an inalienable as well as an indivisible right. This right cannot be transferred to any person, whether in totality (as Hobbes did) or in parcel (as did Locke). Both the executive and the legislative power resided in people, who obviously invoked both powers simultaneously when they enacted the social contract and charged the sovereign with the commission of enforcing the declared general will. The slightest modification in the stipulations of either the social contract or general will would render the sovereign authority illegitimate, in which case the people would regain their natural rights, which they renounced in favor of the now violated compact.[5]

In this form of political organization the conditions are the same for all, and no one individual has any interest in making his rights burdensome to other associates.[6] Rousseau goes on:

> each man, in giving himself to all, gives himself to nobody; and as there is no associate over which he does not acquire the same right as he yields others over himself, he gains an equivalent for everything he loses, and an increase of force for the preservation of what he has ... [I]n place of the individual personality of each contracting party, this act of association creates a moral and collective body, composed of as many members as the assembly contains voters, and receiving from this act its unity, its common identity, its life, and its will.[7]

As such, Rousseau's brand of social contract provides the means through which the members of the community create the condition not of liberal individualism, but of extreme social cohesion guaranteed by adherence to the applicable general will.[8] The institution of the initial social contract requires unanimity: but the majority rule is sufficient for the implementation of the general will.[9] The reason for the weaker condition stems from the very nature of general will, which, as an ever-evolving entity, can only reflect the preferences of the members of majority at a certain point in time in society's life. Put differently, the social contract represents the will of all while general reflects the will of the majority. Subsumed in general will is the assent of the minority, whose members, in conformity with the unanimously accepted stipulations of the will of all, have irretrievably subordinated their private interests to the common interest. The sovereign must carry out the provisions of the declared general will without invoking his own moral sense. For, the fiduciary nature of the sovereign's commission precludes him from making any unilateral changes in the conditions of his service.[10] In other words, sovereign power always rests with the people.

The contract theory of State, while finding favor in Germany, as will be discussed in Chapter 5, came under serious attack in England. David Hume rejected it in a 1748 essay entitled "Of the Original Contract." In it Hume discerned no evidence that the primordial government was instituted by explicit consent: if anything, the original State was instituted by violence, and people submitted to it out of necessity.[11] Another important British critic who participated in the debate was Edmund Burke, who also did not discern in the development of the British constitution, from the Magna Carta of King John to the declaration of Right of William and Mary, "any reference whatever to any other general or prior right" except the inherited rights of the monarch, peers, and common people "from a long line of ancestors."[12] This, according to Burke, belied any argument based on social contract and the concomitant general will. Actually, different societies followed different historical processes and established different social and political conventions. Each of these institutional environments must "be looked on with reverence; because it is not a partnership in things subservient only to the gross animal existence of a temporary and perishable nature: [i]t is a partnership in all science; a partnership in all art; a partnership in every virtue, and in all perfection,... a partnership not only between those who are living, but those who are dead and those who are to be born."[13] In Burke's view, the French were foolish in repudiating their constitutions and acting as if they "had never been moulded into civil society, and had everything to begin anew [in] 1789."[14] So, according to Burke, it was true, as Rousseau had postulated, that societies were governed by a contract: but it was a contract that sanctioned only the society's hard-earned physical and moral patrimony. The first and foremost duty of the sovereign was to protect this heritage from destructive outbursts, such as the one currently raging in France.

Bentham and the rise of utilitarianism

Jeremy Bentham found both Burke's and Rousseau's arguments flawed. As for Rousseau, his view of community revolving around the unifying concept of general will was a myth. This theory contradicted the observed human capability of producing socially beneficial outcomes without the guiding light of the interest of the community. In truth, "the community is a fictitious *body*, composed of the individual persons who are considered as constituting as it were its *members*... [and t]he interest of the community the sum of interests of the several members who compose it."[15] Similarly mythical was Burke's characterization of the State as the guardian of the community's political heritage. It amounted to little more than subjecting the individual will to the will of the sovereign who, in turn, served the interests of some historically consequential groups. Both representations of society failed to discern the fact that human conduct happens to answer to a mightier authority:

> Nature has placed mankind under the governance of two sovereign masters, *pain* and *pleasure*. It is for them alone to point out what we ought to do, as well as to determine what we shall do. On the one hand the standard of right and wrong, on the other hand the chain of causes and effects, are fastened to their throne. They govern us in all we do, in all we say, in all we think... In words a man may pretend to abjure their empire: but in reality he will remain subject to it all the while.[16]

This is not to say that individuals are utilitarian machines devoid of any sense of rectitude and propriety. On the contrary, they are "in the *habit* of paying *obedience* to a person, or an assemblage of persons, of a known and certain description (whom we may call *governor* or *governors*, [and] such persons altogether (*subjects* and *governors*) are said to be in a state of *political* SOCIETY."[17] This habit does not stem from any explicit act of consent. It is the principle of utility which dictates that it will be in the individual's own interest to conform to the rules of society. A contrary action will only serve to inflict undesirable consequences to a person. Accordingly, under the governance of the principle of utility, the individual proceeds with the sole objective of augmenting his happiness and diminishing his unhappiness, and he does so regardless of whether the alternatives under his consideration involve the enhancement of his own interest or the interest of the community. Given that communities cannot have any ends above and beyond those of their constituting members, the interest of the community represents but the sum of the interests of the members who compose it. Consequently, the individual acting to augment his own interest is at the same time augmenting the interest of the community. The problem is that individuals have conflicting needs and preferences, and these differences mitigate the maximization of the total benefit. It is for this reason that there exists in society a place for political authority. The principle of utility does not preclude government intervention. If anything, it welcomes any government policy, no matter how artificial or alien to the established social and political conventions, provided that it is directed at reconciling the incongruity between the private and the public interest. Indeed, it is the duty of government to establish a bond between private and public interests through such measures.

At this juncture, a chasm opens between the views of Jeremy Bentham and Adam Smith. Smith envisages a "natural" identity between private interest and public interest, with laissez-faire providing the common bond. Any "artificial" policy, that is any course of government action that is not in conformity with the principle of individual interest would not serve the interest of the community. This identity arises, not "from the effect of any conscious regulation by the State or society, ... [or] any human wisdom which foresees and intends general opulence, [but from] a propensity in human nature."[18] Smith elaborates on this point:

> In civilized society [man] stands at all times in need of the co-operation and assistance of great multitudes ... In almost every other race of animals each individual, when it is grown up to maturity, is entirely independent, and in its natural state has occasion for the assistance of no other living creature. But man has almost constant occasion for the help of his brethren, and it is in vain for him to expect it from their benevolence only. He will be more likely to prevail if he can interest their self-love in his favour, and show them that it is for their own advantage to do for him what he requires of them. Whoever offers to another a bargain of any kind, proposes to do this. Give me that which I want, and you shall have this which you want: ... it is in this manner that we obtain from one another the far greater part of those good offices which we stand in need of.[19]

Awareness of collective interest is not a necessary condition for socially beneficial results. Smith deems a country gentleman more likely to be aware of the interest of the community than a merchant or manufacturer. Yet, the actions of merchants and manufacturers may be more instrumental in advancing the interest of the community than those of the country gentleman, notwithstanding the former's limited awareness of public interest:

> It is by [the] superior knowledge of *their own* interest that they have frequently imposed upon [the landowner's] generosity, and persuaded him to give up both his own interest and that of the public, from a very simple but honest conviction, that their interest, and not his, was the interest of the public.[20]

Smith thus shows that in a free economy self-interest would come to harmony with public interest and carry society to wealth and prosperity. Hence, political authorities should resort to no other policy but laissez-faire. Socially and politically inspired systems of incentives and limitations will serve only to hamper economic progress:

> Every system which endeavours, either, by extraordinary encouragements, to draw towards a particular species of industry a greater share of the capital of the society than what would naturally go to it; or, by extraordinary restraints, to force from a particular species of industry some share of capital which would otherwise be employed in it; is in reality subversive of the great purpose which it means to promote. It retards, instead of accelerating, the progress of society towards real wealth and greatness; and diminishes, instead of increasing, the real value of the annual produce of its land and labour.[21]

Smith goes on:

> All systems either of preference or restraint, therefore, being thus completely taken away, the obvious and simple system of natural liberty establishes itself of its own accord. Every man, as long as he does not violate the laws of justice, is left perfectly free to pursue his own interest his own way, and to bring forth his industry and capital into competition with those of any other man, or order of men. The sovereign is completely discharged from ... the duty of superintending the industry of private people, and of directing it towards the employments most suitable to the interest of the society.[22]

Bentham agrees with Smith that individuals are essentially self-interested rather than community-minded; but he does not believe that the two sets of interests would harmonize of their own accord. When the two interests clash, as they often do, the legislator must bring about the identification of the two egoisms through direct intercession.[23] The existence of crime is sufficient proof for Bentham that natural harmony is a fallacy. An agent acting under the principle of utility normally chooses a course of action that seemingly augments the happiness of the community: but he does so only to avoid undesirable consequences to himself. As such, a measure of conflict normally accompanies the reconciliation of private and public interests at the individual level, and this disutility can only be removed by transforming the institutional environment into one in which the individual's selfish impulses are channeled as a matter of course into socially useful purposes. For example, by appropriately reforming public education, we can inculcate in young people's minds the perception that such altruistic sentiments as good will, sympathy, and benevolence actually contribute to the happiness of one's own self.

Public education is only one component among the numerous social, political, economic, legal, cultural, and religious institutions of a society. To produce the greatest happiness for the greatest number we must reform each and every institution that stands in the way. This requires a wholesale constitutional reform aiming at creating a political society in which individual motivations are both freely expressed and effectively reconciled with each other. Such results could be obtained only under the aegis of a constitution stipulating a single-chamber parliament, frequent elections, comparable electoral districts, universal suffrage, and secret ballot. Only under such conditions can the different preferences of people be accurately registered and that which appears common be adopted as the basis of public policy. Such a constitutional arrangement would, on the one hand, satisfy the principle of individual egoism, for it would prevent legislators from imposing their will upon the wills of the members of the society in an unwarranted effort to direct them in doing good for themselves. On the other hand, it would comply with the principle of equality, since every person's individual utility, expressed through his representatives, would receive equal treatment in the calculation of collective utility.

Bentham did not subscribe to any particular reform movement. His was call for a wholesale replacement of utilitarian calculus as a means of reformed social and economic conditions.[24] The principle of utility as an overriding social philosophy would put an end to political debate about what kind of government activity would remedy social ills. This would not mark the end of political intervention. Even in a society in which utilitarianism reigned supreme, there would remain some instances where governmental intervention would still be required.[25] But these instances would be far fewer than what is generally thought.[26]

In this juncture, Bentham's theory merges with that of Adam Smith. For, also in Smith's view of a society subscribing to laissez-faire, the individual citizen, under the security provided by the government but without any restrictions on his spontaneous activity, is led by the invisible hand of natural liberty to a propitious equilibrium, which serves not only the agent's selfish ends, but also community's moral ends. Laissez-faire, precisely like utilitarian social philosophy, allows for limited government intervention. In fact, certain services traditionally shunned by private entrepreneurs for being unprofitable, such as maintaining a standing army and providing good communication facilities, are deemed the indispensable features of a "civilized and opulent" society. Smith elaborates on this point in an oft-quoted passage:

> According to the system of natural liberty, the sovereign has ... three duties to attend to: first, the duty protecting the society from the violence and invasion of other independent societies; secondly, the duty of protecting, as far as possible, every member of the society from the injustice or oppression of every other member of it, or the duty of establishing an exact administration of justice; and, thirdly, the duty of erecting and maintaining certain public works and certain public institutions, which it can never be for the interest of any individual, or small number of individuals, to erect and maintain; because the profit could never repay the expence of any individual or small number of individuals, though it may frequently do much more than repay it to a great society.[27]

Smith's dictum that the private entrepreneur will shun the provision of certain activities, which, in turn, will be taken on by the sovereign, leads to a disconcerting outcome, namely that these services will necessarily be overpriced from the point of view of most citizens. This will inevitably cause a burden on the community since the sacrifice inflicted by the collection of the commensurate revenue will exceed the benefit produced by public expenditures. Unable to enhance the benefit emanating from these services, the sovereign has no other recourse but diminishing the burden their defrayment inflicted on private budgets. It is with this apprehension that Smith warns the sovereign to "contrive ... every tax ... as both to take out and to keep out of the pockets of the people as little as possible."[28] Unfortunately, however, exactly the opposite occurs in practice. First, there is the substantial cost of tax collection itself that adds to the unproductiveness of government expenditures. Second, taxes obstruct people's sense of industry, hence lead to the diminution of the funds from which taxes are drawn. Third, taxes create the temptation of evasion and fraud while at the same time requiring the State to punish perpetrators. Finally, frequent visits and odious examination of tax collectors subject people to unnecessary "trouble, vexation, and oppression," which, though not entailing an out-of-pocket cost, are "certainly equivalent to the expence at which every man would be willing to redeem himself from it."[29] In short, as a rule, taxes prove more burdensome to private individuals than they are beneficial to the State. Consequently, statesmen and political economists, instead of deliberating on the benefits of public expenditures and their proper extent, should discuss how to minimize the *sacrifice* caused by the transfer of the tax revenue from the private budget to the public budget.

The origin of the sacrifice view of taxation

Smith devotes a whole book of the *Wealth of Nations* to this end, in which he sets out to explain:

> first, what are the necessary expences of the sovereign or commonwealth; and which of those expences ought to be defrayed by the general contribution of the whole society; and which of them, by that of some particular part only, or of some particular members of the society: secondly, what are the different methods in which the whole society may be made to contribute towards defraying the expences incumbent on the whole society, and what are the principal advantages and inconveniences of each of those methods: and, thirdly, what are the reasons and causes which have induced almost all modern governments to mortgage some part of this revenue, or to contract debts, and what have been the effects of those debts upon the real wealth, the annual produce of the land and labour of the society.[30]

Smith thus sets forth an essential characteristic of British fiscal theory: the government must assume the role of a responsible caretaker and take on the task of providing certain services which, though inherently unproductive, nevertheless provide the essential fixtures of a great society. Because the provision of these services necessarily entails payments exceeding a comparable market price, the government should finance them in such a manner that it causes the least sacrifice to the budgets of contributing citizens.

Precisely with this intention Smith goes on to discuss appropriate taxation policies for each of the three categories of government services that he prescribes: national defense, administration of justice, and public works and services. Stressing that national defense is intended for the benefit of the entire society, he deems it reasonable to defray this expenditure through general contribution, with each member of the society contributing in proportion to his respective ability as measured by his income. As for the financing of the expenses of justice, Smith proposes it to be defrayed by appropriate fees of court (rather than stamp duties, for otherwise judges might be tempted to unnecessarily multiply the proceedings before them to collect as much payment as possible). With regard to the financing of public works and services, he makes a tripartite distinction. The cost of building and maintaining public works, as well as that of the palace and Parliament, should be defrayed by general tax contributions since these amenities are intended to benefit the entire society. When it comes to government services benefiting local users, their costs ought to be covered by local revenue. As for those amenities that serve the needs of only certain users, such as the navigable canals and highways used by private entrepreneurs, the revenue should be raised by tolls.

The main criterion adopted by Smith in the determination of tax policies is clearly whether or not the benefit from a government expenditure program is attributable to a particular user or group of users. He elaborates on this point when in his discussion of public education:

> The expence of the institutions for education ... is ... no doubt, beneficial to the whole society, and may, therefore, without injustice, be defrayed by the general contribution of the whole society. This expence, however, might perhaps with equal propriety, and even with some advantage, be defrayed altogether by those who receive the immediate benefit of such education and instruction, or by the voluntary contribution of those who think they have occasion for either the one or the other.[31]

The fiscal theory that emerges from Smith's discussion is an eminently normative one, concerned mainly with the analysis of alternative tax schemes and their effect on the individual budget. The role of the fiscal theorist should consist of the analysis of alternative tax schemes in order to ascertain the ones that seem most effective to alleviate the fiscal burden. Realizing that the first step in this endeavor would be the measurement of the burden caused by taxation, contemporary political economists turned to Bentham's "moral arithmetic" or "felicific calculus" for guidance.

The essence of the Bentham criterion was that each individual's utility, though thoroughly subjective to himself, was objective data to the community. If every person were allowed to specify his perceived utility vis-à-vis a slate of public expenditures it would be a simple task to choose the alternative that maximized the sum of these utilities. Accordingly, Bentham's social welfare function for n members of the community was in the form of $U = u_1 + u_2 + \ldots + u_n$.

The problem with this equation is, naturally, that it is based not only on the explicit postulate of additivity of individual utilities, but also on the implicit assumption of their comparability. Bentham provided no argument for the existence of an interpersonally valid common unit of utility, except for expounding that money could be used as a common denominator in utility calculations. The task of resolving the problem of quantification and commensurability of individual utilities fell on the shoulders of his two disciples, J. S. Mill and Chadwick.

Mill and the proper bases of social policy

Bentham's vagueness on questions of measurability effectively eluded J. S. Mill.[32] Mill's elaboration on the Bentham criterion was limited to a discussion of the propriety and importance of resting social welfare judgments on individual preferences, but not on the commensurability of different individuals' utilities or on the form of social welfare function.[33] This was because Mill considered the primary use of the sum-of-utilities criterion to be its applicability to social policy rather than economic choice and because the conclusions he arrived at were qualitative, not quantitative, in nature; in other words. Nevertheless, in Book V of his *Principles of Political Economy* (1848) – which remained for many decades the most widely used textbook in Britain until Marshall's *Principles* came out in 1890 – Mill delves in a detailed examination of the proper role and the extent of the influence of government in the economy.

In this book, Mill distinguishes between two sets of government economic activity, necessary and optional. The activities Mill deems necessary are those that are inseparable from the concept of government. They include national defense and civil safety, administration of justice, provision of public works, as well as coinage, collection of taxes, and maintenance of a uniform system of weights and measurements. As for optional government activities, Mill justifies the production of any service that generates "substantial" net utility. In Ekelund's and Hébert's words:

> The key to Mill's philosophical position on the limits of the laissez faire principle lies in his recognition that government interference under capitalism *could be required by some great good.* Thus Mill was able to list several exceptions to the doctrine of laissez faire without compromising on the basic principle. His [numerous] exceptions would allow [optional] government intervention in the areas of consumer protection, general education, preservation of the environment, selective enforcement of "permanent" contracts based on future experience (e.g., marriage), public-utility regulation, and public charity.[34]

Mill draws two other dichotomies in the provision of government services. He views some measures to be restrictive and some others propelling, depending on whether they intend to dampen or enhance market forces. A government intervention envisaging preservation of the environment would constitute an example of the first type of measures. An example for the second category of interventions would be the expansion of educational opportunities to instill productive skills in the general population. Alternatively, interventions might be preventive or reactive. The former entail such ex ante measures as providing sanitation services to prevent epidemics. Reactive measures are designed to undo past mistakes, such as limiting the size of bequests.

Most of the institutional changes proposed by J. S. Mill closely reflect his master's postulate concerning the incongruity of private and public interest, as well as its corollary, planned artificiality of social reform projects. A good illustration in this respect concerns Mill's role in the passing of the new Poor Law Amendment Act of 1834. The proposal stipulated that no public assistance should be given to the destitute unless they agreed to live in workhouses, where the living conditions would be kept deliberately inferior to those of the most poorly paid laborers. The reasoning behind the stipulation was that being poor was the result of one's own failing, except one was mentally or physically handicapped, and that able-bodied poor people should not be rewarded for their indolence. Mill saw a direct reflection of Bentham's teachings in this proposal, in whose support he wrote:

> The condition of a pauper must cease to be ... an object of desire and envy to the independent labourer. Relief must be given; no one must be allowed to starve; the necessaries of life and health must be tendered to all who apply for them; but ... relief must be given only in exchange for labour, and labour at least as irksome and severe as that of the least fortunate among independent labourers.[35]

Mill was deeply apprehensive of the external effects of poverty. He favored an efficient system of relief that, while caring for the handicapped and destitute, discouraged the able-bodied from becoming the wards of the State.[36] He believed that only a centrally run administration would be able to plan, institute, coordinate, and control a relief system which, though patently artificial, would nonetheless provide effective work incentives, hence would contribute to the greatest benefit for the greatest number.

Chadwick and economic efficiency of social policy

There is no mention of any interpersonally valid common unit of utility in Mill's discussion concerning the destitute who might prefer the harsh conditions of the workhouse versus workers accepting the humblest conditions of employment to be independent. This void in "felicific calculus" was filled by another favorite disciple of Bentham's, Edwin Chadwick.

Chadwick was a secretary of Bentham's and a close friend of J. S. Mill's. He was also a pivotal member, with Nassau Senior, of the Royal Commission on Poor Law Reform. Chadwick, a staunch believer of preventive government measures, initiated and implemented a string of reforms in sanitation, health, education, criminal justice, and environmental policy between 1832 and 1854. The measuring stick he applied to these projects was that of economic efficiency. To this end, he amended Bentham's principle of utility to read: Any government intervention is justified provided that it reduces waste in the employment of economic resources. As a capable reformer with a long record of public service, Chadwick found ample opportunity to put a series of cost-cutting schemes to work, and the results were phenomenal:

> Put in charge of improving sanitation and thereby reducing the mortality of British criminals transported to Australia, Chadwick

> noted that the British government paid a flat fee to the ship's captain for each convict who embarked from a British port. The captains, of course, found that they could maximize profits by taking on as many prisoners as could be safely carried without endangering the ship and by minimizing expenses (food and drink, etc.) on the prisoners en route. Survival rates among the prisoners under this incentive system were as low as 40 percent, humanitarian pleas for improved sanitation notwithstanding. After a quick assessment of the situation, Chadwick changed the payment system so that the ship's captain received a fee for each live convict that *disembarked* in Australia. Within a short time the survival rate increased dramatically to $98\frac{1}{2}$ percent. All that was needed was to give the ships' captains an incentive to protect the health of their cargo – thus creating an artificial identity between the public interest (i.e., the safety of the prisoners) and the private interests (i.e., the profit of the shipper).[37]

In achieving this result, Chadwick was accomplishing the grander feat, vis-à-vis J. S. Mill, of giving credence to Bentham's thesis that augmentation of collective utility could be induced by artificial means. As such, he was instrumental in prevailing Bentham's postulate of inequality of private and public interests over Smith's doctrine of natural liberty, which had hitherto taken a stronger hold in contemporary British political economy. Mill and Chadwick both demonstrated that public policy could indeed produce beneficial outcomes if it entailed proper incentives. But Mill, leaning on the Smith argument, rejected extensive government intervention in the public economy. Chadwick, in turn, endorsed any intervention that helped render the economy more competitive. As such, Chadwick proved to be the better Benthamite. For, in his capacity of an a reform-minded public administrator, he demonstrated over and over again that individuals' selfish impulses could indeed be directed into socially beneficial ends to produce the greatest benefit of the greatest number, exactly as expounded by his master.[38]

Henry Sidgwick: the great synthesizer

Yet, Chadwick is not the most acclaimed defender of utilitarianism. That honor belongs to Henry Sidgwick who, in *Methods of Ethics* (1874), demonstrated that the principle of utility could be instrumental in promoting general happiness only when it is employed in conjunction with two other principles of human conduct. On the one end of the social platform Sidgwick rested the natural principle of egoism – natural because it accounted for the innate propensity individuals demonstrated in promoting their self-interest. On the opposite end there stood the principle of intuitionism, derived and buttressed by another natural propensity, moral conduct, according to which individuals accepted as ethically binding only those endeavors that were directed toward attaining socially beneficial ends. Adam Smith was the archetypal defender of the first principle and Samuel Clarke of the second. Smith's theory – set out in *Moral Sentiments* (1759) nearly two decades before the appearance of *The Wealth of Nations* – was based on the premise that human beings, though basically egoistic, are at same time capable of fostering the senses of sympathy, propriety, virtue, merit, and duty. Earlier, Clarke, a firm advocate of rationalist ethics, had demonstrated in *A Discourse Concerning the Unchangeable Obligations of Natural Religion* (1706) that individuals are endowed with a moral sense, that is, an innate knowledge of right and wrong; a logical sense that led them to morally valid courses of action; and a unique virtue that guides them to commit themselves to appropriate courses of action.

What united Clarke and Smith was their belief that human sensibility, or common sense, would be instrumental in creating outcomes that satisfied both private and collective interests. Sidgwick judged this presumed source of rationality to be too vague and weak to serve as a precept of human conduct. He first rejected Clarke's argument of enlightened self-love as the supreme principle of rational conduct. To Sidgwick, this principle was fatally inconsistent for recognizing individual differences simultaneously in the forming and enforcement of the underlying rationality. He then rejected Smith's principle of natural self-interest on the ground that it conflicted with the widely observed phenomenon that most individuals routinely subordinate their private interest to public interest when a clash arises between the two. Finally, he turned to Bentham, charging that one could not necessarily derive from his postulate of psychological hedonism the corollary that an action is right only if it contributed more to the general happiness than any alternative action open to the individual. Consequently, it cannot be elicited from the principle of utilitarianism the result that individuals, either instinctively or as a result of social engineering, will subordinate their private considerations to the general happiness.[39]

Sidgwick's tremendous achievement consisted in bringing the seemingly incongruous arguments of Clarke, Smith, and Bentham into a propitious synthesis. He accomplished this feat by first ridding Bentham's utilitarianism from its psychological-hedonistic trappings and then inserting this artificial construct as an effective regulator between two natural principles of human conduct, egoism and intuitionism. In doing so, Sidgwick conferred upon utilitarianism its ideal form. D. H. Munro elaborates on this point:

> It would seem to follow from the hedonistic calculus that there is no moral difference between a situation in which A benefits (obtains 50 units of pleasure, say) at the expense of B (say 40 units of pain) and one in which A and B both obtain moderate benefits (say 5 units each). The total increase in human happiness (10 units) is the same whichever we choose. To meet this objection Sidgwick modified the greatest happiness formula by making the equal distribution of happiness a requirement as well as its maximization. It would seem to follow that equality, as well as happiness, is good in itself. Ideal utilitarianism does not escape this objection, since we need to amend the "greatest good" formula in the same way. It is, however, easier for the ideal utilitarian to accommodate the change: since he has already admitted a multiplicity of goods, he need not shrink from regarding the equalization of goods as itself a good.[40]

With the advent of marginal calculus, Sidgwick's construct gathered additional weight. An early recognition came from Maffeo Pantaleoni in 1883, immediately after Sidgwick's *Principles of Political Economy* came out in print:

> There enters into the administrative process the ... theoretical requirement of balancing the marginal sacrifice engendered by the exaction of total revenue against the marginal utilities of the various items of expenditure, or, as Sidgwick puts it: "We must regard both expenditure and supply as having at least a margin within which the restriction or enlargement of either must partly depend on the effects of the corresponding restriction or enlargement of the other; within which, therefore, the gain secured to the public by an additional increment of expenditure has to be weighed carefully against the sacrifices inevitable entailed by the exaction of an additional increment of supply."[41]

F. Y. Edgeworth took Sidgwick as his "chief guide" in his endeavor to formulate an efficient distribution of the burden of taxation. In his view, Sidgwick not only best contemplated the crowning height of the utilitarian first principle, from which the steps of a sublime deduction led to the high tableland of equality, but also discerned the enormous interposing chasms that deterred practical wisdom from moving directly toward that ideal.[42] Edgeworth, in his 1897 article, liberally quotes from Sidgwick's *Principles of Political Economy* (1883):

> "In the first place it is conceivable that a greater utility in the distribution of produce would lead ultimately to a reduction in the total amount of to be distributed in consequence of a general preference of leisure to the results of labour on the part of the classes whose shares of produce has increased."[43]

Edgeworth notes that Sidgwick, all the while, did not miss the accompanying danger "that the increase through equalisation of the incomes of the poorer classes will cause the population to increase at a more rapid rate than at present; so that ultimately the increment of an average worker's share will be partly spent in supporting a larger number of children, and partly reduced through the decrease in the efficiency of the more crowded labour."[44] As such, he demonstrated that rational conduct could be enriched by the application of moral consciousness, regardless of whether that consciousness is derived from religion (Clarke), self-interest (Smith), or hedonism (Bentham).

The first principles of British fiscal theory

By the late 1880s, certain concepts had been already established in British fiscal doctrine. For one thing, differences in innate endowment had been soundly rejected as a legitimate source of differences in economic well-being:

> The existence of such inequalities is recognized, but they should not be permitted to determine the state of distribution. To be born with a high- or low-ability level is not due to the will or action of the particular individual. Like social status, this accident of birth is considered as lacking ethical sanction as a basis for distribution. According to this view, some other principle of assignment must be sought.[45]

According to J. S. Mill, the principle of equity in taxation called for a proportional tax on income. Mill, following Bentham, feared the disincentives attributable to progressive income tax rates; yet, diverging from his master, he favored sharp progression in inheritance taxation.[46] His main contribution was to pose the problem of equity in terms of equal sacrifice, thus setting the framework for a subsequent discussion by

Sidgwick and Edgeworth.[47] Sidgwick demonstrated that when a given aggregate of private good available for distribution among two or more comparably endowed individuals was divided among them equally, a further amount of collective good would be created.[48] This principle gave rise to the fundamental impetus of the British theory of taxation to tax similar taxpayers similarly. Dubbed as the rule of horizontal equity, the principle states that under any given tax scheme, individuals with the same ability to pay should pay the same tax.

This concept of equity, as it becomes immediately clear, views the tax problem in and of itself, independent of expenditure determination. In other words, a given tax revenue is needed and each taxpayer is asked to contribute in line with his or her ability to pay as measured by his income.[49] British fiscal theorists largely remained loyal to this line of reasoning. As put by Arthur Cecil Pigou:

> [E]ven if Sidgwick's view that equity is itself a good is rejected, there are available other considerations adequate to establish the principle of [horizontal] equity in its economic applications. First, if £1000 has to be taken from two people of equal wealth and similar temperament, the law of diminishing utility shows that less hurt will be hurt by taking it in equal parts from each of them than by taking it in any other proportion. Secondly, if it is taken in any other proportion, a sense of being unfairly treated will be created in the person who pays the larger amount... Thirdly, unequal treatment... breeds a sense of insecurity all around; for everyone feels that he may be the next victim. This discourages people from working and saving to obtain possession of durable things, and so indirectly strikes a blow at the accumulation of capital much heavier than would be struck by the collection of an equal sum of money on some intelligible non-arbitrary plan... Unfortunately, however, the principle in its barest form, as sketched above, cannot be applied to practice, because in real life no two persons ever are exactly similar.[50]

Edgeworth and the problem of vertical equity

The question that now arose was that of vertical equity, that is, the question of how to determine the tax shares of people with different abilities to pay. The practical difficulty lay in calculating the *different* amounts of taxes vis-à-vis the *different* amounts of incomes in the face of *different* marginal utility of income schedules for *different* people! It was Edgeworth who succeeded in accomplishing this daunting task.

A true Benthamite, Edgeworth was convinced that utility was measurable in terms of its "least perceptible increments" and that a "hedonic" theory of taxation based on such a calculation was in order. When Edgeworth ventured to expound the first principles of the pure theory of taxation, Bentham already had applied the principle of decreasing marginal utility to personal income in *Principles of the Civil Code* (1802), and William Lloyd equated utility with the pleasure of consumption of a commodity in his famous Oxford lecture (1833).[51] In the ensuing decades, political economists, showing a keener interest in consumer demand, began to disassociate themselves from the tradition of Smith and Ricardo and came to recognize consumer wants as the primum mobile of economic exchange. This gave rise to a second flowering of Bentham's utilitarianism. Benthamism became thick in the air as contemporary authors subscribing to hedonistic calculus equated utility with the pleasure experienced by an individual during the act of consumption. The movement resulted in a full-fledged revolution in economic theorizing, which culminated in the works of, first, Gossen (1854), then, simultaneously, of Jevons (1871), Menger (1871), and Walras (1874).

It was pointed out earlier that Bentham, while apprehensive of the problem of equality of income, did not address the question of interpersonal comparisons of utility. The closest that he came to discuss the problem of commensurability of different people's utilities was in a passage in his *Theory of Legislation* (1802):

> It is to be observed in general that in speaking of the effect of a portion of wealth upon happiness, abstraction is always to be made of the particular sensibility of individuals, and of the exterior circumstances in which they may be placed. Differences of character are inscrutable; and such is the diversity of circumstances, that they are never the same for two individuals. Unless we begin by dropping these two considerations, it will be impossible to announce any general proposition. But though each of these propositions may prove false or inexact in a given individual case, that will furnish no argument against their speculative truth and practical utility. It is enough for the justification of these propositions – 1st, If they approach nearer the truth than any others which can be substituted for them; and, If with less inconvenience than any others they can be made the basis of legislation.[52]

Stigler notes that Bentham expounded interpersonal comparisons of utility not by calculation, but by assumption. He then went on to formulate three propositions on the utility of income:

1st. Each portion of wealth has a corresponding portion of happiness;
2nd. Of two individuals with equal fortunes, he who has the most wealth has the most happiness;
3rd. The excess in happiness of the richer will not be so great as the excess of his wealth.[53]

This was the wisdom Edgeworth received from Bentham and the three contemporaneous founders of the marginal utility theory. Of these three political economists, Jevons and Walras explicitly and Menger implicitly, expressed total utility for commodities x_1, x_2, x_3, ... as an additive entity in the form of:

$$f(x_1) + g(x_2) + h(x_3) + \ldots$$

assuming that each commodity yielded diminishing marginal utility and with the implications that the demand curve for each commodity had a negative slope and that an increase in income will lead to increased purchases of every commodity.[54]

Edgeworth in his *Mathematical Psychics* (1881) attributed to the total utility function a general form: $U(x_1, x_2, \ldots, x_n)$. This further abstraction, no longer requiring diminishing marginal utility as a necessary or sufficient condition for convexity, destroyed the pleasant simplicity and specificity of the earlier total utility function.[55] In addition, the shape of indifference curves now depended on the relations between or among commodities. As noted by Edgeworth himself, commodities may be rival – like margarine and butter – if an increase in one diminishes the marginal utility of the other, or they may be complementary – like bread and butter – if an increase in one increases the marginal utility of the other; however, there is no way to reduce the convexity property to a property related to this classification.[56] In other words, the convexity of the indifference curves had to be postulated independently. Only after the appearance of Irving Fisher's doctoral dissertation in 1892 did it become clear that it was not essential to know how many units of utility each indifference curve actually represented: the existence of a map of indifference curves would suffice for analytical purposes.

There is no mention of Fisher's work in Edgeworth's 1897 treatise exploring the foundation of the pure theory of taxation. If anything, Edgeworth reiterates Bentham's tenet that the goal of the fiscal authority is to maximize the sum of individuals' utilities subject to the revenues required. He then explicitly postulates that (1) individual taxpayers have identical utility functions that depend on their levels of income; (2) these functions are subject to diminishing marginal utilities of income; and, (3) the total amount of income in society is fixed. The corollary of these axioms, naturally, is that (1) the fiscal authority can and should redistribute income as long as the applicable taxation scheme increases total utility; and (2) the redistribution process should continue until complete equality is achieved, both in marginal utilities and in incomes.

The essential feature in Edgeworth's model is that:

> [t]axes should be set in such a way that the after-tax distribution of income is as equal as possible. In particular, income should be taken first from the rich because the marginal utility is smaller than that of the poor. If the government requires more revenue even after complete equality has been reached. Then the additional tax burden should be evenly distributed ... Edgeworth's model, then implies a radically progressive tax structure – incomes are leveled off from the top until complete equality is reached. In effect, marginal tax rates on high income individuals are 100 percent. However, ... each of the assumptions underlying this analysis is subject to question.[57]

Marshall: the link between Sidgwick and Pigou

One of the chief founders of price theory, Alfred Marshall, elaborated the postulate of diminishing marginal utility in his treatment of the concept of consumer surplus. Following Daniel Bernoulli's argument that utility increased by lesser and lesser amounts as the amount of income increased after a certain threshold, Marshall suggested that fiscal authorities, too, heed this argument and adopt a graduated system of taxation. The reason for the diminishing character of marginal utilities is due to the human propensity that:

> after a time, new riches often lose a great part of their charms. Partly this is the result of familiarity; which makes people cease to derive much pleasure from accustomed comforts and luxuries, ... [and] [p]artly it is due to the fact that with increased riches often comes either the weariness of age, or at least an increase of nervous strain; and perhaps even habits of living that lower physical vitality, and diminish the capacity for pleasure ... There is some misuse of wealth in all ranks of society ... Laws against luxury have been futile; but it

> would be a gain if the moral sentiment of the community could induce people to avoid all sorts of display of individual wealth. There are indeed true and worthy pleasures to be got from wisely ordered magnificence: but they are at their best when free from any taint of personal vanity on the one side and envy on the other; as they are when they centre round public buildings, public parks, public collections of the fine arts, and public games and amusements. So long as wealth is applied to provide for every family the necessaries of life and culture, and an abundance of the higher forms of enjoyment for collective use, so long the pursuit of wealth is a noble aim; and the pleasures which it brings are likely to increase with the growth of those higher activities which it is used to promote... The world would go much better if everyone would buy fewer and simpler things, and would take trouble in selecting them for their real beauty, being careful of course to get good value in return for his outlay.[58]

Along with the explicit conception of diminishing marginal utility of income based on intertemporal considerations, there is an implicit point in the preceding passage for the preference for consumption rather than income as the basis of taxation. Pigou elaborated on the latter argument expressing his preference of a general expenditure tax over a general income tax because it does not discriminate against saving – hence investment – and accordingly prevents double taxation.[59] As far as Marshall's explicit argument is concerned, it resulted in the problem of efficiency gaining ascendancy over the problem of equity.

It will be recalled that Smith addressed the problem of equity right at the outset, pointing out the harmful effects of taxation, and proposing that the fiscal authority to lighten the pockets of the people as little as possible. Efforts to develop a theory of efficiency in taxation became discernible in J. S. Mill's writings. Marshall took the issue head on and demonstrated with the help of a diagram that:

> if the commodity is one, the production of which obeys the law of constant return, so that the supply price is the same for all amounts of the commodity, consumers' surplus will be diminished by more than the increased payments to the producer; and therefore, in the special case of a tax, by more than the gross receipts of the State. For on that part of the consumption of the commodity, which is maintained, the consumer loses what the State receives: and on that part of the consumption which is destroyed by the rise in price, the

> consumers' surplus is destroyed; and of course there is no payment for it to the producer or to the State. Conversely, the gain of consumers' surplus caused by a bounty on a commodity that obeys the law of constant returns, is less than the bounty itself. For on that part of the consumption which existed before the bounty, consumers' surplus is increased by just the amount of the bounty; while on the new consumption that is caused by the bounty, the gain of the consumers' surplus is less than the bounty.[60]

In doing so, Marshall warned of the underlying assumption of constant marginal utility of income and suggested that welfare may be raised by giving a subsidy to decreasing cost industries while taxing those with increasing cost.[61] He then added in a footnote on the same page that the excess burden of a product tax would be larger for the case of a luxury than for a necessity, since demand tends to be more elastic.[62] With this, he opened up a new vista in fiscal analysis. Namely, he inaugurated partial equilibrium models of price determination, which allowed fiscal economists to analyze the effect of a tax on a particular market while ignoring the repercussions on other markets or the aggregate economy. This kind of analysis soon became the trademark of British fiscal theory affording it a unique problem-solving character in the analysis of the effects of alternative tax policies upon the private economy.

Marshall contributed little to fiscal theory in a direct way; but his indirect influence on fiscal theory has been enormous.[63] His formulation of the economic framework remained dominant in the analysis of the private sector supply as well as in the reconciliation of the two sides of the market mechanism.[64] The task of applying the marginal method to aggregative types of *fiscal* problems fell on his favorite student, Pigou, whose many important contributions in this field are rediscovered periodically.[65]

Pigou: the welfare view of the public economy

Pigou's adherence to utilitarian premises was unmistakable; but he approached them with caution. In his view, when it came to the satisfaction of individual needs, the individual agent was generally capable of maximizing his own utility. But there were numerous exceptions to the rule, which called for government action. As illustrated by Ebenstein:

> the individual has to be protected against fraud and misrepresentation, as in the advertising (which may be false) of drugs and medicines

> (which may be harmful). Moreover, this regulatory function of the state need not always be negative, but also encourage the positive, as in the case of the state supplying school children with free milk and lunches, or selling these items below cost. The case of monopoly is another instance in which the individual consumer is helpless unless he can mobilize the authority of the state in protecting himself against monopolistic exploitation.[66]

There are numerous other manifestations in the public sector that hamper the maximization of an individual's self-interest. These give rise to distortions both in the allocative and in the distributive fields of the public economy. Two categories of such manifestations are alluded to in the above paragraph, namely, that, first, the problem that individuals are often at a disadvantage to ascertain the benefits of certain goods vis-à-vis the suppliers of those goods; and, second, the "well-known disharmonies associated with monopolistic practices which deliberately restrict either directly or by price policy the investment of resources in a monopolist's chosen field."[67] Third, there exists the problem caused by a gap between a person's "wants" and his "needs." Pigou warns: "no normal child *wants* to be educated, and ... a man may want extremely cocaine, heroin and other such drugs that are bound to do him serious harm."[68] Finally, there is the more pervasive problem of externalities, a concept that will be elaborated next. In all cases, it will be to the benefit of society for the government not to stand aside.

This is not to say that the State should take every opportunity to impose itself on the public economy. Pigou warns of the danger that the "Welfare State holds in itself a *cumulative* threat to productivity, which ... should be continuously and carefully watched."[69] The people should also bear in mind that the Welfare State is not a way of getting something for nothing: every piece of welfare has to be paid for, often by increased taxation.[70]

Marshall's coverage of external economies was limited. This was because he was interested only in the positive spillover effects of the technological improvement generated by large firms upon smaller enterprises.[71] As for Pigou, he rests his monumental work, *Economics of Welfare* (1920), directly on the concept of externality. The following passage from a later work is illustrative of this emphasis:

> When people decide to spend their money in certain ways it sometimes happens that their spending yields uncovenanted benefits or inflicts uncovenanted damage on other people whose gains or

> losses do not enter into the calculations of the spenders. There are many examples of this. The social costs involved in the supply of alcoholic drinks includes the provision of police to control the effects of excess, but these costs do not enter into the price that the purchasers of such drinks have to pay for them. Nor does the damage done to people living near smoking factories and the extra washing bills they have to pay enter into the price of the factory's products. If they did, as, with strict social accounting, they ought to do, the price of those products would be higher, less of them would be demanded and less resources devoted to making them. On the other hand, when a good landlord protects the amenities of the neighbourhood man erects a beautiful instead of an ugly house there is a benefit to others for which he gets no payment. These gaps, positive and negative, between private and public costs were not much in people's minds until fairly recently. Now everybody understands them.[72]

It was partly owing of Pigou's efforts that people formed an awareness of this problem, the natural extension of which being that the State should assume a paternalistic role in resolving negative as well as positive externalities. In the case of negative externality, the fiscal authority would resort to taxation and resolve the maladjustment by equating private cost to social cost. In the case of a positive externality, alternatively, it would employ a subsidy, this time equating private benefit to social benefit. To illustrate, if a steel producer polluted the air during the course of production, the fiscal authority would levy a tax upon each unit of the polluter's output in an amount just equal to the marginal damage it would inflict at the efficient level of output.[73]

It did not elude Pigou that the mere existence of an externality does not in itself warrant corrective action. For, a greater loss in welfare may occur from internalizing an externality through a resource reallocation than the gain in welfare deriving from such action.[74] He warns that

> we seldom know enough to decide in what fields and to what extent the State, on account of [externalities], could usefully interfere with individual freedom of choice. Moreover, even though economists were able to provide a perfect blueprint for beneficial State action, politicians are not philosopher kings and a blueprint might quickly yield place on their desks to the propaganda of competing pressure groups.[75]

Pigou was equally aware of the problem that the internalization of an externality, seemingly entailing an allocational consideration only, would necessarily give rise to redistributional repercussions. In the case of a negative externality associated with steel production mentioned earlier, for instance, the legal requirement holding the firm responsible for those harmed by the pollution would invoke a new definition of property rights. This change provides a strategic link between allocational and distributional activities of the fiscal authority.[76] Pigou considers this inescapable link a propitious eventuality, for, in his view, it affords the State an inherent right to interfere with the "natural" distribution of income and wealth: the only question is how far the State should go to do it efficiently.[77]

In Pigou's view, economic welfare as a whole will be promoted if the proportionate share of real income available to poorer classes is increased by proper taxation policy. This view he evidently did not inherit from Bentham or J. S. Mill. Indeed, Pigou remarks that in the early decades of the nineteenth century "it was honestly believed ... that to help poor people in their difficulties was in the long run positively bad for them; that it would only render them idle and thriftless, cause them to produce innumerable offspring for whom they could not provide, and so on."[78] But, thanks to a better understanding of the principle of diminishing marginal utilities of income, it was now realized that the cost of the redistribution of incomes is much smaller than was once supposed. Two reasons account for this change of thought:

> First, a given worsening in the economic situation of a reasonably fortunate person will not usually affect him nearly as much when he has become accustomed to it as it does when [a redistributive tax] was first imposed ... Secondly, whereas for a single person or family to be forced to accept a lower living standard [due to the tax] while their friends – and their enemies – are left as before may be very distressing; but if the whole of their class or group suffer alike, they will scarcely suffer at all ... [So], transfers away from better-to-do persons do not hurt the victims much, while the beneficiaries, whose needs are more elementary and less complex, gain from them a great deal.[79]

Musgrave wonders why Pigou, though having advanced so close to come up with a theory of the provision of public goods, or at least with an explicit linkage between externalities and public goods, gave only scant attention to the expenditure side of the budget in *Economics of Welfare* (1920).[80] Nevertheless, he hails Pigou's 1928 work, *The Theory of Public Finance*, as a major contribution to the theory of taxation.[81] It is here that Pigou, after distinguishing among equal-absolute, proportional, and marginal sacrifice, expounded "the one ultimate principle of taxation":

> [W]e have one ultimate principle, namely, least sacrifice, whose claim is undisputed: and a second ultimate principle, equal sacrifice among similar and similarly situated persons, but not among others, whose authenticity is somewhat less secure. If the second of these principles is recognised as well as the first, there is, for analysis, a conflict of ideals. Both the "ultimate" principles brought before the tribunal of something more ultimate still, *i.e.* the principle of maximum good, and weights must be assigned to them so proportioned that good as a whole, including the good of equality, shall be made as large as possible. In practice, however, as will appear presently, tax arrangements that conform to the principle of least sacrifice always and necessarily conform also to the principle of equal sacrifice among similar and similarly situated persons. Hence, even if the principle of equal sacrifice between similar and similarly situated persons is a true ultimate principle, since it can be deduced from the principle of least sacrifice, it is not a *necessary* one. Though, therefore, for academic persons there may be a more complex esoteric doctrine, for politicians and men of affairs we may properly assert that least aggregate sacrifice is the one ultimate principle of taxation.[82]

While Pigou considered the two forms of state economic activity, allocative and distributive, to be closely intertwined, he still treated the two topics separately for the sake of convenience and clarity. The following passage from Musgrave presents a lucid account of Pigou's view regarding the allocative function of fiscal activity:

> Within a given budget size, the programme mix is to be adjusted so as to balance the marginal benefits derived from various projects; and in determining the size of the budget, the marginal benefits from public outlays are to be equated with those from private outlays. Such would be the simple formula if the community was a unitary being. Since it is not, and since the desire of any one taxpayer to contribute depends on the contribution of others, government, as the agent of its citizens collectively, must exercise coercion upon them individually. This coercion creates indirect costs, which must be allowed for. But though the need for coercion is noted, there is no consideration of the mechanism by which it will inform government how individuals value social goods. Pigou, evidently, was still unaware of what

> had been contributed by the Austrians and Swedes three decades earlier. His contribution, however, was to place the extreme case of "full bounty" [argued by Marshall] into the broader spectrum of externalities, which may differ in degrees and kind, i.e. may range from "mixed" social goods to the polar case of full external benefits.[83]

According to Pigou, there are two kinds of "maladjustments" that prevent society's economic resources from being allocated optimally:

> The first is that, in respect of certain goods and services, the return at the margin which resources devoted to making them yields to their makers is not equal to the full return which the community as a whole receives, but falls short of or exceeds that return. In other words, the value of the marginal private net product of resources so employed is greater or less than the value of the marginal social net product. The second cause is that in respect of certain goods and services, the ratio, so to speak, between people's desire and satisfaction which results from the fulfillment of desire is greater, or less, than it is in respect of other goods and services ... When maladjustments have come about or are threatening to come about from either of the two causes, ... it is always possible, on the assumption that no administrative costs are involved, to correct them by imposing appropriate rates of tax on resources employed in uses that tend too be pushed too far and employing the proceeds to provide bounties, at appropriate rates, on uses of the opposite class.[84]

Pigou delineates in a lengthy footnote how his conclusion differs from that of Marshall concerning taxes subsidies expounded in Book V, Chapter XII (1890), which was mentioned earlier:

> Marshall shows that sometimes, though not always, the payment of a bounty on the production of a commodity obeying the law of decreasing supply price will add to consumer's surplus (measured in money) more than the money cost of the bounty, and suggests that there is a *prima facie* case for a bounty only when this condition is satisfied. My thesis is that there is a *prima facie* case for a bounty *in all cases* where the payment of it adds to consumer's surplus (as measured in money) more than the addition made to aggregate real costs of production (as measured in money); and that, where conditions of decreasing supply price (from the standpoint of the community) prevail, there must *always* – under conditions of simple competition – be

> some rate of bounty that will accomplish this. The amount of money actually disbursed by the State in paying the bounty, being in large part a transfer and not a using-up of resources, is not, as such, a factor in the problem.[85]

To sum, the main preoccupation of British fiscal theorists remains the unproductive nature of public services. That diplomacy, national defense, and fire protection have fallen under the aegis of the State is the result of historical realities. Private entrepreneurs shun these services because they are unprofitable. But, as these services constitute the essentials of any societal life, they must be provided even if their provision entailed a payment that exceeds a comparable market price. Hence, the State, acting as a responsible caretaker, has assumed the task of managing these (unproductive) services in such a manner that their provision causes least sacrifice to household budgets. The State's main concern must be to minimize this sacrifice by devising a scheme whereby the total tax bill is divided among the citizens in a most equitable manner. This entails a distribution system based on each individual's relative welfare position as determined by his assets, inheritance, or income. The benefit approach offers no help in this regard, since subjective valuation, while the prime mover in the private economy, is not applicable in the determination of the benefit shares from public services. Consequently, a quid pro quo solution proposed by the benefit approach is out of question. The only use of subjective valuation in fiscal analysis is in the measurement of the amount of sacrifice that taxation inflicts to individual budgets. Yet, public expenditures are the necessary fixtures of modern society, and their expenditures must be covered one way or the other. Consequently each citizen must honor his respective fiscal obligation as determined by his ability to pay. Citizens generally comply with this reality, as they have come to perceive taxes as a premium they have to pay to maintain their respective welfare position. Fortunately, because the variety and extent of public expenditure is kept to a minimum, the required public revenue, hence the accompanying coercion will be correspondingly small.

4
Italian Fiscal Doctrine*: The Benefit View

As in Britain, so in Italy up to the 1880's, public finance had been regarded as an appendix to political economy dealing with the problems of taxation. The premise that the solution to these problems should be sought in the economics proper rather than in law, politics, history, or philosophy was established in Italy as early as in the 1850s by Francesco Ferrara, the revered teacher of the three founders of Italian fiscal doctrine – Maffeo Pantaleoni, Antonio De Viti de Marco, and Ugo Mazzola.[1]

Ferrara's argument was founded on two postulates. The first was that any economic good, private or public, must necessarily be productive since it was intended to satisfy either a private or a collective want. Second, any economic choice must be based on individual preferences, since it was ultimately the individual who paid for the cost of production and derived the utility from consuming an economic good, regardless of whether the exchange took place in the private or in the public sector of the economy. These two postulates, taken together, gave rise to the premise that suppliers and consumers of public goods would take into consideration, when organizing their respective budgets, the relative productivity of these goods to satisfy collective wants. In other words, tax collectors and taxpayers would act in the public economy exactly like producers and consumers operating in the private economy. That is, they would consider a tax as nothing but a price ascribed by the producer-State for the utility that a collective good imparted to the consumer-taxpayer. As aptly put by Ferrara, "the tax, in its pure significance, would represent neither a sacrifice nor a violence exercised on the contributor by some superior: it would represent a *price*... for all the great advantages which the State provides for us."[2] This tenet, which constitutes the heart of the benefit principle of taxation, set apart Italian fiscal doctrine from the British doctrine of public finance, which, having deemed the activity of the fiscal authority categorically *un*productive, concerned itself exclusively with the problem of minimizing the sacrifice that the financing of public services inflicted upon taxpayers.

Imbued with the teachings of Ferrara,[3] and simultaneously subscribing to the operational framework introduced in the previous decade by Jevons, Menger, and Walras, Pantaleoni, De Viti, and Mazzola proceeded to rest the actions of the consumer-taxpayer and producer-State upon a marginalist foundation. Their collective efforts, which appeared in print in the period extending from 1883 to 1890, proved extremely fruitful as they resulted in the establishment of a distinct fiscal doctrine that influenced not only contemporary Italian writers, but also many important scholars of public sector economics from across the borders. As such, Pantaleoni, De Viti, and Mazzola have come to be recognized, at least by their compatriots, as the founding fathers of pure fiscal theory.

Most Italians are convinced that their ancestors were the unsung fountainheads of the mother discipline as well. As evidence, they point out the many works of some eighteenth-century Italian political economists who expounded original thoughts on value, money, population, and international trade.[4] Nowhere was this claim defended more ardently than in the prefaces Ferrara wrote in a series of textbooks published in the 1850s and 1870s under the rubric *Biblioteca dell'economista*.[5] Also Pantaleoni, in numerous articles he published in Italy's top economic journal at the time, *Giornale degli economisti*, argued that some classical Italian economists were the unrecognized precursors of the neo-classical theory of value. Italian authors were not the only ones to advance this claim. To illustrate, Otto Weinberger pointed out that Ferdinando Galiani (1728–87) had argued for the abolition of interest rate restrictions, Pietro Verri (1728–97) had pleaded for the lifting of trade restrictions, and Giammaria Ortes (1713–90) had preceded Malthus's population studies.[6] Another admirer of early Italian economists went so far as to suggest that Smith's 1776 book had been indebted to Verri and that Smith merely extrapolated on an even earlier work, that of Antonio Serra (1550?–1610?).[7] One can add to this list the names of Filippo Briganti (1780), who almost a century before Stanley Jevons (1871) defined economics as "mechanics of pleasure, or hedonism," and Cesare Beccaria (1771), who discerned over a century before Edgeworth (1881) in the law of self-interest the exact counterpart of the law of gravity.[8]

To assess these claims is beyond the scope of this work.[9] Whether Smith read Verri or Serra, Jevons was familiar with Briganti, or Edgeworth knew of Beccaria's *Elementi di economia pubblica* may never be known. But political economy certainly was an Italian vocation and classical Italian economists no doubt developed many authentic economic arguments. To illustrate:

> First it was Italian writers – namely Ludovico Muratori, Ferdinando Paoletti, [Antonio] Genovesi, and others – who had pleaded for "the greatest happiness of the greatest number" many years before the publication of Bentham's well known books. Second, it is established beyond doubt that [Giammaria] Ortes in his *Riflessioni sulla popolazione* (1790b) had already pointed out the disproportion between the increase of population and that of subsistence – even stating and discussing the geometrical growth of population – twenty or twenty-five years before Malthus. In England M'Culloch afterward went so far as to declare in his *Literature of Political Economy* that what was right in the doctrine of Malthus had been already stated [by yet another] Italian economist, Giovanni Botero, in his book *Della ragione di Stato* (1589). The works of Botero, furthermore, had been translated into English; and it is strange that Malthus did not mention him, although he cited Machiavelli and was accustomed to read Italian texts.[10]

By and large, however, the influence of the Italians on British economists flowed in the other direction. Italian political economists closely followed and did not hesitate to accommodate within their framework of analysis the contributions of English-language authors. To illustrate, when Stanley Jevons developed marginal utility analysis in 1871, Italian economists appropriated it immediately. One reason this operational context found such a fertile ground in Italy might be that the nexus between utility and value had already been established in that country by Galiani, Verri, Ortes, Beccaria, Muratori, Paoletti, Briganti, and Genovesi. Meanwhile, Ferrara vigorously expounded in the preceding 20 years that the value of a commodity derived not from scarcity or cost of production, but from its utility.

The problem for Italian students of the *public* economy, however, was that when they merged the principle of equimarginality with the newly revived benefit principle of taxation they came up with inconsistent results. It was mentioned in the preceding chapter that British public economists found a wholesale solution to this problem by embracing the *other* fiscal precept, ability-to-pay, as the proper basis of taxation. This methodological move allowed British authors to emancipate the fiscal authority from the rules and consequences of the market process.

The Italians, by contrast, were reluctant to dispose of the benefit principle, whose roots in their land traced all the way back to Tommaso Campanella.[11] Ferrara's contribution was to transform Campanella's dictum of heavenly justice into a principle of fiscal equilibrium, and this twist produced a lasting impression on the three fiscal scientists.

Pantaleoni, De Viti de Marco, and Mazzola were conversant not only with the contributions of early Italian benefit-view authors but also with those of Grotius, Rousseau, and Locke.[12] All three were fluent in multiple foreign languages and fully abreast of contemporary economic literature. Mazzola is known to have read Sax's *Grundlegung der theoretischen Staatswirthschaft* and Wieser's *Der natürliche Wert* in their original German. Pantaleoni, whose mother was English and who graduated from University of Potsdam in classical studies before obtaining his law doctorate from University of Rome, was equally well-versed in English, German, and French economic literature. As for De Viti, married to an American woman, he was fully trilingual in English, French, and Italian.

These men followed the lead of their mentor, Ferrara by recasting the benefit principle as a condition of efficiency in the supply and demand of public goods while diverging more and more from the teachings of their British counterparts, who extended the benefit principle to the taxation side of the public budget without any revision. Pantaleoni, De Viti, and Mazzola were of the opinion that the benefit principle needed to undergo a thorough rehabilitation before being applied to the entire domain of public sector economics. They agreed with the British doctrine that the relation between the taxpayer and the tax collector was one of voluntary exchange, and with the Austrian fiscal dictum that individual valuation should be the prime mover of the fiscal process. At the same time, they believed that the determination of the prices of public goods unfolded differently in the public economy than what was being perpetuated by contemporary British and Austrian authors. Specifically, Pantaleoni, De Viti, and Mazzola maintained that while the tax was a price for the consumption of present or future public goods, the equilibrium of supply and demand of public goods was achieved within the parameters of a political market, one in which the suppliers were represented by average parliamentary representatives and the consumers by average voters.[13]

General characteristics of classical Italian fiscal theory

Italian theory of public finance, *Scienza delle finanze*, like *Staatswirtschaft*, its German counterpart, examines the economic activity of the State complete with its political, social, and legal implications.[14] The integrative nature of the *Scienza* is evident in the following definition taken from a pre-War edition of *Enciclopedia italiana* (1929–36):

> the science of public finance, or public economics, taken as a whole, studies the economic principles, political objectives, and legal norms that govern the acquisition, management, and employment of economic resources by political bodies for the satisfaction of collective needs, or, more tersely though less precisely, the economic, historical, and legal distribution of the cost of the production of collective services among the individual members of the political system.[15]

The *Scienza*, owing to its vast scope as displayed in the earlier definition, came to be arranged in the Italian academic environment by the 1880s into three closely interrelated branches of scholarship: *economia finanziaria* (fiscal economics), *politica finanziaria* (fiscal politics), and *diritto finanziario* (fiscal law), each subfield observing the public economy from a distinct vantage point. As noted by Buchanan, *economia finanziaria*, constituting the theoretical core of the discipline, was held in higher esteem in Italy than conventional economic theory to the point that all outstanding Italian economists felt themselves compelled to do some work in the field.[16] But De Viti de Marco, Pantaleoni, and Mazzola, devoted themselves to *economia finanziaria* more than any other Italian political economist. And they served their calling well, since, in the process, they elevated their specialty to a par with the nascent price theory. They achieved this feat by equipping fiscal economics with the same formidable analytical tool, marginal calculus, which Jevons, Menger, and Walras had just successfully grafted onto private economics.

De Viti's involvement generated farther-reaching consequences for the development of *economia finanziaria* as compared to that of Pantaleoni or Mazzola.[17] For, De Viti, after having demonstrated that economic equilibrium could be attained in the public sector in the same fashion as it was achieved in the private sector, ventured to bring about a grander equilibrium, one that complied not only with the principles governing the public economy, but also with those affecting modern polity. This gave an unprecedented impetus to *Scienza delle finanze*, as it motivated both notable economic scientists (such as Benvenuto Griziotti and Carlo Conigliani) to explore the political foundation of the public economy and highly regarded political scientists (such as Gaetano Mosca and Benedetto Croce) to scrutinize the economic underpinnings of the political organization.[18] The result was the establishment of *Scienza delle finanze* as an autonomous field of scholarship with vast interfaces with political science, philosophy, sociology, public law, history, and public administration.[19]

Scienza delle finanze had previously been studied in Italy apart from political economy. But this was done "... merely for the practical reason of division of scientific labour that was necessary by the fact that professional economists found it impossible to include along with general economic phenomena the very numerous ... phenomena which [were] associated with the life of the State."[20] However, in Pantaleoni's, De Viti's, and Mazzola's views, the separation served only to degenerate public finance into an amorphous scholastic entity hopelessly out of place in the face of myriad fiscal problems affecting Italian society. What was needed was to bolster none other than the scientific foundation of this economic discipline. The new fiscal science, as envisaged by Pantaleoni, De Viti, and Mazzola, should be recast against a pure-economic backdrop. This would provide the fiscal authority with more useful guidelines to govern the public sector than those culled from sociological, political, legal, or philosophical inquiry, or, as in the case of ongoing fiscal politics, sheer empiricism. It was with this conviction that these three economists proceeded to expound the new parameters of fiscal science.[21] The product of their endeavor was a refreshingly holistic yet decidedly pure theory of public economics.[22]

Interestingly, the three founders of the new science did not follow identical methodological paths. Pantaleoni was more interested in the supply side of the fiscal act. In the process, he developed a fiscal model whereby the providers of public goods aimed to maximize collective utility by equating the marginal yields of alternative public expenditures. De Viti attributed more importance to the demand side of the public account. What were the properties of certain goods that satisfied the collective wants of the demanders of public goods? How did these properties change over time? What was the process through which the prices of these goods were determined? De Viti's grand design was to accommodate these concerns within the framework of a political market in which the consumers of collective goods initiated the exchange process and the fiscal authority supplied the appropriate public goods under the provisions of a representative-democratic constitution. Mazzola's monumental achievement was to cast the equilibrium conditions within the Walrasian framework, showing that the taxpayer reached equilibrium by, first, determining his perceived need for a public and a private good; second, equalizing the marginal rates of substitution between the public good and the private good; and finally, equalizing these rates to the goods' marginal costs, that is, their marginal rates of transformation.[23]

What follows is a more detailed examination of the contributions of Pantaleoni, De Viti, and Mazzola to the theory of public economics. The exposition unfolds in chronological order to emphasize the developmental path along which Italian fiscal doctrine traversed before reaching the definitive phase characterized by Mazzola.

Pantaleoni and the "Rational" fiscal authority

In the early 1880s, immediately after political economy was placed on a new footing by the introduction of marginal calculus, Italian fiscal scientists proceeded to determine the prices of public goods in the manner in which Walras, Menger, and Jevons determined the prices of private goods. Maffeo Pantaleoni was the first political economist anywhere to have applied marginal analysis in the determination of fiscal equilibrium. He was also the first to apply this calculus to the *expenditure* side of the budget. In his 1883 work, *Contributo alla teoria del riparto delle spese pubbliche* [Contribution to the theory of Allocation of Public Expenditures], he places the fiscal authority squarely within the framework of rational egoism. He deems the State's ends to be basically reconcilable with those of the individual citizen, who, in Pantaleoni's view, is not an egoist acting exclusively to maximize his own happiness, but a "tribal" egoist, who is so constituted as to identify his own maximum happiness with that of his species.[24] Hence, according to Pantaleoni, the fiscal arm of the State is a conduit of individual happiness, as it serves the tribal egoist to attain both sets of wants, private and social.[25] Pantaleoni thus establishes an important dimension of the nascent *Scienza*: social wants and private wants are complementary to each other and *together* contribute to the total satisfaction Economic Man. Consequently, the tribal Economic Man, while making sure that ultimately his own self is satisfied, would voluntarily contribute to social ends to enhance the total utility he could derive from societal life.

The State thus emerges as a fixture of human society neither for any supernatural reasons nor for the sole purpose of laying the ground for Economic Man to promote his individual hedonism. Assuming a surplus, rather than a situation of tradeoff between social and personal wants, Pantaleoni views the former category of wants as an extension of individual wants. This new frame of reference, subsequently formalized by Mazzola, led Italian fiscal economists to develop more auspicious fiscal premises than those advanced by their English-speaking counterparts. For, as was discussed in the previous chapter, in the views of the latter group of political economists the State was a necessary evil, tolerated in human society simply because it fostered individual liberty by preventing internal and external predation and because it provided certain services shunned by entrepreneurs. This paradigm switch would in no way deter economic analysis. On the contrary:

> ... economic problems may be worked out just as easily and correctly by taking as our rule the hypothesis of a *homo oeconomicus* actuated by tribal egoism, who with regard to each act will compare the expected increase of tribal happiness ... [as by starting with] the hypothesis of a *homo oeconomicus* actuated by individual egoism. It must be observed ... that the wider hypothesis of a *homo oeconomicus* actuated by tribal egoism ... is the simpler and truer one, and that by its means the scope of ordinary economic problems is extended to comprise those also which are usually classified separately as forming part of a special class of problems of State economics.[26]

The postulate of tribal egoism does not apply only to the taxpayer. Pantaleoni envisages a society in which the elected representatives of the State also act as tribal egoists. Both groups of individuals are motivated, in the first place, by a given set of immediate interests (say, a taxpayer in need of a serious health problem would seek a nearby hospital whereas a public administrator in need of defraying the current expenses of his bureau would seek appropriate funds). In the second place, the two parties act in conformity with a series of long-term interests, and bring them into harmony with the first by means of complex political processes (say, a taxpayer would demand a new hospital to be built in his neighborhood whereas the public administrator would request a larger budget from the central authority to accommodate the growing demand for the services provided by his bureau).

The complexity inherent in the political process revolving around the demand and supply of public goods should not daunt the fiscal economist. For, first and foremost, the fiscal administrator will be cognizant of the fact that total satisfaction of the citizens will ultimately depend on how well his office has allocated public goods in conformity with present and future demand. To safeguard all current and prospective interests of the electorate, the fiscal authority will assign appropriate weights to social wants when preparing the expenditure side of the public account. What fiscal administrators would need in this endeavor is purely economic, not political, reasoning. And, they have an unerring decision rule available to them in this regard: it is none other than marginal calculus, which requires the allocation of public expenditures in such a way that the marginal yields from equivalent units are equalized. A happy joint product of this simple calculation is that, when the functionaries of the government are maximizing the total utility of public expenditures, they are also maximizing the period of their tenure.

Pantaleoni is not unaware that his model of the public economy manifests an inherent difficulty in attaining equilibrium as compared with private economy. Indeed, the equalization of the marginal yields of public outlays does not come about through Walrasian *tâtonnement*. In this particular market, the allocator of public funds – say, the finance minister – will be continuously sidetracked in that duty by a host of non-economic considerations. The minister's political temptations will not result in substantial divergence from the Walrasian construct, however. For, even a politician of "average rationality," as represented by the typical member of Parliament, will perceive, after reflecting upon the complementary character of public goods from the point of view of the taxpayer, that the best rule for allocating the budgetary burden is marginal, and not political, calculus.[27] Hence, as was remarked by Musgrave,[28] Pantaleoni establishes as early as 1883 the two distinguishing characteristics of Italian fiscal doctrine: (1) the two sides of the government budget are to be determined jointly; and, (2) the satisfaction of social wants are to be tied to the preferences of individual taxpayers, no matter whether the actual valuation of the public good in question is made by the functionaries of the State.

Most English-language students of public finance are probably familiar with the 1883 essay of Pantaleoni, especially considering that it is reprinted in its entirety in Musgrave's and Peacock's *Classics* (1959).[29] But they may not have been acquainted with Pantaleoni's later relevant contributions. Pantaleoni's yet-to-be-translated 1891 work, *Cenni sul concetto di massimi edonistici individuali e collettivi* [Notes on the Concept of Individual and Collective Precepts of Hedonism], in which he elaborates on the concept of complementary nature of public goods, is probably unknown outside Italy.[30] Also likely unknown is his 1913 work, *Atto economico* [Economic Act], in which he expounds the view that the public-economic act, though stemming from the egoistic nature of man, cannot be explained by economic reasoning alone and that no equilibrium in the public economy would be satisfactory unless a political one is simultaneously achieved.[31] Similarly in his *Una visione cinematographica del progresso della scienza economica* [A Cinematographic View of the

Progress of Economic Science],[32] Pantaleoni, as the first proponent of the newly emerging paradigm of Italian fiscal theory, after having distinguished between "political" prices and "economic" prices, warns the politician of the grave consequences of relying on political prices alone and reminds him that only economic prices can be conducive to obtaining equilibrium in the public sector. Another important work of Pantaleoni, his 1889 book, *Principii di economia pura* [Principles of Pure economics], in spite of the fact that it became available in English in 1957, has not yet been referred to in the English-language treatment of classical Italian fiscal theory. And that is rather unfortunate, since that work, though technically belonging to theory of private markets, contains many useful insights of Pantaleoni's germane to public sector economics.

Pantaleoni's interest in fiscal theory was secondary to his involvement with price theory. He was particular in calling this field "economic science" and not "political economy," thus distinguishing himself from most fellow Italian political economists for his belief that economic discourse could not generate satisfying outcomes unless it was based on mathematical characterization. His 1889 textbook mentioned in the previous paragraph, *Principii di economia pura*, precedes Pareto's *Cours* by seven years and rivals Marshall's *Principles* both in scope of coverage and depth of analysis. When he turned his attention to fiscal theory, Pantaleoni naturally retained his mastery of the concept of utility, augmented by his exquisite grasp of marginality, which he had gleaned largely from Walras.[33]

Pantaleoni's view of the "political" market, whereby the Walrasian solution becomes a possibility via the politician's invisible hand came immediately under attack from contemporaneous fiscal economists in Italy and abroad who strove to build a model of the public economy resting directly upon the preferences of the taxpayer. But as these criticisms were more concurrently aimed at De Viti's postulate of a "sentient" fiscal authority than Pantaleoni's proposition of a "rational" allocator of public funds, we now turn to De Viti's views in this regard.

De Viti de Marco and the "Sentient" fiscal authority[34]

The productive life of Marquis Antonio De Viti de Marco – which began in 1879, when his first work appeared in *La rivista europea internazionale*, and ended in 1939, when the last revised edition of his celebrated textbook came out – almost exactly coincides with the life span of the classical Italian theory of public finance, which, as pointed out by the illustrious student of that doctrine, "covered approximately a sixty-year period extending from 1880 to 1940."[35] The fundamental role De Viti played in the development of the *Scienza* needs no substantiation. *Il carattere teorico dell'economia finanziaria* [The Theoretical Character of Financial Economics] (1888), in which De Viti expounded his views on public goods, public debt, and fiscal burden, firmly establishes him as the principal founder of the Italian public finance tradition.[36]

The *Scienza delle finanze*, as it stood at the time of the appearance of De Viti's *Il carattere teorico*, did not intimate a promising future. In the words of Luigi Einaudi, the star pupil – and later the principal collaborator – of De Viti's, fiscal literature in the early 1880s constituted "a sorry batch of loose political, economic, and practical precepts, rambling discussions of philosophic themes and values, and desultory legal comments."[37] As this unpropitious material failed to produce adequate fiscal outcomes in the hands of a string of eminent political economists who, following the unification of the country, served as finance ministers (Sella, Magliani, Minghetti, not to mention the venerable Ferrara himself), serious doubts were voiced in the country's academic circles as to whether economic criteria were relevant for effective fiscal decision-making at all. The criticism persisted even after Pantaleoni (1883), De Viti (1888), and Mazzola (1890) successfully incorporated marginal calculus into *economia finanziaria*.

Giuseppe Ricca-Salerno (1888), inspired by the Austrian fiscal theorist Emil Sax (1883), argued that though the Walrasian model was no doubt conducive to the determination of the prices of private goods, as well as some collective goods whose benefits could directly be imputed to an individual, it would be inoperative in the determination of the prices of ordinary public goods whose benefits were indivisible. Ricca-Salerno did not believe (as De Viti, Pantaleoni, and Mazzola did) that an individual was equipped to array all his private and collective wants in a single continuum and to forego a lower-ranking private want for a higher-ranking collective want. Echoing Sax, he argued that, in the public economy, individuals actually proceeded in accordance with the precepts of "mutualism and altruism," a behavioral pattern plainly observable among the members of private associations. These individuals, having lived through comparable experiences, would readily discern the relative importance of each item in the common agenda and naturally go along with the majority rule in the attainment of common good. In short, Ricca-Salerno was urging fellow fiscal scientists to eschew Walras's *economic* template built upon the ill-fitting axiom of egoism and to espouse a *psychological* construct – that of Sax – which, stemming from the axiom of sympathy rather than egoism, would bring forth fiscal equilibrium in democratic societies.

Another detractor, Vilfredo Pareto (1916) directed his criticism at the second component of the economic axiom – rationality. He started his argument by pointing out that human beings displayed two kinds of conduct, rational and non-rational, depending upon whether or not they employed efficient means to reach their objectives. Pareto found that Walras's characterization of rational behavior, though in full swing in the private economy, was grossly out of place in the public sector.[38] Pareto envisioned the latter environment as part of the sociopolitical realm in which human conduct is governed by myths, taboos, and half-truths, rather than logic. Ruling elites enkindled these atavistic beliefs in order to perpetuate their political privileges. Thus, to put such a powerful construct as Walrasian "rational mechanics" in the hands of a ruling class would only serve to buttress that group's grip on the general population. Pareto characterized the contributions of his fellow "scientists" of public finance as misplaced efforts to straitjacket the multi-faceted, non-rational demeanor of Social Man into the narrowly focused, strictly rational disposition of Economic Man. He exhorted Italian fiscal economists, De Viti in particular,[39] to endow their "art" with a *sociologically* valid operational framework, such as the one developed by himself, which befitted the behavioral constitution of the ordinary citizen as perfectly as the Walrasian model suited the comportment of the archetypal economic agent.[40]

It occurred to De Viti that unless he put Ricca-Salerno's and Pareto's criticisms to rest, the fledgling Science of Public Finance would never arise from the chaos from which he was trying to rescue it. More specifically, De Viti believed that:

> ... to call a fiscal decision rule ["psychological" or "sociological"] amounts to calling it a "synthetic" one, based on a vast number of conflicting interests as between individual classes and parties, or passions, sentiments, and prejudices, which vary from place to place and moment to moment ... De Viti ... saw in all these things – the tangle of facts; the special interest groups, orders, and classes; the variety of tax systems created in various times and places – certain vital points of orientation ... What he did was to study, in a logical manner, what would be the actions – and the consequences of the actions – of those who govern, according as the latter are assumed to be bent upon benefiting themselves, on the one hand, [and] the whole nation, on the other. It is precisely because De Viti wished to remain in the abstract

> field of [economic] science that his [contribution would constitute] a precious guide to the practical man.[41]

De Viti, evidently alluding to Ricca-Salerno's and Pareto's rebukes, emphasizes right at the outset that the relationships that exist between the fiscal authority and individual citizens are governed by nothing but *economic* laws: "Fiscal activity is the economic activity of the State ... [and] economics is the discipline that offers the first necessary and fundamental explanation of the fiscal phenomenon."[42] He goes on to argue that the hedonistic rules applicable to the public sector, once elucidated, would provide politicians and public administrators running this sector of the economy on behalf of the electorate with much more useful guidelines than those that they might cull either from sociological (Paretian) or psychological (Saxist) approaches.

De Viti's model of the political market

De Viti detects a perfect symmetry between conventional economic theory (*economia generale*, or *privata*) and fiscal theory (*economia finanziaria*, or *pubblica*), the former studying the productive activities directed to satisfy individual wants and the latter focusing on the productive activities aiming to fulfil collective wants. Thus, fiscal economics is subsumed by the same theoretical principles governing basic economic relationships. Put in sharper terms, it attempts to solve the ordinary economic problem, namely, the problem requiring the decision-maker to determine what (public) goods to produce and how to distribute among the consumers (taxpayers) the cost of producing those goods. De Viti then posits that the fiscal authority, like any enterprise, will be motivated to produce its goods at minimum cost. Similarly, each taxpayer, like any consumer, will be motivated to maximize his utility from the consumption of (public) goods by paying the least possible price (tax). In other words, the theory of value reigns in the public economy as well, and it is according to the principles of this theory that the producer-State and the consumer-taxpayer will proceed to mutually attain the highest possible level of need fulfillment:

> Our conclusion, then, is that fiscal phenomena belong to the theory of the demand and supply of public goods, just as private-economic phenomena belong to the theory of the demand and supply of private goods. For the individual supplier we substitute the State and for the individual wants we substitute collective wants.[43]

De Viti is keenly aware of two significant differences that nevertheless remain between conventional economic theory and fiscal theory. The first emanates from the complementary nature of public goods.

> So long as man lives in isolation, one can conceive of the existence only of individual wants. But when man passes from a state of isolation to life in society, then there arise, and are added to the individual wants already existing, a series of requirements that did not exist before. For example, the individual will feel the need that his person and his goods should be defended against the attacks of other members of his social group; in addition, he will feel the need of resolving in some way the disputes that arise between him and other individuals to whom he is bound by economic, ethical, or political ties; and finally – as one passes from the communal life of the various social groups within a political aggregate to the communal life of the various political aggregates which make up the larger international community – he will feel the need for national defence and for the systemisation of the relationships which connect him to other nations. Wants, or needs, of this type, which are born in a group from the very fact of social life, we shall call *collective wants*. But in the last analysis, these collective wants are *felt* by the individual. We must not allow the word *collective* to deceive us into believing that we are discussing needs that are felt by the group taken as a whole, as if this group were a sentient organism, capable of feeling pleasure or pain.[44]

The second difference concerns the coercive nature of the fiscal process. Collective wants represent the *conflicting* interests of the various groups that make up the social fabric. One group may demand, say, more national defense and less public education while another may demand less of the former and more of the latter. It is the State's responsibility to intervene and resolve this impasse.

> Hence arises the following difference between … private economy and … public [economy]: viz., that, in the former, every individual want is satisfied in proportion to the demand of every individual, and the total demand is the arithmetic sum of individual demands; whereas in public [economy] the collective demand is the resultant of the conflicting evaluations of various groups and individuals. Thus the hatter produces exactly as many hats as there are individuals requiring them; but he does not take into account those who do not wear hats. The State, however, if it furnishes headgear to its soldiers,

> must produce as many hats as there are soldiers, including those who do not ask for them.[45]

Thus, De Viti transcends Pantaleoni, who expects the archetypal provider of public goods, the finance minister, to act according to standard economic behavior based on rationality. The minister's task, in Pantaleoni's view, consists simply of equating the marginal yields of alternative expenditure projects. De Viti, meanwhile, requires the representatives of the fiscal authority additionally to be sentient, that is receptive to the conflicting collective wants of different groups and to be motivated to produce a fiscal solution that, in the long run, will be in the best interests of *all* key social groups.

The fiscal decision-making process

The theoretical framework developed by De Viti has been aptly termed by some modern critics as one of *histoire raisonée*.[46] What is central in De Viti's work is indeed an unmistakable quest for a fit between some pivotal fiscal-theoretic parameters and some historical landmarks on the path of the development of modern State. We should resist the urge to label this perspective as anachronistic and provincial. For it is likely that today's students of the public economy, imbued with the positivistic orientation of the mother science, stand to greatly benefit from the historical perspective adopted by De Viti. De Viti's model serves to give prominence to the political decision-making process that obviously affects fiscal equilibrium while at the same time accentuating the transformation that this decisional process has undergone as the constitutional parameters have progressed over time from feudalistic to democratic.

De Viti goes on to discuss two polar political markets, monopolistic and cooperative, the first representing the feudal State in which the fiscal authority pays no heed to taxpayer demand and the second the democratic State, in which fiscal equilibrium is achieved by the principle of equimarginality between the demand and supply of public goods. In the monopolistic State, structured as an absolute monarchy or oligarchy, a ruling class makes fiscal decisions single-handedly with respect to the taxation as well as the expenditure side of the fiscal account. In this State the governing elite determines the tax-price in such a way that after the citizens "buy" the public good in question the elite earns an "excess profit" for itself. The monopolistic State is in a more favorable position than the monopolistic firm operating in the private economy, since the fiscal authority can not only set the tax-price as high as it wishes, but it can force citizens to consume the public good under consideration. Additionally, the State may use its administrative and legal faculties to proscribe the use of any substitute (public) goods today or in the future.

Owing to these favorable conditions, the monopolistic political market can last a very long time, but not indefinitely. A glance at the political histories of many nations which started off as monarchies or oligarchies would reveal the fact that over the centuries larger and larger proportions of citizens have come to participate in the affairs of the State, and that this result was attained after considerable struggle. Hence, it is reasonable to envisage the other extreme of the spectrum where the struggle for participation has culminated in a final stage in which *all* citizens are invited to express their judgment concerning the appropriateness of an imminent public project. In this second scenario, which precedes Lindahl's mise-en-scène by a full three decades, the suppliers and consumers of public goods are one and the same. It is impossible in this model to generate an excess profit. The production is undertaken at net cost, which includes, to be sure, a portion that taxpayers would pay for the efforts of their elected agents and to indemnify the sacrifice felt by the members of the minority who deem the public good overpriced.

According to De Viti, reality lies somewhere between the monopolistic and the cooperative State. In modern societies, the valuation of public goods is made by the elected agents of taxpayers within the limits of the mandate given them by the voters under the rules of the prevailing constitution. Except for one important difference, the role these agents play in the public economy resembles that of the management of a modern corporation to which the stockholders have delegated their authority. The difference is that the fiscal authority has at its disposal a power that private managers ordinarily lack, the power of compulsion. Thus, the coercive nature of the fiscal authority emerges as an integrative element of Italian fiscal doctrine. This feature has invited serious criticism, which will be discussed in the next section.

Going back to the spectrum of political markets delineated by De Viti, he discerns that, throughout this historical progression, it has always been the individual citizen who *personally* has experienced both the satisfaction stemming from the consumption of a public good and the burden associated with its financing. De Viti adds that nowhere in history does one observe a State that was totally absolute, that is, one in which the ruling class summarily disregarded the citizens' preferences concerning collective goods. If anything, the State has become more and more responsive to the collective wants of the electorate as larger and larger proportions of constituents have gained the right to give their approval to the public budget. De Viti professes that the democratic trend must eventually culminate in a happy stage in which individual preferences will be *directly* instrumental in producing the fiscal account. Until the direct-democratic ideal is attained, however, within the framework of the ubiquitous *representative*-democratic constitutional system, it will be not the taxpayers, but their elected agents who will decide, within the limits of the mandate granted by the former, what public goods to produce and how to distribute the tax burden among the constituents.

As such, De Viti provides the fiscal arm of the State an invaluable decisional tool. Einaudi stresses this dimension of De Viti's construct of the public economy in following terms:

> The statesman who, when he ... looks not for minute rules of daily life, but for a guide which, like a beacon, will direct him in the choice of the road which he seeks, and which he will later traverse in very different ways according to the changing phases of history, will always be grateful to de Viti for having offered two guiding lights. One of these [the monopolistic State] he will certainly wish to avoid; for no one wishes to govern peoples for one's own sake or for that of the group to which one belongs. The other beacon [cooperative State] flashes a hope of arrival in a port which will represent a gain for all, the attainment of that goal which is best suited to the whole nation.[47]

Tracing the historical development of England from the thirteenth century onward, De Viti concludes that the right of taxpayers to approve the total public revenue and to distribute it among the various public expenditures remains the most important element in the modern State and that this process must be made an integral part of modern theory of public finance. That a politically privileged *class* is entrusted with the task of governing the public economy does not necessarily entail a *collective* choice process. In De Viti's model of the public economy – as in that of Pantaleoni and Mazzola – it is always an *individual member* of the governing group, typically the finance minister, who is entrusted with the task of making fiscal decisions. The minister, in turn, is assumed to be sensitive to the collective wants emanating from the populace and be cognizant of the eventuality that, if he were to fail to satisfy the collective wants of the majority, he and his political cohorts would lose their offices in the subsequent election. Seeking an appropriate decision rule for the accurate valuation of public goods, the minister therefore focuses on the preferences of the *average* voter, not only because such preferences would yield a good approximation of the general demand for public goods, but also because they are easily inferable from ordinary means of mass communication, such as the press, universities, and professional organizations.

The coercive element in Italian fiscal doctrine

Inevitably, according to De Viti, until the society has reached the direct-democratic stage, there will always be a tax-paying minority that will consider the fiscal account overpriced vis-à-vis their personal valuations. The problem for the members of this minority is that they, though finding the fiscal account unproductive, are nevertheless compelled to contribute to it. De Viti is genuinely apprehensive about this problem, though he sees it as a necessary fixture of the contemporary fiscal decision-making process. He remarks that, in modern parliamentary systems, the citizens, conscious of maintaining a balance between private goods and collective goods, have come to proactively delegate to their elected representatives the power of compulsion to be exercised in the event that a particular minority failed to honor its tax obligation as determined by public law.

Pantaleoni did not recognize the problem of compulsion, for he reasoned that a tribal egoist who would find a public expenditure item overpriced from his own vantage point would eventually go along with the majority decision after reconsidering the want-satisfying properties of the relevant public good for the majority of the electorate. Fiscal compulsion was a non-issue similarly for Mazzola, who believed that his model fully complied with the precepts of both economic efficiency and social justice. De Viti, in his turn, squarely addresses the problem of fiscal coercion and aims to resolve it. In the manner envisaged by De Viti, fiscal coercion emerges as the result of a distinguishing characteristic of public goods, non-excludability, whereby the resenting members of the collectivity cannot be prevented from consuming these commodities. As a result of this inevitability, a measure of fiscal coercion would be felt by a minority.

One group of contemporary Italian economists, especially Enrico Barone and Cesare Cosciani, while agreeing with De Viti's overall characterization of the public economy, remarked that he grossly understated the role of coercion in this economic sector. According to these critics, taxpayers obviously do not freely and voluntarily contribute to the financing of public goods. If they did, there would be no need for fiscal authority. Barone argued that De Viti's prefixing of the distribution of the tax burden by the fiscal authority was essentially equivalent to choosing a social welfare function. However, once such a function was chosen, and action taken in accordance with it, no pretense of voluntary choice needed to be maintained.[48] Similarly Cosciani stated that no fiscal theory should deny that two sets of individual behavior were involved in fiscal decision-making: that of the ruling class and that of the taxpaying group in responding to the alternatives put before them.[49] Thus, no fiscal theory should make light of the compulsory nature of the public revenue raising process.

The second group of economists strived to find ways to make the coercive element in De Viti's fiscal construct more palatable. Puviani, and later Fasiani, allowed the fiscal authority to use certain measures conducive to creating a "fiscal illusion" to bring the perceptions of a given group of taxpayers in line with the majority's wishes. To these economists, such artificial measures would be preferable to resorting to sheer compulsion. Writing in 1897 in his *Teoria della illusione nelle entrate pubbliche* [Theory of Illusion in Public Entries], Puviani stresses that the fiscal authority might create illusions to lead various categories of citizens to think that the tax burden are lighter than what they seem and that the benefits expected from the proposed public expenditure greater than they look like.[50] As for Fasiani, true to his De Vitian roots, he studies fiscal illusion in two limiting cases of political constitution, monopolistic and cooperative, deriving certain acceptable rules of conduct for the fiscal administrator operating in each form of political market. The interesting aspect of fiscal illusion as discussed by Fasiani and Puviani is that while the fiscal administrator consciously influences voter behavior through fiscal illusions the voter continues to behave consistently.[51] In other words, the individual confronting fiscal illusion acts in the same way on two identical instances in different points in times, showing that his learning has not dispelled the illusion and that his utility function has not shifted in the meantime.[52]

De Viti, anticipating the criticism against the compulsory character of his fiscal theory, reacts by formulating a fiscal precept we have encountered earlier and we will elaborate later whereby the governing body adopts the goal of minimizing the fiscal dissatisfaction felt by the minority. The reason De Viti supplies for this condition is that, for entirely selfish reasons, no parliamentary government would risk to alienate any sizeable group of dissatisfied voters.

More on De Viti's view of the public economy

The Devitian edifice is precarious for two reasons. In the first place, there is nothing in "the grand design of De Viti ... to cause the marginal-productivity criteria to be met."[53] Second, De Viti's treatment of the rights of the dissenting minority is uncharacteristically too nonchalant for such an otherwise eminent liberal.[54] De Viti, countered these criticisms by cutting across both of them in a single stroke: the fiscal administrator, discerning that the deviations from the principle of maximum economic advantage will only serve to increase the prices to be imputed to all tax-payers for the production of public services, is likely to conclude that an economically unsubstantiated political gain in the short run would give rise to a graver loss in the long haul.[55] As a result, he will eschew any temptation of political opportunism and will try to serve the economic interests of the largest possible majority of the electorate.

At this juncture, De Viti, evoking his trademark historical constructivism, adds that, in modern public economies, individual taxpayers already have demonstrated a propensity to make appropriate judgments concerning the advisability of various public expenditure projects. In fact, the ordinary citizen has become quite savvy in deciding which of the two alternatives, say, additional hospitals or additional schools, would be more conducive to promoting collective welfare. De Viti calls this cognitive process the "determination of the value to the *community*."[56] A taxpayer will, at the same time, compare the marginal utility he would expect to derive from the public good under consideration with the marginal disutility that the corresponding tax would impose on his budget. This De Viti calls the "determination of the value to the *individual*." Thus, the problem of the distribution of the tax burden is settled at the very moment that the decision is made with respect to the value to the community – that is, the productivity – of the public expenditure. Now De Viti, obviously aware of the eventuality that not all individual citizens will unanimously find a given public good equally productive, expounds yet another fiscal precept: the fiscal administrator must deduct, when determining the utility of a public expenditure from the point of view of the community, the measure of unproductiveness felt by the minority from the measure of productiveness felt by the majority. Unfortunately, however, De Viti does not provide a full explanation as to just how the finance minister is to achieve such a calculational miracle. Instead, taking a sweeping tangent, he reiterates that the valuation of public goods is not essentially different from that of a private good and that, under the provisions of contemporary constitutions, the relationship between the State and the individual citizen already has progressed into a fortuitous partnership, not unlike the kind that has always been thought to exist in the private economy between the producer and the consumer. In fact, according to De Viti,

> the State can be likened to a private citizen both as a legal subject and as an economic agent. This means that the psychological drives and the economic ends, as well as the legal constraints within which the individual is allowed to operate, are identical for both the State and the individual so that a substitution of one for the other can be made, though only in a hypothetical sense and for the sake of reasoning.[57]

Reminding the reader that in economic exchange it is not important *which* of the two partners, the consumer (taxpayer) or the producer (State), does the actual valuation of economic goods, De Viti admonishes the critics of the *Scienza*

> against the common error to the effect that individual valuations of the utility... of [ordinary] public services are impossible because the share of utility which each citizen derives from military defense, ..., the maintenance of highways, [etc.,] is unknown and unknowable. This – it is said – has no counterpart in private economics... [Let us] take a concrete example precisely from private economics: when Jones buys a ticket for a theatrical performance, could it be said that the share of utility which he derives from the performance is known or knowable? Yet no one can doubt that there does exist an economic-exchange relationship between the price of the ticket and the enjoyment that the buyer hopes to derive from its use.[58]

Having asserted that in the public economy valuations of this sort just happen to be typical, De Viti concludes that it is not necessary for the citizen to weigh the tax that he is expected to pay against the portion of the collective good that he is expecting to consume. It is enough simply that the individual compare the tax he is required to pay with the *conjectured* evaluation of the benefit of the collective good in question, with the only condition that the evaluation is made by the same person.[59]

De Viti de Marco: a precursor to the modern theory of public goods

The reflection of De Viti's theory of public goods upon the modern fiscal theory is plain. But why has this reflection not been fully discerned by the international community of public economists? The two universally sanctioned founders of the modern fiscal theory, Wicksell and Lindahl, while professing familiarity with Mazzola's theory of the demand and supply of public goods,[60] did not intimate any affinity with De Viti's work. Worse for De Viti, among the international readers of his main opus, one rarely finds a convert: Samuelson terms De Viti's work downright confusing;[61] Musgrave identifies him as a mere figure among the many followers of the doctrine of voluntary exchange;[62] and Buchanan finds him important only within the flawed political market framework De Viti expounded.[63] What is worse, Musgrave and Peacock (1958), while incorporating the works of Montemartini, Barone, and Mazzola, omitted the work of De Viti altogether. Finally, as for the two English-speaking economists who have reviewed the 1936 translation of De Viti's book, Benham and Simons, only the first was impressed by it while the second found it utterly worthless.[64]

If the occasional non-Italian student of contemporary public finance demonstrates some affinity to De Viti's work nevertheless, the credit should go to Luigi Einaudi who made it his life's goal to bring the views of his mentor to the attention of the international community of fiscal economists. It was directly the result of Einaudi's efforts that De Viti's main work was translated, first into German (in 1932), then into Spanish (in 1934), and subsequently into English (in 1936). It was Einaudi again who supervised the compilation of the second German edition, which came out in 1935. Oskar Morgenstern, the editor of this expanded edition, also was a close collaborator of De Viti's.[65] Yet, Einaudi's and Morgenstern's efforts proved insufficient to generate a good measure of enthusiasm in international academic circles toward De Viti's teachings.[66]

Yet one must admit that De Viti's vision of the public economy, in which the politico-economic motivations of the fiscal bureaucracy are rendered instrumental in the determination of the public budget, provides an apt operational framework in the study of the fiscal process in today's society. Also, nearly 70 years after the appearance of the English translation of De Viti's *Principii*, and in the wake of many a collective choice-oriented model of the public economy that appeared since then, the supply component of the public sector elaborated by De Viti still remains largely undeveloped. On another plane, the constitutional framework envisioned by De Viti, notwithstanding the disconcerting overtone resulting from his concept of the ruling class, is a close representation of the representative-democratic system that, for better or for worse, is the rule rather than an exception in post-modern society.

Accordingly, De Viti, by rendering the fiscal authority an endogenous element in the determination of fiscal equilibrium, acted only as a precursor of the modern theory of public choice.[67] Indeed in De Viti's vision of cooperative public economy, in which the individual is both a consumer of collective goods and a contributor to the expenditure side of the fiscal account, many of the elements of modern public choice are readily discernible. To illustrate, De Viti's use of the "average" voter as the determinant of supply and demand of public goods is but a stone's throw away from Bowen's concept of the median voter that appeared six decades later.

The question as to why Italian fiscal doctrine represented by De Viti has remained outside the reach of the English-language student of public finance is still not answered in a satisfactory manner. It is hoped that once some lingering misconceptions of Italian fiscal doctrine established by Pantaleoni and De Viti and formalized by Mazzola are cleared up, the much-needed unification of Continental and Anglo-Saxon fiscal theories will be closer at hand. It is with this mission that the rest of this chapter deals with the contributions of Mazzola, who is even less known among the fountainheads of the pure theory of public finance.[68]

Ugo Mazzola and the "Efficient" public economy[69]

Mazzola focused directly on the nature of public ends and public wants and the capacity of certain goods for satisfying such ends and wants. He devoted his entire life, which came to an abrupt end when he was only 35, to elevate fiscal economics to an autonomous discipline, whose subject matter, according to Mazzola, radically differed from that of conventional microeconomics. Mazzola fully appreciated the low regard in which fiscal economics was held in Italy in the 1880s when while price theory was taking tremendous strides, *Scienza delle finanze* was in search of a positive foundation. Mazzola agreed with Achille Loria, who complained in 1886 that fiscal economics was falling seriously behind the general progress other social sciences were making and that, unlike them, it was not being rejuvenated from the fount of historico-positive method.[70] Mazzola's answer to Loria was that price theory, too:

> was treated initially only as a political "art." But it made progress continuously, and has only now taken the shape of a "science." The change occurred because price theory has adopted the objective method of analysis. The efforts exerted in the field of theoretical research have resulted in the discovery of certain laws according to

> which economic events actually proceed. Thus, it is now possible to account for the influences underlying conflicting interests in the private economy. Because price theory did not limit research only to everyday problems taking place in the market, it has provided new theoretical insights so that it is now possible to analyze effectively the problems associated with money, banking, insurance, transportation, etc. In the discipline of fiscal theory, in contrast, the search for general principles was either accorded a secondary place or was mingled with extraneous judicial and political elements. For example, the discussion of the problems of the "most equitable" taxation was not preceded by an investigation of the casual links on which certain facts were based. We do not harbor a prejudice against applied work. On the contrary, we are in favor of generating practical solutions to urgent fiscal problems; but we would like "pure" scientific research to have a major part in illuminating the true state of fiscal phenomena.[71]

With *I dati scientifici della finanza pubblica* [The Scientific Elements of Public Finance] (1890), Mazzola attained his goal splendidly. He demonstrated for the first time in Italy and elsewhere that the Science of Public Finance was capable of attaining the dual goals of fiscal optimum, efficiency and justice, by following a purely positive algorithm.

We have seen that when Mazzola set out to systematically analyze the public economy, some key premises of Italian fiscal doctrine already had been set forth by two close colleagues of his, Pantaleoni and De Viti.[72] To reiterate, Pantaleoni (1883) had extended the concept of valuation to the expenditure side of the fiscal account and De Viti (1888) postulated that since there always existed an economic exchange between the State and the citizens, to each service offered by the State must correspond a tax claim. It behooved Mazzola to meld the two parts of the fiscal account into a single product within the marginalist framework.

Like Pantaleoni and De Viti, Mazzola rests his pure theory of public finance directly upon the behavior of Economic Man. The *homo œconomicus* that emerges in *I dati . . .*, however, is radically different from that imagined by contemporary Anglo-Saxon and German political economists. Mazzola explains:

> There exists, in the first place, the aims of the individual. To attain these aims, however, it is necessary [that the individual] first accomplish other aims . . . [M]an does not set aside as his ultimate or direct aim such things as national defense or general security. He wants to

> accomplish his material aims in life or his spiritual aims in the field of moral and intellectual improvement. He cannot arrive at these ends, however, unless he is able to live in such a way that he feels secure against his foreign and internal enemies and is prepared to cooperate with other men for the attainment of aims denied to men who live in a state of isolation. Therefore the "public" aims are distinguished as being "conditional" to the attainment of the ultimate aims of man and as being attainable only through political cooperation. The voluntary association of private individuals would not serve the purpose; what is needed is rather a political cooperation.[73]

Mazzola thus reiterates an important feature of collective goods, that is, they are complementary to private goods. He then emphasizes another key characteristic: the benefits of public goods are indivisible. It is because of the latter feature that price theory cannot be extended to the public economy directly. In Mazzola's usage, the term "indivisibility" also encompasses non-excludability and non-rivalry. The following passage may help illustrate this point:

> The utility of most public goods is complementary and indivisible. The services of law and order, public health, etc. are contributory causes to private satisfaction. But although their consumption produces individual satisfaction, the quantities consumed by each individual cannot be divided up and measured. What is known is simply that public goods enter into individual satisfaction in certain proportions. The indivisibility of consumption constitutes the technical reason preventing the formation of a single market price in the public economy. In the case of a private good, anyone who cannot pay the price is excluded from consumption. But if a public good had a price exceeding its marginal utility for some classes of consumers, their unwillingness to pay the price would not effectively exclude them from consuming the good. To prevent this outcome, the public good must be withdrawn from the market altogether – even from the use of those who are willing to pay the price – for, otherwise, those who wish not to pay would still reap the benefits of the public good in question. This occurs because the market price is the maximum the consumer would pay for the amount of marginal utility that the good would offer. The concept of indivisibility of public goods also explains why the public economy sometimes resorts to a device very similar to private prices – namely, duties or fees – whenever the quantity of a public good consumed can in fact be imputed to the individual.[74]

Consequently, Mazzola postulates that in some instances the price theory can be extended directly to the private economy:

> Fees, or fixed charges, as we have had occasion to observe, represent a price phenomenon in the public economy resembling private prices. For example, the delivery of mail may have different marginal utilities for various users, but the price is uniform. The reasons underlying public fees are well known. The fee is a price, and most often a monopoly price, fixed by the government in conformity with certain purposes.[75]

The prices of pure public goods, meanwhile, are determined in the following manner:

> In the private as well as the public economy, utility-maximizing behavior dictates that the available resources be allocated among various uses in such a way that the marginal utilities of all the goods are, after the allocation, equal. The prices of public goods too are formed in this way, that is, by equating the marginal utilities of public goods after considering the accompanying fiscal burden. This price formation process is different from that of the private market, however, in that it [results in multiple prices].[76]

That multiple prices existed in the public economy is by no means an original idea. Mazzola agrees with Wieser, who remarked in his 1889 work that if, as argued by Sax (1883), the laws of price theory indeed governed both the private and the public economy, then *everyone* would pay a price commensurate with the intensity of the need one felt. The corollary of such an argument would be that wealth would then cease to offer any ascendancy and poverty would cease to constitute a hindrance. Wieser notes, however, that only in the public economy can this result be observed.[77] At the same time, gross inequality in the satisfactions affects the private economy. He is appalled by the spectacle of a society governed by two contradictory laws, one applicable to the private economy which spares the rich, except where they come into competition with each other, and the other applicable to the public economy where the goods possessed by the rich are put at a lower figure.[78] Wieser concludes that such a deeply rooted divergence between the two economic organizations can only be explained by the fact that each serves different purposes. As for the purposes of the public economy, they require that we leave the sphere of the theory of value and trespass into the sphere of justice and philosophy to undertake their analysis.[79]

> Mazzola disagrees with the last part of Wieser's conclusion and replies: The analysis of this matter does not lie outside the limits of the theory of value. We do not need historical or philosophical study: we simply need to know why the prices of certain goods are formed in one way while the prices of certain other goods in another way. This is a question of economics pure and simple, and not of philosophy or jurisprudence.[80]

Mazzola finds that, the overall allocation of resources between private and public goods is governed by nothing but the principle of utility maximization. It is the amount of the complementary utility accorded by the individual to the available public goods that determines the share of the private resources the individual would be willing to allocate to the consumption of the public goods. Mazzola states:

> It will be readily appreciated that [in the public economy] differential utility can arise only from faulty valuation...or when the equilibrium of the scale of utilities is disturbed.[81]

The first problem specified in the preceding excerpt is not endemic to the public economy. In the private economy, too, marginal utilities are not always known. It was precisely in this connection that De Viti had made the famous comment concerning Jones buying a ticket for a theatrical performance without necessarily knowing the share of utility that he would derive from the performance.[82] It is simply that in the public economy goods and services of this sort happen to be typical. Consequently, there will be occasional divergences between the benefits expected from and the price attributed to a public good. It is the *second* problem that fiscal theory has to concentrate on, that is, when there exists a disturbance affecting the scale of utilities. For, it is quite conceivable that the finance minister, after all an elected politician, will alter the average valuation of public goods to favor a given constituency. Mazzola is aware of this possibility though not overly disconcerted by it:

> Such a disequilibrium will occur when agencies to which the valuation is entrusted will decide to serve the interests of a predominating class or person. If they indeed do so, some members of the

> community would be obliged to allocate a larger part of their private resources to public goods than would correspond to the complementary utility that these goods would provide for them, and hence obtain inadequate satisfaction. Some other members, in the meantime, would have at their disposal a larger quantity of private goods obtained at the expense of other economic agents ... Apart from these deviations, however, the law remains valid for the entire [range of public goods].[83]

Wicksell finds that, despite Mazzola's serene attitude about it, fiscal coercion is grossly present in his theory and that it would be a flagrant injustice to force someone to contribute to the financing of a collective expenditure which did not enhance that individual's own interest.[84] Mazzola's economic "law" obviously glosses over this problem and Wicksell's trepidation in this respect is well warranted. Still, it would be an injustice to compare Mazzola's contribution to fiscal theory with that of Wicksell, who, after all, directed all his effort to the rehabilitation of Mazzola's model. A more appropriate comparison can be made between Mazzola and his contemporary Anglo-Saxon counterparts, namely Marshall, Edgeworth, and Sidgwick, in whose hands fiscal theory was reduced to "little more than utilitarian ethics applied to certain economic problems,"[85] not to mention German and Austrian authors, such as Wagner and Sax, who either dispensed with marginal analysis altogether or applied it to the public economy rather clumsily.

In this connection, Mazzola's model of public economy, presented in the Appendix at the end of the chapter, constitutes a rich example of marginalist workmanship. Within that particular operational framework, Mazzola's model exhibits a level of vigor superior to Marshallian–Pigovian construct. The coeval British fiscal doctrine, as described in the previous chapter, relied heavily on taxation theory, concentrating on the development of fiscal policies to help secure economic stability at the expense of omitting the expenditure component of the public account entirely. Only in past 40 years has the British public finance literature taken a turn toward a prescriptive theory of public expenditure, following the contributions of such influential authors as Samuelson, Musgrave, and Buchanan, whose theories were based on the discovery of public goods as a positive element of fiscal analysis. By and large, the Italian concept of public goods still has not penetrated the Anglo-Saxon fiscal doctrine, "and it remained, for the most of the English-speaking economic world, yet another mystery in the Pandora's box of Continental esoterica."[86]

The Italian concept of ruling class

Considering that the English translations of De Viti's and Pantaleoni's main works were made available some time ago and that a pivotal chapter of Mazzola's work was included in Musgrave's and Peacock's *Classics* (1958), it is no longer possible to explain away the apathy by "the linguistic barrier," as it was by Buchanan.[87] It seems that the apathy arises from a conceptual platform. For, when the essential features of the classical Italian fiscal theory were brought by Buchanan, Musgrave, and Peacock to the attention of English-speaking students of the public economy in the late 1950s and early 1960s, that audience had already been exposed to more palatable models of the public economy – such as those expounded by Wicksell, Lindahl, Johansen, Myrdal, and Bowen – whereby the consumers and suppliers of public goods brought about fiscal equilibrium directly and spontaneously. The three Italian authors, meanwhile, were invoking the not-so-invisible fiscal arm of the ruling class in the attainment of fiscal equilibrium.

Yet it must be understood that, despite the unfortunate misnomer "ruling class," what was introduced by Pantaleoni, and was perpetuated in the Italian fiscal science under that rubric, was no means an oligarchical prescription. It was the sociological school, the main rival of the theory of public goods in Italy promoted by Pareto, that adopted the concept of a rotating oligarchy serving its own objectives with little or no feedback from the citizenry. This was precisely the political constitution that De Viti wanted to avoid. In De Viti's terms, modern human society had come a long way from such an unadulterated form of monopolistic State. Under current conditions, the ruling elite, even if it came to power not by a democratic rule, but by chicanery, as envisaged by Gaetano Mosca and Vilfredo Pareto, would want to extend its tenure for as long as possible. And in order to do so, it would constantly compare the utility and the cost of its actions. As such, De Viti's view of a society run by a "sentient" ruling group of politicians elected by a majority for a given term to accomplish a set of economic tasks in the future, while certainly not in agreement with a direct-democratic political construct *à la* Lindahl, does not differ in any substantial way from today's representative-democratic systems, especially those where political parties follow the tradition of adopting and publicizing their official economic programs. Second, if the decisions concerning the supply and pricing of public goods were explained by the Italians largely by the behavior of the politician or bureaucrat rather than the voter, this must be viewed as a happy occurrence, since the supply component of the public economy only recently has attracted the attention of certain public choice-oriented scholars. In the broader view of these scholars, politicians are regarded neither as selfless lawgivers nor as selfish political actors exogenous to the economic happenings in society. They are considered as self-interested competitors trying to maximize returns (power, position, votes, etc.) under certain constraints (reelection, for instance),[88] exactly as construed by the founders of the *Scienza*. Third, before attempting to criticize the Italian theory of public goods on its own merits, it should be recalled that what the Italians had in mind was evidently not an "active" voluntary exchange process whereby the citizens' preferences were translated into votes each time that a fiscal decision was made, but one which can be called a "tranquil" voluntary exchange process, one that took place within certain boundaries recognized by the electorate as well as the politicians, and formalized in a constitution of "consent."[89] Further research would be worthwhile in this connection, for it is conceivable that Pantaleoni, De Viti and Mazzola were read as harboring collectivistic concepts, and their views summarily dismissed, by those who, having subscribed to absolute individualism, have categorically opposed any political scheme in which a voter's status is reduced to that of an acquiescent partner.

Yet, many aspects of the Italian theory deserve criticism. Pantaleoni's concept whereby the pricing of public goods is delegated to an "average" member of parliament, or De Viti's belief that the ruling class would concentrate on "average" voter demand are but two specific examples of these debatable aspects.[90] Even more seriously, the very assumption that the politician's behavior must be rational – or, for that matter, sentient – appears to be entirely evangelical. The exceedingly normative nature of this pivotal assumption was rightly noted by Einaudi (1936) and Buchanan (1960), who, agreeing with Cosciani, argued that De Viti's construct of the public economy could only be rescued if it could be considered a wholly normative one.[91]

Such criticism is well taken. However, it should also be borne in mind that the Italian fiscal theory is not made up only by Pantaleoni, De Viti, and Mazzola, but merely begins with them – very much as the Swedish theory initiated by Wicksell did not stop with Lindahl.[92] In the decades that followed, the main features of the collective choice framework set forth by the founding fathers have been criticized and refined by Italian authors belonging to each and all the three branches of the *Scienza*, as well as those belonging to political and other social sciences. Einaudi, Cosciani, Fasiani, Montemartini, Barone, Conigliani, Borgatta, have all made important contributions in this regard.[93] What emerges from these efforts is a framework that, albeit its salient positive methodology, is surprisingly reconcilable with the normative optimality conditions applicable to the public economy. The Italian theory of public goods enriched with these later contributions appears to be capable of providing public choice-oriented students of modern public finance a much-needed bridge between the positive and normative modes of analysis.

Appendix

In an attempt to render the contributions of the three classical Italian fiscal scientists more accessible to students of modern public finance, this appendix presents a mathematical exposition of the Italian theory of public goods.

According to Pantaleoni, the complementary character of public goods requires that

$$B^1 = B^1(X_1^1, X_2^1)$$

where B^1: total benefit of individual 1; X_1^1: benefit of private good to individual 1; X_2^1: benefit of public good to individual 1.

Similarly, the total cost to individual 1:

$$C^1 = C^1(X_1^1, X_2^1)$$

where X_1^1 and X_2^1 represent the prices for the individual 1 of the private and public good, respectively.

As expounded by Pantaleoni, the fiscal authority must apply "marginal calculus in the allocation of public expenditures in such a way that marginal yields from equivalent units are equalized" (1883, p. 11). Thus:

$$\frac{\partial B^1/\partial X_1^1}{\partial B^1/\partial X_2^1} - \frac{\partial C^1/\partial X_1^1}{\partial C^1/\partial X_2^1} = 0$$

where the ratio on the left is the marginal rate of substitution between the public good and the private good for individual 1, and the ratio on the right is the marginal rate of transformation between the public good and the private good for the same individual.

Because of the summative nature of the benefits emanating from the public good – as discussed by Mazzola in great detail (1890) – taking two individuals, 1 and 2, together:

$$\frac{b^1x_2}{b^1x_1} + \frac{b^2x_2}{b^2x_1} = \frac{cx_2}{cx_1}$$

where the lower-case *b*'s and *c*'s indicate partial derivatives. This shows that the sum of the marginal rates of substitution between the public and private good is equal to the goods' marginal cost. Hence, it can be demonstrated that the Italian theory of public goods preceded the seminal contributions of Samuelson (1954) and Buchanan (1968) by at least 60 years.

5
German Fiscal Doctrine: The Organic View

The roots of this doctrine can be traced directly to the eighteenth-century German cameral science, *Kameralwissenschaft*, which entailed the preparation of the royal fiscal account and the management of royal properties and monopolies by specially trained functionaries. In the larger sense, usually expressed in the plural, *Kameralwissenschaften* denoted the theory and practice of the entire economic and administrative activity of the State. In 1727, the first professorships in *Kameralwissenschaften* were established by Friedrich Wilhelm I at the universities of Halle and Frankfurt/Oder with the express purpose of training public administrators in economics, statistics, finance, and public law.[1] *Kameralwissenschaften* encompassed three closely interrelated specialties, *Wirtschaft*, *Polizeiwissenschaft*, and *Hausewäterschaft*, which dealt, respectively, with problems that pertained to the public economy, public policy and administration, and commercial, industrial, and agricultural management.

The French beginnings of German theory of State

The Cameralist orientation envisaged the State as a complex organic entity composed of various sub-entities, each operating within its respective channel of authority and not necessarily in conformity with the actual preferences of its subjects. Most Cameralists were not impressed by the laissez-faire doctrine advanced by Adam Smith whereby the notion of wealth was traced back to a single source, namely, the egoism of the individual.[2] They were more affected by the concepts of State elaborated in the works of Montesquieu, Voltaire, and Rousseau under the rubric of General Spirit,[3] National Genius,[4] and General Will,[5] respectively.

Montesquieu stresses that individual action falls under the powerful control of General Spirit, which exhibits distinct manifestations from one society to another. This is so because it rises from different causes, climates, religions, laws, maxims of government, precedents, morals, and customs.[6] This spirit affects every aspect of societal life. Indeed:

> [i]f in any part of the world there had been a nation whose inhabitants were of a sociable temper, open hearted, pleased with life, possessed of judgment, and a facility in communicating their thoughts; who were sprightly, agreeable, gay, sometimes imprudent, often indiscreet; and besides had courage, generosity, frankness, and a certain point of honor;[7] no one ought to endeavor to restrain their manners by laws, unless he would lay a constraint on their virtues ... It is the business of legislature to follow the spirit of the nation, when it is not contrary to the principles of government; for we do nothing so well as when we act with freedom, and follow the bent of our national genius.[8]

Even the most tyrannical despot is helpless before the distinctive spirit of a nation. The King of Persia may force a son to slay his father or a father to slay his son: but he cannot make them drink wine.[9] Ideal polity is one in which individual rationalism, that of the ruled as well as the ruler, is duly tempered with the prevailing social, economic, legal, and historical institutions at a given point in time. Some societies have fared better than others in this respect. Montesquieu finds the contemporary British political system to be more in line with the requirements of ideal society vis-à-vis many other regimes, including the coeval French, not because the British political system is based on loftier principles, but because the British Parliament has continually examined itself and has remained attuned to the ever-evolving British General Will.[10]

Voltaire, too, emphasizes the influence of the accumulated spirit of past generations upon individual development and action. Terming this accumulation National Genius, he warns that without its guidance the individual would be reduced to a hollow entity, a stranger to himself, not knowing from where he has come and to where he is going.[11] He finds contemporary French society to be rife with these sorts of souls among those frequenting the elegant Parisian *salons*. For these skeptical, nonchalant, and ultimately inarticulate members of the leisurely class the only link with National Genius is provided by workers, peasants, and untutored servants.[12] This indicates an unfortunate element in the development of French society. For, the precepts embedded in the larger realm of national custom would have been much more conducive to accomplishing great deeds and ensuring a more durable existence than the morals and manners of the ruling minority.

While collective spirits of nations are often compared to each other, none could be held superior to another:

> There is no single good code in any country. The reason for this is evident: laws have been made by degrees, according to times, places, needs, etc. When needs have changed the laws that remained became ridiculous. Thus the law that forbade the eating of pork and the drinking of wine was very sensible in Arabia, where pork and wine are pernicious. [But] it is absurd in Constantinople.[13]

Voltaire is critical of a political system based on monarchy, but he does not deem democracy categorically superior to it. A benevolent despot enlightened enough to protect intellectual liberty and personal property suits Voltaire's taste best, as he finds that the rule of a fine lion would be better than that of 200 rats.[14] However, as a matter of practical consideration, he places his preference on constitutional monarchy:

> The English nation is the only one on earth which has succeeded in controlling the power of kings by resisting them, which by effort after effort has at last established this wise system of government in which the prince, all-powerful for doing good, has his hands tied for doing evil, in which aristocrats are great without arrogance and vassals, and in which the people share in the government without confusion.[15]

Rousseau, a firm believer in natural law, while expanding on Montesquieu's and Voltaire's ideas, rejects the notion implicit in their writings that it would be possible to strike a compromise between General Spirit or National Genius and contemporary Western social institutions directed to promote the interests of the aristocratic class. Rousseau, deeming virtuous even the pre-reason, pre-social man actuated solely by self-preservation, postulates that no single individual should be forced by any social institution to part with any fraction of his natural liberty. Natural liberty does not exist only in a state of isolation, however. And the problem is not that there is an inherent incompatibility between two models of man, one in the state of nature and the other under the dictates of a political constitution:

> The problem is to find a form of association which will defend and protect with the whole common force the person and goods of each

> associate, and in which each, while uniting himself with all, may still obey himself alone, and remain as free as before.[16]

In other words, the individual is in need of a collective mechanism that will protect him against crime and exploitation. That is, the individual *wills* a covenant directed to promote both his individual interest *and* the social interest, a social contract that combines security, which comes from collective association, and liberty, which the individual possessed before the making of the contract.[17] In other words, this compact not only renders tangible the moral attitude fostered in the hearts of various individual citizens, but also protects it from misuse by members of government. General Will thus emerges as a call for collective action aiming to transform the prevailing contrivances into social institutions, which, while promoting individual interest within the established political constitution, inspires shared responsibility in the attainment of common interest.

Internalization of the ideas of the *Philosophes*

These thoughts found a strong reflection in the discourses of influential German Cameralists. The first of these authors was Friedrich Carl von Moser who, in his *Von dem Deutchshen national-Geist* (1765), gave Montesquieu's concept of National Spirit an unmistakably patriotic twist. Calling it *national-Geist,* Moser formulated it as a platform of social institutions upon which to erect the economic, political, and cultural policies of a unified Germany. He contended that the rifts that separated one group of Germans from another – Catholics versus Protestants, Prussians versus Bavarians and so on – could be filled only to the extent that German governments aligned their public policy with an overarching collective spirit.[18] The argument was subsequently picked up by Hegel, who, giving the concept a new name, *Volksgeist,* correlated it with the cultural accomplishments of a society in conformity with its religious, ethical, social, political, and legal institutions.[19] Hegel reminds that in each stage of development of a State, we discern a particular "form of reality in which the individual has and enjoys his freedom, but only on the condition of his recognizing, believing in, and willing that which is common to the Whole."[20] The State is nothing but the actualization of the particular collective will that a people (*Volk*) possesses in its self-consciousness and which it formalizes as the constitutional basis of their State. In other words, a people does not begin as a State, but becomes one in the course of its life cycle, during which "it blossoms, grows strong, then fades away and dies."[21] In each stage of this cycle a different national spirit becomes manifest. Finally F. K. von Savigny, rechristening the term as *Volksbewusstsein* to emphasize "the common conviction of a people," viewed collective spirit as a general agreement culminating in a distinct framework of political, social, and legal institutions, notwithstanding the fact that the constituents gave it only tacit support.[22] Thus, the organic concept of State gained a central place in Cameralist literature, with Moser buttressing the pragmatic, Hegel the phenomenological, and Savigny the cohesive foundation of it.

The German theory of the public sector

A series of liberal reforms initiated in the nineteenth century – such as the dissolution of the guilds and regulatory bodies and the emancipation of the peasants from manorial labor services and dues – provided the impetus for an unparalleled economic growth in German states. In the second half of the century, rapid progress in agriculture and industry, bolstered by the customs union (*Zollvereign*), increased German states' bargaining power in their trade relations with other countries.[23] Around the same time, simultaneous with the expansion of private and public economic activity, and the improvement in bookkeeping records and statistical methods, *Kameralwissenschaft* was transformed into *Staatswissenschaft*, Science of State. The specific aim of this emerging field of scholarship was to articulate the laws that were thought to govern the behavior of both the individual and the State that pertained to the accomplishment of private- as well as public-economic goals.

German scientists of the State did not view these laws as timeless. To them, the laws governing economic behavior stemmed from special circumstances along the historical progress of each national community, hence were applicable only with respect to the specific problems affecting a given society at a particular point in time. The solutions to these problems required the analysis of not only economic, but the whole gamut of pertinent social, legal, political, ethical, cultural, and technical conditions. Put differently, *Staatswissenschaft* was a context-bound science, one that precluded its practitioners from abstracting the economic act at the expense of the special conditions affecting the allocation of economic resources among various goods and services. This premise held for both private- as well as public-economic decisional environments.

By the middle of nineteenth century, *Staatswissenschaft* brought under its rubric various branches of scholarship, including economics, statistics, politics, public policy, banking, and public law. In this period lively taxonomic discussions filled the air, especially those concerning the economics proper of *Staatswissenschaft*. In the end, three overlapping spheres of economic activity were discerned, *Privatökonomie*, *Nationalökonomie*, and *Staatsökonomie*, the first referring roughly to business economics, the second to political economy, and the third to public economics. The first two economic realms were different from the third in that they abided by the dictates of the voluntary exchange process. The third realm allowed for a coercive process enforced by functionaries of the State, who made economic decisions on behalf of individual citizens. In both economic realms, private or public, the appropriateness of the economic act was judged with respect to the applicable circumstances and events. As for the private-economic act, the axioms of self-interest and rationality would suffice to give rise to an optimal solution between a consumer and a producer. The social relationship between the two economic agents is impersonal and mechanical. The opposite occurs in the public economy where the two participants, the taxpayer and the State, sustain each other *organically* under the tutelage of a collective spirit determined by an array of variables endemic to each national community. *Staatswissenschaft* provides appropriate norms under which a people, acting as a collectivity rather than a mere conglomeration of individuals pursuing their respective interests, could come up with fiscal policies in conformity with that society's pertinent stage of development and applicable ideals.[24]

German political economists found that the basic economic postulate did not work well in the private economy either. One of the most vocal proponents of economic historicism was Karl Knies, who, arguing that any economic phenomenon was relevant only in the context of place and time, urged his colleagues to submit to the basic methodological premise that economics laws were essentially laws of analogy and not laws of causality.[25] Knies's argument was elaborated by Gustav Schmoller, who found that the failure of economic science in solving real problems stemmed from its unfortunate reliance on "the naive optimism of laissez-faire ... and unhistorical rationalism, the stale last remnant of eudaemonistic enlightenment of the 18th century."[26] Schmoller, arguably the most eminent *Staatswissenschaftler* in Germany before the rise of Adolph Wagner, pointed out that, despite the enormous effort expended by the adherents to Smith's argument of self-interested rationality, economic scholarship had not progressed beyond Comte's second stage, the metaphysical, and, was centuries away from being a truly positive science.[27]

Wagner and his theory of communal economy

Adolf Wagner, disagreed with Schmoller's judgment. He believed that the reason for the lowly status of economics within the larger framework of *Staatswissenschaft* stemmed from an unwarranted effort to collapse three distinct domains of economic science into one amorphous whole. Wagner reminds that the economic act unfolds differently in each different organizational environment. At the one extreme lies *Nationalökonomie,* an economic milieu in which the individual strives to promote his self-interest. At the other extreme is situated *Staatswissenschaft,* the altruistic economic domain in which the propelling motivation is one of duty and righteousness. In between there lies a ground where the individual acts to accommodate both sets of motivations. It is in this interface that the State coexists with the individual economic agent. In Wagner's opinion, the economic relationship between the citizen and the State should be studied neither within the framework of *Nationalökonomie* based on individual preferences nor within *Staatswissenschaft,* a murky domain consisting of practical aspects of fiscal administration. A new field of economic scholarship is in order, one that duly recognizes the special character of the fiscal economy based on the significance of the State in the life of the social organization and the compulsory nature of the collection of public revenue. This socio-economic realm may be called *Sozialökonomie* and the discipline that studies it *Finanzwissenschaft.*

Wagner was certainly impressed by the views Albert Schäffle articulated in the 1860s that in order to make sense of the complex economic relationships occurring among individuals, families, and communities one needed to go beyond the operational framework dictated by individual rationality and self-interest, What needs to be explored is "communal" economy, *Gemeinwirtschaft,* where the economic act refers not to that of an abstract individual, but of an actual person, who is the product of a particular array of social, cultural, moral, and ideological traditions prevailing in his community. This communally inclined individual would be motivated to allocate his income in such a way that both his private needs and his collective needs are reconciled in a satisfying synthesis. The goods serving to satisfy collective needs are provided by the State, who has its own income, made up of two kinds of revenues: that which it collects as a result of a commercial exchange, such as the sale of timber from State forests, and that which it collects as taxes. The first category of State income, composed of fees and royalties, come from an entirely voluntary transfer of private funds to the public budget, akin to the voluntary exchange process that takes place in the market economy. It is the second category of revenue collection that requires an analysis befitting the special characteristics of communal economy.

Gemeinwirtschaft differs from voluntary exchange economy in that the exchange relationship between the taxpayer and the tax collector is not quid pro quo. Smith's principle of enlightened self-interest is out of place in this economic organization, where special needs are experienced:

> These needs are felt subjectively by the competent public authorities, and by individuals in so far as they think as members of the community. The public economy thus rests on the sacrifice of its members. The individual feels as a member of the community; and where this is not the case, coercion forces him to act as if he felt in this fashion.[28]

As such, social cohesion, and its compelling arm, fiscal coercion occupy a central place in *Sozialökonomie,* and hence in its theoretical framework, *Finanzwissenschaft.* Lorenz von Stein, agreeing with Wagner, elaborates on this point:

> What I am, what I have and what I do belongs in some part to what I have received through the community. The strength of the community resides in what each individual surrenders to it from his personal life ... [T]he State personifies this society and endows it with the power of volition and action. Everything that constitutes the essence of community is comprised by the State, by its will and deed, its constitution and its administration. The State confers measure and order on all things, including the economic interaction of individuals and community, which is inherent in the very nature of community. The relevant intentions of the State are expressed in legislation and enforced upon the individual by public administration. This is the genesis of taxation.[29]

Despite this crucial difference, a close collaboration exists between private and communal economy. Hans Ritschl explains:

> In the principle of cohesion lies the primary fundamental difference between communal economy and market economy. But neither of these systems exists today to the exclusion of the other, and they meet and interweave in a host of ways. It is of the essence that the

> member of an exchange society is at the same time a member of the community, that the member of a community is also a member of an exchange society. Indeed, in the old city economy with its autarkic nature, to some extent in the manorial economy and again in the economy of nation State, the group of persons forming the exchange society coincides with that forming the national community.[30] Community and society today carry each other. Sociologically, the community is interwoven with the component elements of the exchange society; economically, the community today mostly rests on the exchange society; and juridically, the community in its turn, carries and provides the foundation for the exchange society. But let us not forget that the more important than the individual's juridical bond with the collectivity, is his spiritual, emotional, and cultural bond with the community and its forces.[31]

Ritschl thus points out the centrality not only of social cohesion in German fiscal doctrine, but also the treatment of public economy along historical and social lines. This view is perpetuated in Wagner's process of determination of fiscal equilibrium, in which process the existing public expenditures are taken to reflect the requirements of a given historical situation, and where changes therein are taken to reflect underlying changes in collective will.[32]

Some other German fiscal scientists took a different tack and framed the historical development of a national community's fiscal institutions within the standard argument of class struggle. Rudolf Goldscheid construed the development of tax policies as nothing more than a series of tax struggles from medieval times to modern society. In his view, it is the sociological, rather than historical, analysis that befits the study of communal economy. The justification of a public expenditure exclusively on the basis of a historically relevant fact – say, an established policy of slavery – would pass the muster of historical scrutiny. But the appropriateness of such a policy can be examined effectively only by scrutinizing the real aims behind ongoing fiscal action. Subjective evaluations, usually implicit in traditional fiscal decision-making, are justifiable solely within the parameters of the prevailing social order. Thus, according to Goldscheid:

> [i]t is perfectly possible to praise the virtues of the feudal State or absolute monarchy or the capitalist economy; but is absurd to believe in the possibility of just taxation within these social systems. Equally, one may regard it as utopian to want to do away completely with

> warfare; but then one must not accept the illusion that there is some way of creating a secure financial order in a world torn by wars. It is possible, on some subjective grounds, to approve of the growing indebtedness of the State to private capital; but it is foolish self-deception to believe that the dispossessed and heavily indebted State is capable of fulfilling major social tasks. Nor is it, finally, impossible to view with sovereign neglect the contradiction between social and economic structure and its juridical and financial superstructure; but it would be an altogether unrealistic misrepresentation to regard the defects which necessarily result from this contradiction as accidental disturbances or as ineluctable evils due to human nature or to the nature of society and economy. All this goes to prove that a sociological approach is the fundamental condition of any objective theory of public finance... It alone can show up the part played by the origin and composition of public revenue in the development of society as a whole and thereby in the destiny of nations and individuals alike. It depends on social structure and upon the internal and external political constellations whether taxes in kind or money taxes are preferable, whether and to what extent indirect or direct, personal taxes or taxes on objects, income and profits taxes or land, investment, property and death taxes are to be chosen, whether the tax screw should be tightened or relieved, what groups of population are to bear the heavier or the lighter burden, whether more reliance is to be placed on customs and excise or on loans, whether internal or external borrowing is preferable, whether expenditure is to be reduced or revenue raised, how taxation is to be combined with economic incentives, and so on.[33]

The aim of the preceding argument is not to establish the mechanism of efficient fiscal action: it is to develop a framework for explaining why certain fiscal action has taken place and for predicting what action will result under what conditions.[34] As such, the sociological approach formulated by Goldscheid grafts onto German fiscal doctrine a much-needed layer of operational insight, that of partial equilibrium analysis. Hence, Goldschied, unlike Pareto, demonstrated that the economic and sociological approaches to the public economy were not only compatible, but also mutually strengthening. Goldscheid's aim was not to determine what would be efficient fiscal action, but to explain why certain fiscal action had occurred and whether similar actions could be predicted under given conditions.[35]

General characteristics of German fiscal doctrine

The most distinguishing feature of German fiscal theory is its generality. This theory encompasses the entire range of state economic activity, which revolves around the central principle of social cohesion. The goods provided by the State, in the form of non-material commodities, aim to foster and perpetuate collective interests rather than individual interest. Wagner expounds the general characteristics of communal economy and fiscal theory in following terms:[36]

I. The fiscal economy, an independent economic unit controlled by a juridical entity, very much resembling that of a joint stock company, referred to in this case as the fiscal authority.
II. Like the management of a successful corporation, the fiscal authority conducts its business through its highly qualified and well-compensated functionaries.
III. The fiscal authority supplies, against a payment, such non-material goods as public institutions and services that are indispensable to the economic life of the entire community. As such, this entails a production process whereby material (private) inputs are transformed into non-material (communal) outputs.
IV. Since the life of the State is perpetual, the fiscal authority cannot be precluded from certain transactions, such as contracting perpetual debts, that are not available to individual businesses.
V. The charges for non-material goods provided by the fiscal authority are determined not by individual valuation, but unilaterally by the functionaries of the State. The fiscal authority is free to define its own tasks, the manner of their discharge, and thus the amount and kind of services to be provided for the people, without reference to their demand for these services.

To summarize, the goals pursued by the State in the communal economy are entirely different from those pursued by the individual in the private economy. Collective utility and individual utility are undoubtedly complementary to each other; however, in the sphere of communal economy, individual utility is subsumed by collective utility. The valuation of this sort of utility transcends the cognitive limits of the individual taxpayer. The task is delegated to the competent functionaries of the State, who have a keen understanding of the economic as well as political, social, and historical exigencies confronting society and have access to the information conducive to effective fiscal decisions.

Thus, in German fiscal doctrine, state economic activity proceeds under the commanding principle of maximization of collective utility, which is quite akin to what is referred to in welfare economics as social utility. But the determination of this magnitude depends more heavily on historical variables than economic ones.

German fiscal theorists were aware of the advent of marginal calculus and did not have any prima facie aversion to incorporating it in the determination of the prices of public services. They also duly noted that the financing of public expenditure lines obviously caused a burden on individual citizens' budgets and that this burden had to be minimized. Accordingly, the examination of individual preferences for the services provided by the State was indicated. As such, marginal valuation was clearly an appropriate method of fiscal analysis. In fact, equilibrium was established in the communal economy when "when a dollar's tax load upon each economic entity deduct[ed] from social utility an amount equivalent to that added by a dollar's expenditure in each line."[37] But this view of tax burden is not of the Edgeworth–Pigou variety. For, the relevant criteria of comparison are reductions from social, rather than individual utility.[38] This comparison fully agrees with the organic view of the public economy where the individual taxpayer and the fiscal authority are construed as two parties acting collectively rather than confronting each other, as envisioned by the subscribers to the individualistic view. Consequently, in German fiscal doctrine the problem of coercion is severely understated. Indeed, there is nothing in the German doctrine to prevent coercion from reaching large proportions. For, the sacrifice principle that is in operation here is directed not to minimize individual sacrifice, but to minimize collective sacrifice attributable to specific expenditure lines.

6
Austrian Fiscal Doctrine: The Subjective Valuation Approach

Austrian fiscal doctrine stems directly from one of the three originators of the marginalist revolution, Carl Menger. His *Grundsätze der Volkswirtschaftslehre*, appearing in 1871 simultaneously with Jevons's *Theory of Political Economy* and before Walras's *Éléments d'économie politique pure* (1874), strongly challenged the existing Austrian economics curriculum that was based on the German historical tradition. In his characterization of the market process, Menger eschewed any aggregative patterns of economic activity. Instead, he represented economic exchange as an introspective, interpretive, as well as rationalistic cognitive process adopted by agents towards the attainment of optimal outcomes.[1] Writing in uncomplicated prose and without resorting to mathematics, Menger demonstrated in *Grundsätze* (*Elements*) how the notion of utility provided the only causal connection between need and value in face of scarcity. He discussed at length the want-satisfying properties of goods as well as their complementary role in the enhancement of personal satisfactions showing that it did not matter whether these needs and satisfactions were real or imagined. Economic agents, thanks to their keen cognitive capabilities, would fully comprehend (*verstehen*) the exact nature of their needs and proceed toward their satisfaction regardless of whether the appropriate goods were situated in the private- or the public-economic sphere. Menger conceived of the latter form of economic organization not as an organic entity subsuming the "collective" interests of the entire community, but as the sum of of individual citizens pursuing their respective interests as determined by their introspective valuations.[2]

Menger: the father of Austrian theory of subjective valuation

Menger disagreed with the main premise of the historical school that, since the social organism was governed by continuous change, any effort to formulate universal laws in this sphere of human activity would be misdirected. The historicists maintained that the best an investigator could hope for in the analysis of such a dynamic environment would be to discover some situational laws that might enlighten the emergence of a given social institution. Menger countered in a later work, *Untersuchungen über die Methode der Socialwisswenschaften* (1883), that the existing social structure could be explained in the same manner and on the same principles as, for instance, the change or the emergence of a price structure.[3] The foremost historicist of the day, Gustav Schmoller, immediately rose to challenge. He characterized contemporary economic theory "too young a science" and Menger's *Untersuchungen* "too rudimentary an intellectual effort" to elicit the universal laws of communal economy. The debate, dubbed *Methodendstreit* (Method Struggle), turned exceedingly personal, ending some 30 years later with the general acceptance of Menger's subjectivist approach by Austrian academics. Menger's ideas with respect to the public economy were elaborated by two of his followers, Friedrich von Wieser and Emil Sax, whose contributions were picked up by many fiscal theorists in Italy, Sweden, and England, in addition to Austria.

Menger, while explicating how introspective economic agents directed their scarce resources to their greatest satisfaction in the private economy, did not supply any pronouncements specific to public finance. The reason for this was mainly institutional. Specifically, in larger nineteenth-century German-language universities there existed not one, but two professorial chairs for the subject of economics, one for economic theory and the other for economic policy.[4] As to which of the two professors would teach the theory of the public economy, it was left to individual circumstances. In 1873, when Menger was invited to fill the chair of political economy at University of Vienna, his senior counterpart in the chair of economic policy was Lorenz von Stein,[5] who had already established himself as the professor in charge of public finance. Menger went along with the status quo and remained silent on the topic in spite of the fact that the responsibility for teaching public finance formally belonged to his chair, not Stein's.[6] This responsibility was claimed back by Friedrich von Wiser, when he was called to fill his mentor's chair in 1903.

Wieser: a worthy disciple of Menger's

Friedrich von Wieser rested Menger's framework of marginal utility upon a firmer, broader analytical platform. He attained his goal on two fronts. First, he expanded Menger's vision of private resource allocation via the concepts of "imputation" and "alternative cost." In Wieser's model of economic exchange the supply side had no independent role in establishing values: the primum mobile of the economic exchange mechanism consisted of the marginal calculation of the utilities of final goods. That is, the values of inputs were calculated by imputation to the utilities that finished products accrued to their ultimate users. This was a stab at the heart of Marshallian Neoclassicals, who continued to believe that the source of value resided in "real" costs, as determined by the combined effects of inputs *and* outputs.

According to Ekelund and Hébert, Wieser's imputation theory:

> might best be described as a marginal-utility product theory of input valuation ... [whereby] the value of an additional unit of input applied to production was determined by the marginal utility of the additional units produced ($MUP_i = MP_i \cdot MU_x$) rather than by the traditional marginal-*value* product, which is found by multiplying the marginal *revenue* to the firm by the marginal product of the input ($MVP_i = MP_i \cdot P_x$). [When] one views the Austrian approach in contrast to the traditional Marshallian system, it is clear that the Austrian value theory reached a high point in von Wieser's *Natural Value*. Von Wieser's explication of the system must, in sum, rank as one of the high theoretical achievements of the Austrian school.[7]

Wieser's expansion of Menger's ideas to the provision of goods and services in the public economy was no less momentous. Book VI of Wieser's *Natural Value* (*Der Natürliche Wert* [1889]), devoted to the determination of utility and prices of public goods, opens with a searing critique of the British fiscal doctrine with respect to its omission of subjective value in the sphere of State economic activity. The followers of Adam Smith explained the economic activity of the State simply by the presumed exigencies of societal life. These writers, while paying the due attention to the taxation side of the fiscal account by elaborating on such issues as progressivity, ability to pay, exemption for minimum subsistence, and so on, failed to relate any of these phenomena to the fundamental notion of price theory, that is, the individual valuation of the want-satisfying properties of public goods. It is true that these authors talk about some value: but what they invoke is objective or exchange value rather than subjective or use value. Any peculiar value intrinsic to goods provided by the State is not discussed in the British literature at all as though economic concepts borrowed wholly from the private exchange process would be sufficient to explain the fiscal act.

Wieser is more sympathetic toward German theorists of the public economy. He credits German fiscal scientists for having recognized the one-sidedness of the British doctrine, and having rehabilitated the concept of exchange value by tracing it back to the general conception of individual use value, and then recasting it as national use value. With this transformation, the German organic theory of the public economy became "more rounded and adaptable" though simultaneously "more indefinite and inexact."[8]

Wieser envisions two spheres of economic activity, individual and communal (or, alternatively, private and public). In the first economic organization, the goods are provided for the satisfaction of those wants that an economic agent experiences as an individual. In the public economy, the goods provided by the State are directed to satisfy the wants experienced by the same individual as a member of the community. Because the same individual is situated in both economic organizations simultaneously, it would be inappropriate to consider the two economies independent of each other. Actually, the two spheres of economic activity are fully intertwined and work in a spiral fashion:

> National interests, which are undoubtedly to be reckoned under the head of collective interests, are frequently furthered by personal sacrifice and expenditure. And more numerous instances may be adduced of the contrary case – the individual interests are fostered by collective efforts. The desire to possess a means of coming and going to one's business is undoubtedly personal in the highest degree; but the highways of traffic have been included among the concerns of the commonwealth almost since the beginning of time ... It must, therefore, be some circumstance[s] which ... determine the division of the economic sphere. (1956 [1889]: 220–1)

One reason individuals form communal economies is that in some instances they cannot carry out an endeavor acting singly. One individual cannot ward off the onslaught of a foreign power, fight crime in the larger community, or lay down laws. These actions must be executed collectively and the ensuing burden carried by the community as a whole. The benefit produced by these joint actions cannot be imputed, nor a commensurate price charged, to each individual citizen. The second instance in which the State engages itself in an economic activity is when consumers feel an intense, immediate need for a certain service while entrepreneurs are unwilling to produce it for lack of adequate profit in the foreseeable future. The task of providing this productive service for the demanders would then fall on the State. Third, some undertakings that would normally lie within the purview of private economy are taken over by the State to prevent the accumulation of power into the hands of a single private producer. While it is true that in the end the State emerges as the monopolist, there is an important difference between a State monopoly and a private monopoly. The private monopolist determines the price of the commodity by using ordinary, private-economic valuation in order to maximize his gains. The public enterprise, by contrast, makes use of *public*-economic valuation, which takes into consideration an inherent characteristic of collective goods – indivisibility of their benefits. Wieser goes on:

> In the [first], or private economic group, where goods are capable of being measured very accurately as to their amount and utility, the main endeavour must be to obtain from every practically measurable portion of goods the greatest amount of generally recognized utility. This endeavour must find its expression in an estimate of value which takes its measure, for each single good, from the margin at which the most perfectly utilised supply meets the most perfectly sifted demand ... An exact economic calculus [is thus] established, the advantage and disadvantage of every sufficiently familiar process being put in figures; and it must be regarded as the triumph of economic art to exactly ascertain and exactly realise that plan which the value calculation indicates as the best. In the [second], or national economic group, the first principle must also be to secure the greatest amount of utility, the highest well-being of the citizens. But the utility and its amount will not be exactly estimated ... The estimate of value will often be very vague, and in many cases unanimity of opinion regarding it is not be expected ... [Here,] in place of the quantitative estimate of the value of goods in masses, will emerge the vague and disputable valuation of interests, influenced by inclinations and passions ... It is a matter of the first importance ... to recognize that there is a sphere within which the estimate of exchange value is applicable, and another in which it is not.[9]

From the earlier remark Wieser reaches the conclusion that while in the private economy the exchange price is the same for every consumer, multiple prices will prevail in the public economy, the variability depending on such factors as wealth, income, and the intensity of the need felt for the public good in question. Wieser remarks: "the greater the wealth and income, the greater the degree of the want, the smaller will be the subjective [monetary] equivalent or the taxation, [which makes] a progressive rate of taxation ... justifiable."[10]

In the private-economic exchange, only the marginal purchaser pays the maximum price: all other purchasers whose valuations of the commodity are higher, enjoy a surplus benefit since the exchange price is established for all and no one is required to pay more than the equivalent of the marginal purchaser.[11] In the consumption of public goods, conversely, the contribution toward meeting the costs of these commodities are obtained by consumers in full monetary equivalents, that is, by the maximum amount these individuals are *able* to pay:

> Hence is derived a peculiar law of national economic valuation – [that] of collective valuation generally. In every [private] economy equal quantities of goods have an equal value ... But it is different in the case of the national economic body ... which binds together several otherwise independent economic subjects to carry out distinct purposes. Here the goods which belong to the individual economic subjects, and from which the taxes are to be drawn, are valued as unequal – equal taxes have unequal value, the same value is expressed by unequal taxes ... The fact that, when levying taxes, a government, in contrast to the general law of ordinary economic life, rates economic property differently according to the individual circumstances of those who are taxed, has ... beneficial results. It allows that the public burdens of the poorer classes be put at a lower figure; it allows the ability of the wealthier to bear taxation to be more fully utilised; and it thus places the taxes where they will cause least injury to the satisfaction of private needs. Were the State to act otherwise, [that is,] impose equal contributions, like poll taxes, on every citizen, it would inflict on the poorer classes [de]privations in no way compensated by the extended indulgence in luxury that would be possible to the richer.[12]

Wieser wonders why the same principle of valuation could not be extended to the private economy, that is, why should each individual purchaser not pay according to his purchasing power. If each person were obliged to pay a price according to his means, a universal equalization of satisfactions would be attained in the private economy. In that case, riches would offer no advantage and poverty no deprivation, and, all would have in the long run the same satisfactions."[13] But this cannot be possible as long as private markets remained free and individual agents continued to direct their activities to maximize their respective utilities. While it is true under the prevailing conditions that private property gives rise to great inequalities in the satisfaction of wants, it simultaneously secures, even to those who receive the smallest share in the general distribution, an enormously enhanced satisfaction of wants on the whole due to the great increase in productive return that it allows.[14] There is not much else an economist theorist can contribute to the explanation of this strange turn of events, namely that the same community allows two diametrically opposite market organizations within its borders, one favoring and the other penalizing the rich.[15] Perhaps one day a general theory of society will shed light on this remarkable phenomenon. But such theory will be based not only on economic principles, but the whole gamut of social, political and legal considerations.

Wieser then proceeds to address this task. His *Social Economics* (*Theorie der Gesellschaftlichen Wirtschaft* [1914]) presents a full-fledged theory of economic welfare, combining the essentials of the newly established Austrian economic theory of individual valuation with an authentic theory of political power. Wieser picks up from the point Menger's *Untersuchungen* left off, namely, whether economic concepts applied to the public economy should be regarded as (1) empirical theories, (which are decided by experience); (2) systems of implicit definitions (which share the status of logic and mathematic); or (3) a system wholly *sui generis* (which would lack any epistemological stature at all).[16] Wieser argues that the evolution of social economy reflects a characteristic inherent in human nature, which is the propensity to amass power and acquire leadership. This condition leads to stratification of economic, political, and social relations in each society with the resulting layering of utilities, incomes, and prices.[17] Wieser condemns such stratification for inhibiting the maximization of social welfare and detects a countervailing fulcrum of power in labor unions to remedy market imperfections in the product and resource sides of the social economy. Ekelund and Hébert remind us that Wieser,

> in addition to active unionization, also called for an expanded role for the state in fostering the spirit of the social economy. Where the supposed results of unbridled freedom do not obtain in the economy, as von Wieser put it, "The state alone has a call to protect the weak."

> Further, the state must be recognized as an "indispensable factor in the national economic process." Essentially and broadly, the role of the state is to increase economic welfare in the face of power and capitalistic domination as vis-à-vis historically justified rights to private property. Utility theory must serve as the basis for the state's assessment of economic power. Specifically, von Wieser favored energetic state regulation and/or control of imperfectly competitive firms whenever the profits of "mammoth capital" were unearned, e.g., realized without the efforts of true and enlightened leadership ... In addition, ... the state was to undertake certain projects that would produce only a small marginal exchange value, but that – when the public's interest is taken into account – would be productive of great total utility. Most "social goods," including ... railroads and canals, fall into this category ... Market valuations, in short, may be misleading, and it is part of the legitimate function of the state to seek out and to encourage by subsidy or ownership projects productive of high total utility.[18]

Wieser did not share Menger's enthusiasm for progressive taxation. He saw progressive tax rates a direct impingement on individual freedom and private property. This adversity is based on purely economic, and not political or ethical, considerations:

> The State should not use its sovereign powers of taxation to level out the existing inequality of income and wealth; what it should do when assessing the contributions levied from the citizens, is to take account of the scale of personal values which express the inequality of income and wealth. The State would violate the economic principle if it treated all private economic units from which it levies contributions as having equal valuations ... The heavy pressure which the rising demands of the modern public economy make upon the weaker economic units can be alleviated only by a comprehensive assessment of the citizens' compulsory contributions so co-ordinated that the stronger are taxed relatively more than the weaker. This sort of tax distribution allows the public economy to extend its frontiers as widely as possible without impinging at any point upon the limits of the private economy.[19]

Wieser then offers an interesting analogy. He sees the decision-making process of state economic activity akin to that of a club or private association providing common facilities in the interests of its members and incurring common expenditures for this service.[20] He elaborates:

> Just like the expenditure of an association, the State's spending is not covered by any income of its own. Like an association, the State has to collect membership contributions, which the members must defray out of their private incomes. The revenue side of the state economy is not independent; state revenue, which consists of citizens' contributions, is a special form of derivative income. By virtue of its sovereign power, the State is in a position to make the contributions which it requires compulsory, but it may not assess them arbitrarily ... The ideal State, which we must theoretically postulate, will distribute the compulsory contributions with economic justice among the citizens ... We shall have more to say on how ... the distribution of the compulsory contributions ... must be carried out in order to fulfill the economic principle.[21]

The preceding quotation encapsulates all the distinguishing features of Austrian theory of the public economy. First, it emphasizes that the payments citizens make for the provision of public goods are essentially voluntary, very much like the dues paid by the members of a private association. Implicit in this postulate is the assumption that public goods are inherently productive and that individual citizens fully appreciate this quality. This feature on the one hand separates the Austrian fiscal theory from the British theory based on the sacrifice principle of taxation and brings it in harmony with the Italian theory founded on the principle of benefit. On the other hand, it indicates the emphasis placed by Austrian fiscal theorists on developing an *economic* principle in the attainment of equilibrium in the public economy. This distinguishes the Austrian theory from the German, which turns to historical reasoning, within the framework of the prevailing system of social institutions, to glean insight into a workable paradigm to mete out the fiscal burden among citizens. Third, implicit in Wieser's pronouncement earlier is the concern for an equitable distribution of compulsory contributions made by the citizens. This feature brings Austrian fiscal theory closer to the Swedish fiscal theory based on fiscal justice and separates it from the Italian, British, and German theories based on fiscal coercion. No wonder all the key representatives of these national doctrines have referred to Austrian contributions to the theory of the public economy.

Still another concept inherent in Wieser's analysis of the public economy is his tri-partite analysis of public goods. The first group of goods encompasses those whose financing is covered by fees and direct charges. A State tobacco monopoly, for instance, produces and sells a commodity whose utility is readily identifiable and fully ascribable to its users. What we have in this case is a business undertaking of the State whereby the producer determines the exchange value applicable to its product according to the method adopted by private entrepreneurs. Specifically, the State caters to the composite result of need and effective demand, very much in line with Marshall's representation of the demand and supply of private goods. The second category encompasses those goods that are also provided by the State and whose benefits can also be imputed to individual users. But the determination of the prices of this second category of public goods challenges the exchange value concept. To illustrate, I may prefer to relay a message by mail rather than calling on my friend personally and be willing to pay the commensurate price for the applicable postage stamp. The fact that my neighborhood post office is owned by the State would have no bearing on my decision. It seems, accordingly, that the State, as the owner/operator of postal service, should determine the exchange value of the stamp by the same method as in the first case. After all, postal service is essentially a business enterprise, established and administered by the State either to prevent a monopoly or to supply a service shunned by private entrepreneurs for requiring an immensely large investment without a commensurate profit. These contingencies are not sufficient in construing postal service as a business enterprise: what we have here is an *administrative* enterprise, whose pricing policies substantially deviate from those of an ordinary business firm. In fact, post offices do not charge a price for official letters, they apply reduced tariffs to certain individuals or groups, and they deliver mail to remote locations at ordinary rates, suffering a seemingly meaningless loss. Put differently, the price charged for postal service is the result of a valuation process alien to that which occurs in private markets. In fact, it is based on social use value rather than private use value. It is this fact that, despite the apparent similarities between this and the previous case, renders postal service a public rather than a private good. Goods of this nature lie in the interface between pure private goods and pure public goods, the latter offered by the State to the citizens free of charge.

Wieser takes a public road as an example of this third and last category of public goods. A road produces no profit hence has no exchange value as income-producing capital; but evidently it has a private-economic value for the persons using it. Yet, the State does not resort to determining the price of this public good by exchange value: it chooses to offer the good for free allowing all economic agents to use it in accordance with their own utility preferences. The State is not interested in calculating the utility that this good provides each user individually: it would suffice for the purposes of State to enable private economic units to have access to the highest possible extent of the good in question. This is the case in which the assumption of divisibility cannot be made, hence its total value of utility cannot be calculated by adding up the partial benefits accrued to every individual economic unit. Yet, in this and other cases where government is engaged in an economic activity, the principle of value still remains in effect, either in the form of exchange value (in the first instance) or in the form of social use value (in the last two instances). Wieser recapitulates:

> The economic principle requires that the State's economic plan provide, within the means available, for the most important public interests at the expense of the less important ones. The greater the available funds, the more public services can be undertaken and the more benefits included. The richer State can afford its citizens more effective military protection, the poorer State has to be modest in its military expenditures. Even where the State's economic plan is determined by total value [of utility], it is [still] directed to the same end as an economy concerned with partial values, namely to extend the limits of utility as far as possible.[22]

Emil Sax's contribution to the Austrian theory of the public economy

Writing about the same time, Emil Sax expanded on Wieser's concepts regarding the representation of the State as a voluntary association and the categorization of public goods. Like Wieser, Sax held that the psychological aspects of want determination were basically the same regarding the selection of private and public goods. Like in the private economy so in the public economy individuals are motivated to satisfy their self-interests. However, in the public economy the maximization of a citizen's self-interest necessitates the simultaneous achievement of a socially acceptable economic equilibrium. In other words, economic agents acting in the communal sphere are motivated by mutuality and altruism as much as egoism. Put differently, Economic Man is a social egoist striving to strike a balance between self-interest and collective interest.[23]

Sax's theory was a direct assault on to the so-called "political" theory of the fiscal economy championed by Gaetano Mosca, who asserted that a society, no matter if it had a constitution based on majority rule, is actually governed by a small group derived from the military, hereditary, religious, economic, or intellectual oligarchy. These groups use fiscal policy to promote their own economic welfare within the given structure of political power and resort to compulsion to achieve this end. Sax counters this line of reasoning by asserting that the economy of the State is based not on the political maneuvering of a minority, but on the economic will of the community. The community is the sum of individuals acting in conformity with the principle of social egoism. Truly, not all individual members of the community are actively involved in public-economic activity. However, most citizens make their preferences known to the group of people running the fiscal authority on behalf of the community. This ruling group may be tempted to tilt the balance in its favor; but it would realize immediately that it should not deviate from a communally acceptable economic equilibrium. Otherwise the community will protest this deviation and will cease to support the ruling group. To sum, while it is true that the community incorporates a political structure based on self-serving authority and compulsion, these elements do not suspend the principle of economic efficiency.

Thus, Sax reaches the same conclusion reached by Italian fiscal scientists, especially De Viti de Marco. For, Sax, too, envisions a fiscal environment administered by a responsive ruling group striving to maximize its utility as well as the social utility of an acquiescent electorate. Under these conditions, the majority of individual citizens would pay their tax shares voluntarily. Fiscal compulsion would be applied only to a minority of citizens who find the majority decision unproductive with respect to their needs. The main difference between the two theories is that Pantaleoni, De Viti, and Mazzola explicated the valuation processes of public goods from a rationalistic point of view whereas Sax established a psychological process of want determination in line with the valuation framework set forth by Menger and Wieser.

Sax follows a path similar to Wieser's in terms of classifying goods. To begin with, state economic activity directly influences the individual welfare of an individual agent. This occurs because the fiscal act ultimately requires the withdrawal of private goods from individual economic units and the transfer of these goods to the State. From the point of view of the individual economic agent, this withdrawal represents the cost of the public-economic act and the sum of these goods used in the ensuing collective activity corresponds to the total cost to the community:

> For the process to be economic, the goods in question must be so used that they satisfy a need of higher priority than that from the satisfaction of which they were withdrawn, that is the lowest in the order of private needs to be satisfied... If we say that the value of the goods withdrawn from their prior use is their cost value, and the value of the same goods in their intended use their use value, then we can formulate this theorem: use value must exceed cost value and may never be below cost value, and when this is not so the intended [public-]economic activity is to be abandoned... The extent to which goods are to be transferred from the private to the state economy, ... is determined by individual value. The lower the value which anyone attaches to a unit of his property, the more such units (money) he will be prepared to spend for some particular purpose, if necessary. In addition, the amount of goods to be transferred is also conditioned by the social relations between the members of the community, as the subjects of action, and those individuals who benefit by it. These social relations derive from the degree of selfishness or altruism which individuals within the community [simultaneously] display towards each other, or from the peculiar mixture of "mutuality."[24]

Sax then turns to the classification of public goods and their corresponding prices. He envisions four categories of public goods. The first encompasses those goods whose consumption leads to some identifiable personal benefit to their users. Sax ascribes these goods to the *partikulare* sphere of collective activity. In this category, normal self-interest prevails in the communal market and occasions the same behavior as that which occurs between a private consumer and entrepreneur. Fiscal activity of this kind might be labeled "public enterprise" and the prices at which such goods are supplied to individual economic users "tax prices."[25] The second category of fiscal activity may be called "public services," which comprise those "immaterial" public goods that are used by the public on specific occasions, such as those involving the administration of justice. The prices of these services are determined irrespective of their cost, so that even those who cannot afford to pay them at their full cost value can still benefit from them, with the community bearing the deficit. The payments for these services are called "fees." The third group of fiscal activity entails goods and services, that are both "material" and "immaterial" commodities, whose effects are meant for the community as a whole, although some individuals receive direct benefits from them. To illustrate, if I fall sick and receive treatment from a public hospital, the benefit from this public good is directly imputable to me. Yet the hospital where I was treated was established to serve the entire community, whose members agreed to jointly bear its cost in the future. The relationship underlying this phenomenon is one of mutuality, a kind of altruism propelled by the need for joint action towards a common end:

> This common feeling is a bond of formal equality uniting the community. With respect to the cost there remains a divergence between the members' self-interest to the effect that no-one is to receive an advantage at the expense of anyone else: the total cost having to be met by payments of separate amounts, any deficiency in the contributions of one side would entail an increase in the amounts to be paid by the other side. This is excluded if everyone contributes for his share of benefit the full measure of goods he would use in his own economic unit in equal circumstance, that is, what he would be prepared to spend according to his individual valuation. [And] this is indeed what happens in free "mutualistic" associations.[26]

The State, rather than treating these services as those described by Sax under the rubric of the second category of public goods – that is, rather than having to ask the citizens to pay a fee each time they use the services of a hospital – would prefer to finance that service by a lump-sum tax graduated scheme according to the users' incomes. The distribution of the burden of the financing of such a public service according to this yardstick would give each individual a share of benefit, the value of which is in excess of his cost value. Sax calls this particular kind of fiscal contribution an "assessment" (*Umlagen*). Finally, there are those public goods whose benefits are not identifiable, measurable, and attributable to a particular individual. These goods constitute the pure collective goods proper, and their treatment requires a more detailed analysis. In Sax's words:

> Collective activities of this kind intend and create conditions of welfare which extend to all members of the community and benefit each alike as if they existed for each alone. We can think of any example we choose, such as the control of epidemics: everybody is saved from infection, nobody more or less than anybody else. It is right therefore to speak of these benefits as indivisible. The State supplies these activities for all, and by virtue of its coercive power they

> become an essential need for each person, that is, a need which is given the same subjective rank by all. This situation has certain consequences for the economic intentions of the members of the community and for their resulting economic actions.[27]

Pure collective goods are ordinary "material" goods, for they serve either as consumption goods (although they satisfy the entire community's immediate needs, such as inoculation against smallpox) or as capital goods ultimately leading to that end (such as ports facilitating overseas commerce).[28] The prices of these goods must be determined collectively, and the question is how to achieve an efficient pricing solution notwithstanding the non-identifiability and non-measurability of individual benefits. Sax provides a way to achieve this task.

The total tax revenue for pure collective goods are determined in the same way as are *partikulare* goods proper, namely, by equating the marginal disutility of the commensurate taxation with the marginal benefit of the collective good. It so happens that here we have *aggregate* public expenditure and *aggregate* public benefit. In the pure-collective goods proper, total tax ("absolute" tax, in Sax's parlance) and tax shares of the individuals ("relative" taxes) are determined through a choice process resembling the one that is adopted in clubs or private mutualistic organizations. In such organizations, members are not actively engaged in the day-to-day decision-making. Similarly, in the public economy ordinary citizens acquiesce to the collective decision-making process to achieve a common purpose. In this economy the individual is motivated not only by egoism, but also mutuality and altruism. Each citizen, out of a continuous interaction with other members of the community, readily perceives the saliency of a certain common interest to other citizens – say, controlling epidemics – and goes along with the majority's decision regarding the determination of both the total and the relative tax shares with respect to the financing of a public good apt to serve that interest. As in the *partikulare* realm, in that of the pure-collective goods proper, economic efficiency is attained since the individual citizen acts like his own tax assessor and decides how much he would be willing and able to pay for the given public service. The difference is that in the pure-collective goods sphere, he makes a valuation only after considering the intensity of his need, the needs of his cohorts, and the magnitude of his wealth or income. However, in this economic sphere as well, citizens determine absolute and relative tax shares by forsaking a lower-ranking private want for a higher-ranking public want until the marginal yields are equalized. Ultimately a balance is achieved in the economy between the citizens and the State, one that is both efficient and equitable.[29] Sax goes on:

> Taxation is thus ... an economic process with two aspects which condition each other. Individuals are prepared to pay the cost of state activity on condition that their cost shares be equivalent and overall cost valuation determines the sums to be used for collective activity on the assumption that they be raised by taxes corresponding to that principle. No overall valuation would be possible without determining the amount of the individuals' taxes on the principle of equivalence, because the effects of taxation on the satisfaction of individual needs cannot be otherwise ascertained. We can summarize the result of our investigation as follows: Taxation for the purpose of satisfying [purely] collective needs is a collective cost valuation on the basis if equivalence of individual cost shares, as conditioned by the relationship of mutuality.[30]

Sax's theory suffers from two problems. The first is the unnecessary parallel he draws from the private economy involving "material" and "immaterial" goods. Unnecessary, because Sax's theory would hold even if this dichotomy were discarded. The second problem is more serious. Sax is ill at ease with the concept of marginalism. He holds that the marginalist approach, while applicable in the determination of "relative" taxes, would not be applicable in the determination of "absolute" taxes, that is, in the calculation of the utility of public services for the group as a whole. This confusion seems to have stemmed from his systematic clustering of "group" with "total" on the one side and "share" with "marginal" on the other.[31]

Sax senses an inherent problem in his model in producing an efficient solution. He laments that collective activity often fails to fully attain the desired allocative and distributive objectives. He remarks:

> The individuals involved are too numerous and the process itself too complicated, not to speak of the political disturbances to which it is exposed. One of the major contributing reasons is the practical difficulty of measuring in each single case the wealth and needs which determine individual values ... Furthermore, the effect of taxation on individual economic units may have harmful consequences for the national economy as a whole or may counteract equivalence: it then becomes necessary to take measures to prevent such consequences ... Finally, we cannot overlook anti-collectivistic

> individual egoism, which leads to the attempt, by stealth and falsehood, to evade due taxation, even when it is of the right amount. This is a violation of the canons of mutuality within the community ... If [this] ever becomes a significant factor in any given situation, it must, by collective decision, be controlled by appropriate measures.[32]

Sax thus comes full circle. In the end, he all but admits that the simultaneous determination of both sides of the public budget calls for a coercive approach similar to the German and Italian concepts of State, rather than the Swedish model based on the assumption that individuals can accurately determine their tax shares subjectively exactly as they do in the determination of prices in the private economy. It is on this note that we now turn to the marginal utility approaches of Wicksell and Lindahl, according to which relative tax shares are determined simultaneously with the supply side of the public budget with little or no fiscal coercion.

7
Swedish Fiscal Doctrine: The Collective Choice Approach

There is an unmistakable affinity between Austrian and Swedish perspectives of the public economy. On may add that the Swedish fiscal doctrine is a natural extension of the principles set forth by Wieser and Sax. The two Austrian political economists were responsible for resting the entire fiscal process on the platform of subjective valuation, thus making the theory of the public economy an integral part of political economy. To Sax, collective valuation had its full explanation in the general, that is, individual nature of value. In his characterization, both Robinson Crusoe as a single soul and an entire nation of a hundred million people would obey one and the same law in their economic transactions, that of subjective value.[1] For, all goods, private or public, derived their value from whatever uses they were intended to serve. This is not to say that there exists a perfect parallel between the two categories of goods. In the public economy, due to the variability in personal wants and incomes, the same amounts of collective goods are valued differently. Alternatively, the same amounts of value are expressed in different quantities of collective goods. Wieser expands on Sax's point:

> [E]very intending purchaser who goes on to the market calculates to himself, or ought to calculate, the money equivalent of the goods he wishes to buy, i.e., the sum of money whose value to *him* will equal the value of the goods, so that it is not economically permissible for him to go beyond it. Now a similar money-equivalent must be calculated for the value which the services of the state have to the individual citizen. More than this money equivalent it cannot, economically speaking, be the duty of any citizen to pay in taxation, but, on the other hand, it is the duty of everyone to pay taxes up to this amount in order to meet the costs of the public service. This acknowledged,

> the next matter is the more exact estimate of the individual equivalents. The circumstances which decide are [individual] wealth, income, and want. The greater the wealth and income, the greater will be the subjective equivalent of the taxation; and the greater the degree of want, the smaller will be the subjective equivalent of taxation.[2]

Wieser points out that the fundamental principle laid out by Sax, "equal justice for all," rested upon the legal assumption of the inviolability of private property. This principle required that every taxpayer pay the full money equivalent according to his own valuation. The provenance of this precept lies not in economic reasoning, but in a sense of justice, one that relates to a special dimension of an individual's subjective evaluation process, namely that fiscal equilibrium cannot be achieved in an equitable manner in the face of inequality of economic means and wants.[3] The problem with this obviously meritorious principle has to do with its application. For, there is no economic mechanism that affords a common measure of the different interests of individuals who are differently situated in communal economy with respect to wealth, income, and wants. Such an operational framework has yet to be formulated. This objective constitutes the Holy Grail for two important Swedish fiscal theorists, Knut Wicksell and Erik Lindahl.

Wicksell: towards a just theory of taxation

Wicksell and Lindahl sought a fiscal equilibrium that complied not only with the dictum of economic efficiency, but also the demands of political and social justice. That such a requirement would meet daunting methodological obstacles did not escape them. Yet, they committed themselves with full enthusiasm to the formulation of an economic paradigm that afforded a just distribution of the tax burden within the marginal framework. Put differently, Wicksell and Lindahl sought a fiscal equilibrium that was simultaneously just and efficient. Wicksell noted:

> The difficulty rests, first, on the ambiguity, the relativity, and the changeability of the concept of justice itself. Each attempted solution of our problem will necessarily be coloured more or less by the general social and political philosophy of the writer, by his station in life, and by his personal sympathies and antipathies. As has been correctly observed, there can be justice only among equals... Even apart from all this, and even if one is or believes oneself to be

> completely clear concerning the goals to be attained, it is no simple matter to encompass the infinitely varied and here relevant mutual relations and interrelations between individuals, classes, and the State in one single formula which is comprehensive, rigorous, and susceptible of application in practice... [T]he sacrifice theory... can determine only the distribution of taxes but has nothing whatever to say on the absolute amount of the total tax bill (and hence of the individual's tax bill). Either this last question must be entirely left out of account, which would certainly be very convenient but in my opinion hardly scientific, or the benefit principle must be reintroduced, as best it may, in any attempt at a theoretical determination of the actual amount of the taxes to be raised, or at least of total taxation.[4]

Wicksell's brilliant doctoral dissertation, which he defended at University of Uppsala in 1895, was inspired by his deep concern for these and other social questions. "Now I shall set to work on my... book covering the whole subject of taxation," he wrote a friend in 1894, for "I am truly shocked to see how confoundedly unfair it is to the little man."[5]

Wicksell concurred with Sax's position that the determination of the "relative" shares of the cost of public goods must be based on subjective valuation within the purview of the benefit principle of taxation. But Wicksell disagreed with Sax's application of the same premise to the determination of "absolute" tax, that is, the total tax bill. Wicksell believed that the direct application of the voluntary exchange process resting upon the benefit principle would fail to determine a full reconciliation between the expenditure and taxation sides of the public account. To achieve this result some sort of collective choice mechanism was in order. Wicksell turned to Italian fiscal theory for insight only to find that Italian fiscal scientists applied the benefit principle too loosely. German scientists of State, who used the benefit principle only when they discerned a specific and measurable interest applicable to individuals or social groups, conversely, limited this principle too strictly. In Wicksell's view, the benefit principle should be applied to all those activities of the State that entailed the problem of rational delimitation of separate state expenditures, except those cases in which public expenditures were based on something other than the interests of actual citizens, such as expenditures which resulted from obligations undertaken by the State at an earlier point in time.[6] Austrian and Italian writers who applied marginal utility and value not just to relative shares but also to the total tax bill committed an error. For, they failed to see that when individuals and groups ascertained that the marginal utility of a given collective good did not equal or surpass the marginal utility of the private good that they must forsake for the provision of the public service in question, they would feel overburdened even if they realized that the utility of the public service as a whole exceeded the total value of individual sacrifices.[7] Accordingly, Austrian and Italian writers' propositions concerning an economically optimal equilibrium failed to lead to an *ethical* solution to taxation.

Wicksell singles out Sax and Mazzola as the archetypes of the flawed Austrian and Italian theorists of the public economy. Wicksell finds Mazzola's "supreme law of the fiscal economy [whereby] the degree of [marginal] utility of public goods is always equal to their price" hardly in agreement with the observed experience in all those cases in which fee financing remains impractical.[8] An individual intent to spend his money for private and public uses to maximize the satisfaction of his complementary needs will pay nothing for the consumption of the public goods provided by the fiscal authority. Similarly, Sax's rejection of any state activity whose total utility exceeds the sacrifice that it imposes to individual taxpayers is not acceptable since it would lead to collectivism. For, any comparison between the value to the community and the burden upon individual budgets will necessarily result in extracting money from wealthy individuals to improve the welfare of poorer classes, since the total utility to the community will normally exceed the total sacrifice of the individuals. To illustrate:

> If *A* has an income of 10,000 *mark* and *B* an income of only 1,000, then any "state activity" which, for example, takes 100 *mark* from *A* and only 10 from *B*, and subsequently divides the sum of 110 *mark*, say, equally between *A* and *B*, would cause an excess of sacrifice for *A* and an excess benefit for *B*. In absolute terms both are 45 *mark*. But the sum of 45 *mark* probably has smaller subjective value for *A* than for *B*, both before and after the transfer. Therefore, the excess sacrifice is bound to be smaller than the excess benefit or utility and consequently the total sacrifice smaller than the total utility – *q.e.d.*[9]

Wicksell laments that neither Mazzola nor Sax has envisioned a collective choice process in the determination of fiscal equilibrium. Mazzola's theory is based squarely on voluntary exchange mechanism between an acquiescent taxpayer and a benevolent tax collector. In this model of the public economy the executive and legislative branches are collapsed into a single fiscal authority represented by a single decision-maker. Such a fiscal process is not encountered in any contemporary political constitution. What we normally have is a monarchical executive pursuing selfish, dynastic ends and a parliament interested in the general welfare of the electorate. The executive has delegated his authority more and more to the parliament while the parliament has addressed more and more the interests of the majority. The common constitutional arrangement exhibits intense political activity, which should not be left out of any workable theory of maximization of social utility.

The ultimate values of contemporary political societies have come to center around the principles of equality before the law, greatest possible individual liberty, maximum economic well-being, and peaceful co-operation of all citizens.[10] These objectives need to be balanced against the overall desire for society's continuity and stability. The majority rule, which is embedded in most contemporary constitutions, is routinely invoked to reconcile the conflicting goals pursued by different social groups. But this rule flagrantly disregards the interests of a minority of citizens who oppose the majority on the relative value of the utility and the corresponding sacrifice in the financing of collective activity. Wicksell considers it a blatant injustice if even a single individual is coerced to contribute toward the costs of a government activity that does not further that individual's own interest. So, a new principle of taxation is called for, one that is based on the principle of unanimity and fully voluntary consent in the making of fiscal-economic decisions. Only this new fiscal precept would provide a guarantee against injustice in tax distribution; otherwise, the whole discussion of tax justice remains suspended in mid-air.[11]

The political parameters of Wicksell's theory of the public economy

The first rule in a just distribution of tax burdens is simultaneous determination of both sides of the public account. No collective activity should be initiated without securing its financial means in the aftermath of a valuation process entailing a correct calculation of the benefits and costs of alternative projects and the corresponding ranking of the contemplated projects. Only those alternatives that pass the muster of full or approximate unanimity should become law and those that do not should be rejected. Wicksell rests this rule upon a new interpretation of benefit principle which, formulated within the framework of unanimous parliamentary decisions, would prevent any group of citizens from paying a tax-price greater than the benefits of the collective activity under consideration.

This process of collective choice would work relatively simply when applied to the provision of new public goods and the determination of their absolute and relative tax shares. The mechanics would become more difficult to implement when a reduction of expenditures and revenues is involved. The difficulty arises from the ordinary fiscal practice where individual expenditure and revenue items do not necessarily correspond to each other, hence it is not pre-established what revenue item should be abrogated with the cessation of what expenditure item and vice versa.[12]

Wicksell is well aware that all economic analysis is abstract and schematic, and all results correspondingly hypothetical, hence valid only under certain simplifying assumptions.[13] Yet he does not consider his analysis of the public economy unrealistic, since it reflects the essential political elements with respect to progressive parliamentary regimes of contemporary society. He reminds his readers that Public-Economic Man is activated by personal as well as social impulses.[14] Protected by the principle of unanimity and voluntary consent, this voter-consumer will come to regard taxes as what they really are: the sources of special benefits to himself as well as to his fellow voter-consumers. Each individual member of the electorate would be happy, in spirit of good citizenship, that the goods that taxation withdraws from his private use are destined for purposes which he recognizes to be useful for other people.[15] Wicksell elaborates:

> There would no longer be occasion for the many devious devices by which the true magnitude and significance of the tax load have in the past been concealed from the people. The fiscal principle would have to yield to the economic principle; the direct method of raising state revenues should become the rule and the indirect method the exception ... Special consideration should be given to those public expenditures which today are still formally finances on the basis of the so-called fee principle ... If ... the principle of Value and Countervalue ... were reinstated ... in the manner I have proposed, then there would no longer be such a dividing line between the alleged business method and the fiscal method of financing state expenditure, between the fee and the tax principle. ... [I]t is often better to cover the costs of public activities in some way other than by levying fees or direct charges. This reason is of a purely economic sort and is closely connected with my discussion ... of monopoly

> prices ... If such enterprises [as] ... railways, postal and telegraph administration etc ... were to be run on the fee principle and total production costs [were] ... to be spread over a relatively small number of service units, the unit price would normally have to be much higher than the marginal cost ... Such a pricing policy would allow the public service to satisfy the demands of only those persons who rate its subjective value higher or at least as high as the fee which is charged. The entire range of demand [that] is less intensive than this objective level must remain unsatisfied.[16]

The variability of the use value and subjective value between wealthier and poorer social classes stems from the fact that the members of the latter social class value money more highly vis-à-vis the perceived utility of public goods and services. The fiscal authority should not fall prey to this valuational attitude, however, and should make every effort to secure wider participation in the collective choice process. For, each letter, each telegram, each piece of railway freight which is not sent, each journey which is not made because more is charged for it than it would cost the community, constitutes an unresolved economic problem which can and must be solved in a rational manner, specifically, according to the principle of unanimity and voluntary consent in taxation, preferably incorporating the veto right of the minority.[17]

The essential condition of Wicksell's principle of unanimity and voluntary consent is that expenditures and the means of their financing be voted on simultaneously. This condition does not necessarily require changing a society's constitution: the various political parties need only make use of the right extended to them under most modern constitutions, namely to make the approval of each budgetary demand, or at least of each new one, contingent upon a specific, initially defined manner of financing that expenditure.[18] The incorporation of the veto right of minorities within the larger principle of unanimity would follow naturally if communities espoused the principle of unanimity. When public expenditures and revenues are decided upon separately, the rule of simple majority would appear as an adequate fiscal principle. But it would cease to appear so if public expenditures and revenues are decided upon simultaneously. In that case the political parties would have to make a choice among many possible alternative packages of collective activity, which would result in the selection of the bundle of public goods that would satisfy everybody. This bundle must be imbued with more justice than any other that might appeal more to an accidentally greater half of those interested, but that would be at the expense of the others.[19] As a result, the veto right for the minority emerges as a necessary ingredient in Wicksell's model of the public economy.

The allocationally efficient political process proposed by Wicksell is intended to eliminate the free rider problem. To Wicksell, absolute unanimity, that is 100 percent approval in the allocation of resources in the public economy, is analogous to the efficient competitive solution in the private market.[20] Only under this scheme would an individual cease to act as a free rider and willingly pay the price of the public good in question. Put differently, the individual would feel that his own selection among alternative public expenditures would directly influence the consumption of other individuals in the group, as is true in the two-person exchange of pure private good.[21] Under these circumstances, the individual would consider the rest of the group as a unified block of traders whom the individual could deprive from benefiting from the public good in question if he chooses to void the trade.

The problem with perfect unanimity is that it would lead to total breakdown even if a single individual acted irresponsibly, since a single negative vote would block an entire budgetary policy. It is for this reason that Wicksell explored alternative schemes of "relative" unanimity, say, a five-sixths or seven-eights approval rule, whereby the veto right of a small group of dissenting minority cannot block a budget proposal:

> This means that an individual in a large group situation ... will not be as strongly motivated to exploit others through a negative strategy as he would under an absolute unanimity rule. If a proposal promises some benefits for him, he may accept it even though under a benchmark of absolute unanimity he might be tempted to strategically block the same policy. Thus, under a five-sixths relative unanimity rule, it is more likely that a sufficient number of individuals in society would follow nonstrategic behavior so as to allow an acceptable number of collective decisions to be made.[22]

Richard Musgrave terms Wicksell's *Finanztheoretische Untersuchungen* "the most creative book in public finance ever written," one that "bypassed the formal apparatus of welfare conditions" to offer "a normative approach to voting procedures which links the efficiency problems of social goods provision to the applied issues of how an efficient solution can be achieved in practice."[23] Similarly James Buchanan hails Wicksell for effectively demonstrating to contemporary political economists that fiscal equilibrium emerges from a political decision-making process rather than from the mind of a benevolent despot.[24]

All that one needed, after the appearance of "A New Principle of Just Taxation" was a model of public choice which provided an optimal quantity of a public good such that, for each single quantity produced, a corresponding tax burden may be found that equated the marginal valuation of the good to the marginal tax share of the voter-consumer.[25] This task was attempted by Erik Lindahl.

Lindahl: the principle of unanimity revisited

Lindahl studied at Lund when Wicksell was Professor of Political Economy and Fiscal Law. Though not a student of Wicksell's, Lindahl was immensely impressed by *Finanztheoretische Untersuchungen*. In fact, it was this work that stimulated him to write his own doctoral dissertation on the principles of justice in taxation, though he followed an entirely different methodological path.[26]

Lindahl's model of public economy complied only with the minimal conditions of public choice. Its characterization of voting process, involving only two groups of voter-consumers, lies somewhere between ordinary bilateral voluntary exchange framework and large group collective choice. Lindahl first tried to see whether the sharing of the costs of a public good could be accommodated within the conventional framework of demand and supply relationship. He knew that Wicksell was particularly adverse to any analogy to private-economic exchange process in the determination of fiscal equilibrium. Wicksell was certain that consumers of public goods would never reveal their true preferences for these goods as they would in the private-economic exchange since that would entail paying the corresponding tax-price. It was for this reason that he termed Mazzola's model of demand and supply of public goods as "a really meaningless" construct.[27] Wicksell believed that the only possible way for a given distribution of tax burden to be instrumental in creating the condition of equimarginality would be by asking citizen-consumers to vote on alternative bundles of public services and determine the corresponding total and relative tax burdens unanimously.

Lindahl came up with an ingenious solution. He developed a model of the public economy that complied both with Mazzola's two-party voluntary exchange process based on demand and supply *and* Wicksell's multi-party collective-choice construct resting upon the principle of unanimity. Lindahl's model of the public economy entailed two groups of citizen-consumers, *A* and *B*, the first relatively well-to-do and the other relatively poor. Hence, his model formally complied with the minimum requirements of collective choice for involving more than one group of voter-consumers. However, Lindahl presented his model as a special case of voluntary exchange whereby the two parties intended to reach an equilibrium that was efficient in collective rather than individual terms. He called this particular economic organization as an "isolated exchange," in which one party's demand for a certain collective good at a certain price is perceived by the other party as a supply of this good at a price corresponding to the remaining part of the total cost – since the collective good can only be undertaken if the sum of the prices paid is sufficient to cover its cost.[28]

Lindahl assumed that both groups had equal political power and were intent to approve both the extent of the collective activity – that is, the total tax bill – and the share of each group in the financing of that level of activity. In other words, the supply side of the public account was to be determined simultaneously with the demand side in accordance with the subjective valuations of the two parties. All that was called for in this special economy was the conventional calculus of marginal utility. Lindahl goes on:

> If one party succeeded in getting the cost of the more important public services distributed in a more favourable way than the cost of the marginal ones, this would indicate that that party has defended its own interests better than the other part[y] and hence that political power is not distributed evenly. It must surely seem unjustified from the point of view of the existing property order that one party secures precisely those expenditures which it values most at a lower price than the less important ones. If the economic rights to which the individuals are entitled under a given property order are to be safeguarded in equal measure, everyone should pay the same price for the same units of cost both in the area of the private economy and of Public Finance. On these assumptions the question of distribution really means how big a share of certain total costs each party has to bear. Since the extent of collective activity is not given a priori, but is one of the variables of the problem, the absolute amount of taxation has to be determined at the same time of its distribution. The economic aspect of the problem thereby becomes a good deal more determinate, even though not fully so: the extent of collective activity desired by the taxpayers becomes largely decisive for their cost share.[29]

Lindahl then presents his well-known (Figure 7.1), which shows that, under the assumptions of unequal distribution of economic resources

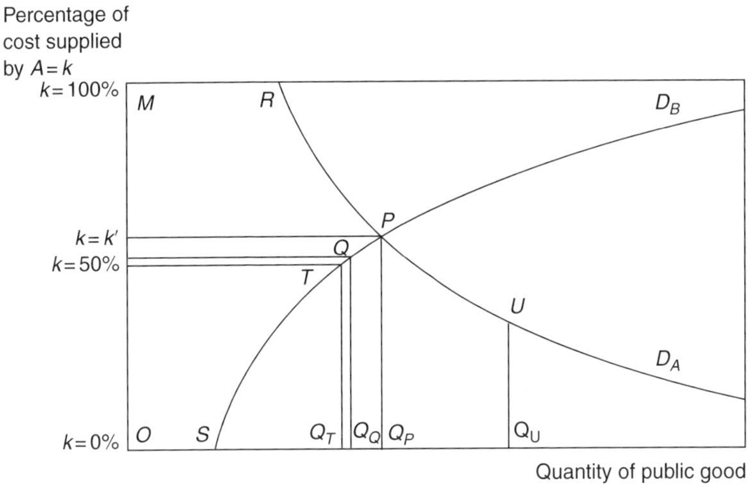

Figure 7.1 The two-party Lindahl solution

but equal distribution of political power, the two parties will determine the price of collective goods with respect to their respective marginal utility: [30]

Lindahl explains his diagram

> Our figure shows on the [ordinate] the relative share of one party (*A*) in total cost at various distribution [percentages]. At point *O* part *A* pays nothing at all towards total cost, leaving the entire burden to the other party, *B*. The further we move away from *O*, the greater becomes *A*'s share and the smaller *B*'s. At point *M* the situation is completely reversed; *A* carries the whole burden and *B* none. On the [abscissa] we indicate the amount of public expenditure which each party is prepared to sanction at the various distribution [percentages]. As in the private economy, so here too demand rises up to the point where marginal utility equals price. On the basis of the curves of individual marginal utility we have drawn two curves representing the monetary expression of the marginal utility of total public activity for the two parties. The two curves [D_A and D_B] show immediately how demand for public goods varies according as the parties have to shoulder a greater or smaller part of public expenditure. At the distribution ration most favourable to itself, party *A* is obviously prepared to approve a maximum of public goods and *B* a minimum, and *vice versa* when the distribution is most favourable to *B*. The intersection

> point [***P***] of the two curves indicates the only distribution of costs at which both parties agree on the extent of public activity [$\boldsymbol{Q_P}$]At the different positions of distribution the two parties will approve public expenditure only to the extent that one party's demand is matched by the other's "supply." The possible equilibrium positions therefore lie on the curve *SPR*, but we may be able to define them more closely. Let us suppose, for example, that the two parties initially agree to split the cost in equal parts. A provisional equilibrium will be established at point *T*. But only [a portion] of *A*'s demand is satisfied and this party will insists on an expansion of public activity. Party *B* can agree to this only if it can secure a more favourable distribution of costs, and *A* will have to face the fact that it must take on a greater share of the cost burden. The equilibrium position is thereby shifted closer to the intersection point of the two curves.[31]

This is not to say that *A* and *B* have to settle at point *P*. The distribution of the tax burden may be altered, through mutual agreement, at any point on the curve *SPR*. The only condition for the equilibrium is that one party's incremental sacrifice as a result of expanded public service is more than compensated by the additional utility gained. The movement from point *T* towards *P* will be possible only as long as *A* is willing to make more sacrifice to gain net utility:

> Once these two factors become equal, as for instance at point *Q*, *A* has reached the equilibrium position most favourable to itself. At an unchanged distribution of cost, it would still be more advantageous for *A* if public activity increased yet further, but *B* will not agree to this ... *B*'s agreement to an expansion of public activity is thus contingent upon *A*'s shouldering a greater share of total cost; but such a shift of the equilibrium position towards *P* means that the difference between utility and sacrifice diminishes for party *A*, which will therefore try to remain at the distribution we have indicated ... Since the most favourable position for one party is for the other the least favourable of all the *possible* equilibrium positions, each party naturally tries to shift the equilibrium ... to its advantage. Which of the possible positions – which lie on the curve *QPR* – will eventually lead to equilibrium, is mostly a matter of the extent to which each party is able to defend its own interests.[32]

Lindhal thus demonstrates that prices of collective goods as well are determined by the marginal utility that afford to their consumers,

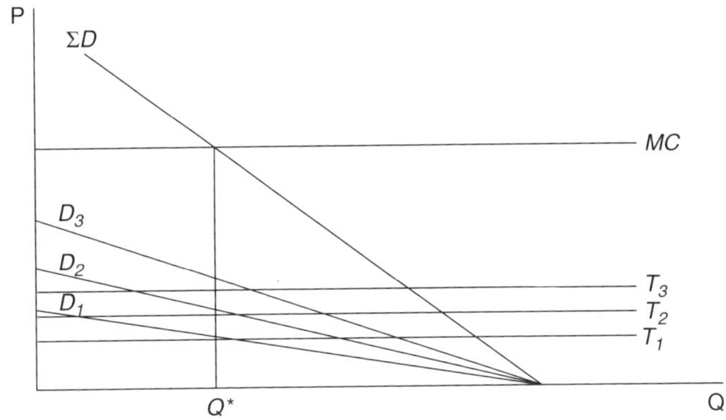

Figure 7.2 The multiple-party Lindahl solution

at least in the case of bilateral voluntary exchange. The next step is to expand this model to more than two parties. To do this one only needs to sum up the demand curves of all the economic units interested in a particular collective activity and determine the marginal utility of this activity for each of these groups. In fact, one can render the scenario even more general by assuming that each of these parties wields different measures of political power. The diagram given above (Figure 7.2) would help explain Lindhal's view in this more general case:

> The market demand for a collective consumption good is found by vertically summing the individual demand curves. The optimal level of output is the level at which the marginal cost equals the sum of the demands. T_1, T_2, and T_3 are the Lindahl tax shares for the three individuals whose demands are depicted in the diagram [as D_1, D_2, and D_3] ... At quantity Q^* the marginal value of the good to consumer D_1 is T_1, T_2 to consumer D_2, and T_3 to consumer D_3. If those prices are charged to the individual demanders, then each individual is paying a marginal price equal to the [his] marginal value of the good.[33]

This diagram demonstrates that an efficient total output of a collective activity is decided at the intersection of ΣD and MC curves regardless of the distribution of income and wealth.[34] Consider that D_1, D_2, and D_3 represent three groups of citizens where D_1 encompasses those with the least income, D_2, those with average incomes, and D_3 those with high income. If the overall tax rate is established at T_2, that is, at the rate of those with average incomes, those with high incomes would welcome this tax scheme and, assuming they have adequate political clout, would force it upon the poor. If, conversely, the low-income group had political power, they might force upon the other two groups a much lower quantity of collective good.

Naturally, this leads to the conclusion that, in the face of unequal political power, Lindahl's tax-prices will be inherently unfair. Lindahl has anticipated this criticism and duly considered the case in which bargaining power is divided unequally. He did not overlook the eventuality that when a party is able to defend its interests better than other parties, the standard equilibrium will shift in direct proportion with the preponderance of power.[35] Referring to his original diagram Lindahl remarks:

> [w]ith due qualification, the actual equilibrium position can still be determined according to the same principles we have used above. If we are dealing with only one given category of public goods and have to determine the amount and distribution of the tax burden, the coercive element due to the preponderance of power obviously has the same effect as if the weaker parties now attached greater values to the public goods. In our diagram, the new equilibrium position is best found by moving the old one along *A*'s price curve, say to point *U; B*'s net gain decreases in proportion with the magnitude of the coercive element. In the face of several alternatives, the dominant party will be able to make that prevail which offers it greater positive advantages than does the "standard" case. If a budget surplus is available or a deficit to be covered, the distribution of benefits and sacrifices will be more favourable to the dominant party than to others.[36]

Lindahl then shows how a dominant party can alter the fiscal equilibrium in its favor:

> First, the dominant party can abuse the other's ignorance and mislead them into believing that the budget is more favourable to them than it really is... If the ruling party cannot achieve favourable finance arrangements by [fiscal illusions], it uses its predominance to impose openly upon the others higher taxes then they want to pay of their free will... [Fortunately,] as the weaker classes succeed in giving currency to their own sense of justice, so their political power grows and so, also, diminishes the ruling classes' preponderance of power and their ability to secure by force special benefits at the expense of others. In the last resort, the views about what is just in taxation determine its actual shaping.[37]

Lindahl eventually tempered his unflinching adherence to fiscal justice. In his 1928 treatise, "Some Controversial Questions in the Theory of Taxation," he states: "I may in the past have expressed myself too categorically in favour of just taxation; now I have revised my opinion to the extent of admitting the theoretical validity of the *economic* postulate."[38] In this new work, Lindahl reiterates that individual taxpayers' subjective valuations are sufficient for the determination of fiscal equilibrium, even whether benefit of collective activity is indivisible. Indivisibility of the benefits of a public good does not render its cost invariable. Public expenditure is often variable. Hence, if the public budget is reduced by 10 percent the fiscal authority organizes its activity less effectively, and if public expenditure were increased by 10 percent the extra money would be used for improvements in public services.[39] So, as was previously remarked by Sax, individual taxpayers construe each successive increment in public expenditures as the marginal utility of public services and evaluate each of these increments more or less accurately in terms of money.[40] What needs to be stressed is that what is being measured is not the *total* utility of the public budget to the individual, but the *marginal* utility of incremental public expenditures to him. In other words, it is not the total utility of each different bundle of public goods, but the marginal values that are elicited by the individuals asked to choose between alternative bundles of public goods. Taxpayers never have been given the opportunity to make such a choice and therefore not aware of the evaluation on which they would base their choice; nevertheless, these values are not altogether unknown quantities.[41] These values can be constructed theoretically as the resultants of those factors that would in any given case determine the evaluation.[42]

Is it indeed possible to attain justice in taxation?

Subjective valuation is not limited to the assessment of public expenditure lines that provide measurable personal benefits. The same concept applies to those cases where the benefit is intended to serve the undifferentiated interest of the entire community. The evaluation still remains individualistic, not in the sense that it deals with the tangible personal advantages to be derived from collective activity, but in the sense that its analysis stems from physical persons.[43] Lindahl concludes:

> If our argument is correct, then ... individual values ... ultimately do determine the actual tax burden, because the men who take decisions base their financial calculations on an estimate of these individual

> values. The estimates can of course be wrong. People's interest in the expansion of some public service may, for instance, be overestimated. [Nevertheless, when] any voter registers his vote for one particular solution ... he thereby discloses his own evaluation, and since the election result naturally has its bearing on the actual solution of the budgetary question, this solution rests directly on individual values. There are, thus, direct as well as indirect links between the individual evaluation of public services and the actual decision on the amount of taxation ... It is a matter of indifference that these calculations are often highly subject to political ideas and prejudices – just as every single person's private spending depends very much on what other people do.[44]

Lindahl thus brings private- and public-economic choice together under the aegis of individual valuation. He judges the private-economic choice to constitute the general case and the public-economic a special case. He has a similar judgment on the two principles of taxation, benefit and ability-to-pay. Both principles are conditioned by the existing distribution of property, regardless of whether it is equitable. A taxpayer's current income and assets certainly influence his valuation of the want-satisfying properties of collective goods and their corresponding prices. Hence, the benefit principle is in full effect in the public economy. However, ability-to-pay is also operative in this economic sphere since the prices of collective goods derive partly from the means a taxpayer can dispose of for their acquisition. So, there is no contradiction between the two principles, but rather a relationship of rank: the benefit principle is the general one, applicable in the determination of objective advantages, while the ability principle is a practical norm for meeting the cost of subjective advantages.[45]

As mentioned in Chapter 2, contemporary authors have tended to ascribe Lindahl's model of the public economy to one principle of taxation or the other. Dual conclusions in this matter arise because the roots of Lindahl's model can indeed be traced back both to the benefit principle (considering that each party pays a price that equals their respective marginal benefit at the efficient output of the public good) and to ability-to-pay (since the equilibrium reflects the given distribution of income affecting the demands of the two parties). This is not to say that Lindahl actually fused the two tax principles into one whole principle. On the contrary, he held them consciously apart, resorting to one rather than the other, depending on the degree of equity prevailing in the distribution of incomes and property:

> If we assume a property order which leaves nothing to be desired from the point of view of social purposes, then the economic principle in public finance will obviously lead to taxation according to benefit – the latter, as we have said, being conducive to maximum satisfaction of wants as expressed in money terms under the prevailing [equitable] property order. On this point there is full agreement between the claims for [socially correct] taxation and for economically correct taxation. It is, however, more likely that the existing property order is not regarded as the best possible one. In that case it is at least theoretically possible to split the tax postulate in two: the property order is to be improved by [corrective] taxation and the remaining tax burden is to be distributed in proportion with the new distribution of wealth.[46]

Lindahl thus develops a two-tiered taxation scheme whereby the central government is responsible for organizing an ability-oriented tax system to move the distribution of wealth in the desired direction, while local authorities, going along with the existing property order, arrange taxation according to the benefit principle.[47] He considers the two-tiered fiscal structure as one of modest limits, accounting for only a small part of the total tax bill paid by a household. All in all, the benefit principle constitutes the heart of the public economy, where the given property order, no matter how equitable, influences individual valuations.

8
Epilogue

Economists differ from other social scientists in that they do not tackle human problems as they present themselves in the real world. To deal with complexities, economists severely restrict decisional variables, especially those that pertain to the behavioral makeup of the decision-maker. This framework was challenged by the proponents of, first, the administrative theory,[1] and, subsequently, the behavioral theory of choice.[2] Price theory has absorbed many of these concerns, shedding many a positivistic layer in the process, but still remaining a unified theory based on a singularly axiomatic foundation that the purpose of human life is to satisfy selfish wants in a rational manner.

Fiscal theory is not monolithic. We have a *set* of fiscal theories, each based on a different axiomatic platform. The benefit approach is based on the assumption that public goods are inherently productive and taxpayers willing to pay the commensurate price. The sacrifice approach, deeming public expenditures unproductive yet necessary fixtures of societal life, considers taxes as an inevitable burden that must be distributed in a least intrusive manner. Other fiscal theories are based on such platforms as historico-organic dimensions of the communal economy, subjective valuation of individual and collective utility, and social consensus. That each one of these fiscal theories can actually be ascribed to a national rubric has been the main point of the present work. A secondary point is whether these theories can be brought together under the rubric of a single fiscal theory.

Some efforts toward such integration certainly have been noted. While a full-fledged hybridization is far on the horizon, Lindahl's model of political market has been largely accommodated in the modern public economics curriculum. Under this system, where each group of voters pays a marginal cost commensurate with its marginal valuation of the collective good under consideration, efficiency is achieved in the Bowen–Samuelson sense because the single quantity of the good that is produced corresponds to the equation of total demand and the marginal cost of production.[3] Unfortunately, another Continental body of fiscal theory espousing an equally propitious construct, the Italian theory of public goods, still remains largely outside the English-language curriculum of public economics. The main reason that Wicksell and Lindahl, and not De Viti and Mazzola, enjoyed some success in the Anglo-Saxon world was that the collective choice process prescribed by the two Swedes was designed to produce a fiscal equilibrium that not only was in accord with individual taxpayers' preferences, that is, was efficient, but also satisfied the precepts of equitable taxation, the main thrust of British public economics. The Italian model of public goods, in contrast, summarily delegated to a group of politicians equipped with the power of compulsion the task of evaluating individuals' collective wants and determining the prices of public goods apt to satisfy these wants. A fiscal construct based on the behavior of a ruling elite was evidently not palatable to English-language scholars, who, thanks to Wicksell and Lindahl, already had developed a taste for a political market mechanism based on a direct-democratic voting scheme that produced a just *and* efficient distribution of the tax burden.

What accounts for the continuing disregard of the contributions in the same community of scholars of the father of the concept of political markets, De Viti de Marco? The constitutional framework envisioned by De Viti, meanwhile, carried a disconcerting overtone resulting from his concept of the ruling class. What was lost in the comparison was that De Viti's model of the political markets was based on a more realistic political constitution, that of representative-democracy, which, for better or for worse, characterizes the typical postmodern polity. By rendering the fiscal authority an endogenous element in the determination of fiscal equilibrium, De Viti acted as no less than a precursor of the modern theory of public choice.[4] Many of the elements of modern public choice are fully discernible in De Viti's vision of cooperative public economy, in which the individual is both a consumer of collective goods and a contributor to the expenditure side of the fiscal account. Accordingly, there is nothing to prevent the grafting of the Italian theory of public goods onto the modern public economics curriculum.

There is much to gain by integrating fiscal theories along behaviorally descriptive parameters. Fiscal exchange – unlike the private-economic exchange, which entails only the assessment of relative prices between the consumer and the entrepreneur – evokes a rich repertoire of variables, including ideologies, alliances, and attitudes, which evidently affects the decisional behaviors of the payers and the collectors of taxes. It should follow from readily observable evidence that the fiscal act encompasses not only the economic, political, and legal circumstances, which are normally included in fiscal theorizing, but also such variables as perceptions, values, and information processing abilities that were found to influence the economic exchange mechanism in the public sector. As noted in Chapter 1, empirical literature offers a wealth of insight in this regard. All that is needed is an effort to meld these behavioral variables with the economic, political, and legal constraints already used by the followers of Buchanan and Downs in their analyses of the public economy. This extra step will also comply with an adage long heeded by most politicians, but not by most fiscal theorists, that there is a *human* element (habit, confidence, fear, and so on) in the economic affairs of the State that defies mechanistic applications.[5]

Evidence warrants a new behavioral foundation for fiscal theory. As a first step, fiscal economists should accommodate in their discourse certain cognitive-psychological findings attributable to all economic agents, such as the human inability to ascribe complex probabilities to future events, the tendency to include sunk costs in the calculation of utility, or the propensity to weigh out-of-pocket costs more heavily than opportunity costs. As a second step, they should concentrate on variables specific to public choice. Ordinary voters obviously display a richer variety of such variables as values, expectations, perceptions, and expectations in determining their preferences than ordinary consumers. These variables should be elicited, measured, and tested before being applied to the fiscal decision-making process.

Fiscal economists have at their disposal a substantial amount of empirical evidence to develop a behavioral theory of the public economy.[6] We learn from this vein of research that:

> [Fiscal] attitudes and preferences can be studied, and they can be more accurately predicted when variables besides those normally employed in neoclassical micro-economic assumptions are used. These additional variables include age, occupational status and job experience, and of particular importance is an appreciation of fiscal knowledge or fiscal awareness. [A]ttitudes, opinions, and fiscal preferences ... are not "facts;" [nevertheless, they] ... have an exploratory function and improve both predictions of behaviour and our understanding of the causes of behaviour.[7]

If economists, fiscal theorists included, genuinely believe that their methodology will one day constitute the heart of a general theory of society,[8] they should not turn their backs to empirical knowledge accumulated in behavioral sciences. An operational framework enhanced by behavioral parameters is likely to elicit the true relationships that exist between taxpayers and tax collectors, hence to be more instrumental than conventional fiscal theory in predicting as well as explaining the public-economic act.

A Synopsis of General Characteristics of National Fiscal Doctrines

This section briefly presents the essential characteristics of national bodies of fiscal thought according to the following plan. Each section opens with a list of the names of the most important representatives and a brief description of the general characteristics of the given national school of fiscal thought. This is ensued by a five-part analysis. The first concerns each theory's treatment of the two sides of the fiscal account. Some theories simultaneously determine both the tax and the expenditure side of the budget while some others determine one side independently of the other. Again, in some national schools of fiscal thought both sides comply with the principle of equimarginality while in some others marginal valuation is reserved only for the tax side. The second analysis concerns the treatment of the problem of economic efficiency. How is the efficient level of output thought to be attained in each theory in face of conflicting individual demands of public goods? How, in each theory, are the votes of individuals translated into the demand for public sector output? The next area of analysis, concerning the handling of the problem of coercion, is closely linked to the preceding one; namely, considering that the majority rule is adopted as the basis of collective choice, what protects the minority in whose valuation the public good appears unproductive? The treatment of subjective valuation is the ensuing area of analysis. Not each and every national body of fiscal thought accommodates this concept. The German school, for instance, flatly rejects it by presuming that individual taxpayers are devoid of the requisite cognitive faculties to discern collective utility. The final section presents some issues specific to the particular national body of fiscal thought. For example, the overriding concern of the Swedish fiscal doctrine is how to avoid coercion in the determination of fiscal equilibrium while Italian theory, decidedly sanguine in this respect, proceeds to investigate how to determine the prices of public goods in accordance with a mechanistic interpretation of marginal valuation. It is hoped that this synopsis will provide help not only in accentuating the different dimensions of each national doctrine, but also in challenging the student of public economics as to whether and how these disparate theories could be fused into an integrated theory of the public economy.

British fiscal doctrine – sacrifice view

Important contributors: Sidgwick, Edgeworth, Marshall, Pigou, Dalton.

General framework: That certain services such as diplomacy, national defense, and fire protection have fallen invariably under the aegis of the State is the result of historical realities. Private entrepreneurs have shunned these services because they are unprofitable. Yet, these services constitute the essentials of any societal life and they must be provided even if their provision entails payments that exceed comparable market prices. Hence, the State, acting as a responsible caretaker, manages these (unproductive) services in such a fashion that their provision demands the least possible sacrifice on household budgets.

Expenditure side: Since the caretaker-State limits its economic activity to a minimum variety and scope of public services, public expenditures do not affect citizens' welfare substantially. As a result, little knowledge can be acquired from the analysis of the expenditure side of the public budget. The task of public economics is to develop ways to minimize the sacrifice that *taxation* imposes on individuals.

Tax side: The State's main concern must be to minimize the burden of taxation, and this task can only be achieved by devising a scheme whereby the total tax bill is divided among the citizens in a most equitable manner. This entails a distribution system based on each individual's relative welfare position as determined by his assets, inheritance, or income. Hence, the ability-to-pay principle, not benefit, emerges as the appropriate principle of taxation.

Subjective valuation: It is the prime mover in the private economy. But since the benefits stemming from public services are indivisible, it is not possible to impute to individual citizens any benefit shares. Consequently, the quid pro quo solution proposed by the benefit approach is out of the question. This is not to negate subjective valuation summarily. It has use in fiscal analysis, especially in comparing the amount of sacrifice that alternative forms taxation inflict on individuals.

Economic efficiency: It is a moot issue. State economic activity is by definition unproductive. Subsequently, the fiscal authority should aim at an equitable rather than efficient equilibrium. The principle of justice requires that fiscal burden be distributed equitably, not only among citizens who have the same income (horizontal equity), but also among those who have different levels of income (vertical equity). This is another reason for the resorting to the ability-to-pay principle rather than benefit.

Fiscal coercion: The cost of public services must be covered one way or the other. This requires that each citizen honor his respective fiscal obligation as determined by his ability to pay. Citizens generally comply with this principle, as they have come to perceive taxes as a premium they have to pay to maintain their respective welfare position (insurance view of taxation). Fortunately, because the variety and extent of public expenditure is limited, the required public revenue is also small, hence the commensurate coercion minimal.

Specific issues: Public economics is a normative economic subdiscipline concerned mainly with the analysis of the effects of alternative taxes on individual budgets and the selection of the particular tax alternative expected to produce the least sacrifice. But first, the concept of sacrifice must be clarified. One can invoke three relevant concepts of fiscal sacrifice (equi-absolute, equi-proportional, and equi-marginal), each relying upon the dual hypotheses of declining marginal utility of income and comparability of interpersonal utilities. Robbins criticized these hypotheses as the "new" Welfare Economics gained momentum in Britain thanks to the contributions of Bergson, Hicks, and Kaldor. Pigou and Dalton, meanwhile, extended the welfare argument to the expenditure side, transforming the public budget into a general plan to produce maximum social welfare.

Italian fiscal doctrine – benefit view

Important contributors: Pantaleoni, De Viti De Marco, Mazzola.

General framework: Taxes are but prices of public goods as determined by taxpayer demand. The goods provided by the State are either consumed by the members of individual households or employed by individual entrepreneurs in the production of private goods. Thus, in either case the State has a tax claim for the citizens' use of public goods. The relation between the taxpayer and the tax collector, accordingly, is quid pro quo.

Expenditure side: Since the purchase of public goods (i.e., paying taxes) entails a transfer of resources from private use to public use, the producer of these goods, the State, must consider both sides of the fiscal account in order to secure maximum social utility. As per the expenditure side, the State would determine the composition of public expenditure lines in such a way that the marginal yields from all equivalent units are equalized.[1]

Tax side: There is always an economic exchange relationship between the fiscal authority and taxpaying citizens that ultimately benefits the latter. However, the quid pro quo solution should not be taken to mean that the tax paid by the citizen exactly matches the share of the public good he actually consumes jointly with other citizens. It is enough for the individual to compare the burden of the tax that he has to pay today against the benefit he expects to extract from the given public good in the future. In this way, taxes resemble season tickets, purchased by citizens for a series of future public-economic performances.[2]

Subjective valuation: The Italian theory is certainly based on subjective valuation. But whose valuations are De Viti, Pantaleoni, and Mazzola actually talking about? The economic agent doing the valuation is not the taxpayer, but a functionary of the State characterized by the finance minister. The taxpayer perceives him as his elected agent. The minister, cognizant of the fiduciary character of his duties, remains receptive to the public needs emanating from his principals, on whose behalf he conducts public economic activity. At the same time, he is apprehensive of the eventuality that if he failed to address these needs fully, he would lose his post in the next election. Unfortunately for the minister, the fulfillment of *everybody*'s collective wants is an impossible task. Therefore, he elicits average voter preference, and takes it as a good approximation of actual collective wants. The minister never loses track of the overarching economic principle that income has a declining marginal utility for individuals, hence he prefers progressive taxation over other schemes of raising revenue.

Economic efficiency: Owing to the complementary character of public goods, fiscal equilibrium is reached at the household level when individuals allocate their resources between private and public goods in such a way that the two marginal utilities become equal.[3] But because another characteristic of public goods is non-excludability, multiple tax-prices must govern the public economy, the differences in these prices reflecting various citizens' different utility valuations, but not different abilities to pay.

Fiscal coercion: Despite the efforts of the rational and sentient fiscal authority represented by the finance minister, the public economy may not attain equilibrium. First, there is the problem of faulty valuation by the fiscal authority. Second, the fiscal authority may favor one constituency at the expense of another. Mazzola dismisses the first problem by stating that it is not endemic to the public economy: Economic Man, too, is known to make faulty valuations. As to the second, Mazzola argues that the finance minister would refrain from any such misstep, as he would realize that the resentment of a suppressed class may eventually jeopardize his tenure. Fortunately for the politician, taxpayers are accustomed to giving their judgment concerning the advisability of a given level of public expenditure *in advance*. They are also used to delegating to the political class the power of compulsion to be exercised when some citizens failed to honor their tax obligation as determined by public law. All in all, fiscal coercion will be small in practice since a rational and sentient fiscal authority will try to minimize the fiscal dissatisfaction felt by the minority bearing in mind that its success will ultimately be measured by the degree to which it achieved this result.

Specific issues: As in Germany so in Italy in the last decades of the nineteenth century, public finance (*Scienza delle finanze*) has evolved into an autonomous discipline studying the public economy in its entire range of manifestations, namely, those that pertain to economics, politics, and law. While this perspective gave Italian fiscal theory a holistic character, the emphasis on systemic analysis diluted considerably the theory's problem-solving prowess.[4]

German fiscal doctrine – organic view

Important contributors: Schäffle, Ritschl, Stein, Wagner.

General framework: The goals pursued by the State in the communal economy are different from those pursued by the individual in the private economy, and the difference is one of kind, not degree. Collective utility and individual utility are certainly related; however, the former subsumes the latter in the sphere of communal economy. The valuation of collective utility transcends the cognitive limits of the individual taxpayer. It is the fiscal authority that through its appropriately trained professionals makes proper fiscal decisions taking into consideration the economic as well political, social, and other realities confronting society at a given stage of its historical development.

Expenditure side: The fiscal authority reaches equilibrium by carefully considering the two parts of the public account. It first ascertains the appropriateness of each expenditure item with respect to historically valid variables, and then determines the proper extent of each of these items.

Tax side: Since the two sides of the budget are determined simultaneously,

> the principle of taxation which is appropriate in this theoretical framework [appears to be] of the Edgeworth-Pigou variety. The relevant criteria of comparison are reductions from social utility...The principle of equimarginal ... subtraction ... provides an acceptable rule for the apportionment of the total tax burden For each allocation of public expenditure the satisfaction of this principle will define an apportionment which will minimize the subtraction of social utility. It should be emphasized, however, that subtraction [is] used only with reference to a social, not an individual, concept of utility.[5]

Subjective valuation: Only the fiscal authority is endowed with appropriate decisional capacity (expertise) and proper decisional resources (e.g., clerical, informational, financial) that are necessary to reach a correct determination of collective utility. Put differently, the situation is one division of work. The citizens readily appreciate the State's assumption of such a formidable task and show the due compliance.

Economic efficiency: The state economic activity proceeds under the commanding principle of maximization of some quantifiable magnitude, presumably one that indicates social utility.[6] However, the determination of this cardinal value depends more heavily on some non-economic variables than on economic ones. Also, the principle of sacrifice that underlies German fiscal theory, "equimarginal subtraction," precludes any reference to subjective valuation.

Fiscal coercion: In the organic view of the public economy, the individual taxpayer and the fiscal authority are seen as two parties acting collectively rather than as adversaries, as is assumed in the individualistic view. As a result, the problem of coercion is severely understated. In truth, there is nothing in German doctrine to prevent coercion from reaching large proportions. For, the equi-marginal sacrifice principle that is in operation here is directed to minimize not individual sacrifice, but collective sacrifice attributable to specific expenditure lines.

Specific issues: The German fiscal doctrine holds that the direct extension of the marginalist approach to the public economy would lead to erroneous conclusions. Fiscal analysis should comply with the methodology applicable to *communal* economy (*Gemeinwirtschaft*), not private economy. Public economics should be separated from price theory and be studied as an autonomous Science of State (*Staatswirtschaft*), complete with all the applicable requirements of societal life, including economic.

Austrian fiscal doctrine – subjective value approach

Important contributors: Menger, Wieser, Sax.

General framework: The psychological aspects of want determination are basically the same for both private and collective wants. Collective wants – like private wants that require either material or immaterial goods for their satisfaction[7] – require either a "*partikulare*," mixed, or pure collective good, depending, respectively, on whether or not the given public good allows the imputation of specific, measurable benefits to its user. The tax shares of *partikulare* public goods are determined by the rules applicable to the market economy. But a different process of choice is required in the determination of the tax shares of pure public goods. Yet, in either case these shares are determined directly by subjective valuation, within the framework of marginal calculus, and without the intervention of the fiscal authority.

Expenditure side: Public expenditure is highly productive. *Partikulare* and mixed, that is non-pure, public goods very much resemble those immaterial goods that are called services in the private economy and whose prices are functions of the intensity of the need felt by the individual. The prices of these public services are determined by the taxpayer's willingness to pay. But the State, rather than having to ask the citizens to pay a fee each time they use a certain service may prefer to finance that service by a lump sum tax graduated according to the users' incomes. Pure collective goods, by contrast, are basically material goods, for they serve either as consumption goods (although they satisfy the entire population's immediate needs) or as capital goods ultimately leading to the same end through the process of imputation elaborated by

Böhm-Bawerk, another disciple of Menger's.[8] The prices of both categories of normal public goods as well are determined by subjective evaluation.

Tax side: Like in the private economy so in the *partikulare* public goods proper tax shares are determined in such a manner that the marginal disutility of the tax-price is equal to the marginal benefit of the public good. The total tax bill is similarly determined by equalizing total aggregate public expenditure to aggregate wealth or income. In the pure-collective goods proper, however, the "absolute" tax – that is, the total tax bill – as well as "relative" taxes – the actual amounts of tax paid by citizens – are determined through a valuation process resembling the one adopted by mutualistic private associations, where members are not actively engaged in everyday decision-making. Similarly the members of the public economy assent to the results of the collective choice process directed to fulfill a common purpose. In the private as well as the public economy the individual is motivated not only by egoism, but also by mutuality and altruism. The difference between the two spheres of activity is that in the public economy the citizen, out of a continuous interaction with his cohorts, more readily perceives the importance of the common interest for his peers and goes along with the majority's decision regarding the determination of absolute and relative tax bills.

Subjective valuation and economic efficiency: Economic efficiency is obviously achieved in the *partikulare* realm since the individual, acting as his own tax assessor, decides how much he would pay for a given public service after considering the intensity of his need and the magnitude of his wealth of income. But also in the pure collective goods proper, where benefits are not divisible and attributable to individual use, economic efficiency is attained by individual valuation, when citizens act collectively to determine absolute and relative tax bills by forsaking a lower-ranking private want for a higher-ranking public want until the marginal yields are equalized. Ultimately a balance is achieved between the citizens and the fiscal authority, one that is both efficient and equitable.

Fiscal coercion: Coercion is obviously not an issue in the *partikulare* realm and for non-pure collective goods. But it is also irrelevant in the sphere of pure-collective goods, since, in this sphere, too, the equilibrium closely reflects a citizen's willingness to contribute to the financing of the given public service. Hence, the fiscal authority is not a necessary fixture of the public economy. However, it is still preferable, on purely practical grounds, to entrust the planning and delivery of this important category of economic goods to such a useful and enduring social institution.

Specific issues: The thought that the individual is his own tax assessor, at least in the *partikulare* realm, is undoubtedly a very handy one. Yet, the theory suffers from two practical problems. The first is the unnecessary parallel Sax and Wieser draw from the private economy involving material and immaterial goods.[9] The second problem is more serious. Sax and Wieser are ill at ease with the concept of marginalism they inherited from Menger. They hold that the marginalist approach, while applicable in the determination of relative tax shares, would not be applicable in determining the absolute taxes, that is, in calculating the utility of the public goods for the community as a whole.[10]

Swedish fiscal doctrine – collective choice approach

Important contributors: Wicksell, Lindahl, Johansen, Myrdal.

General framework: A fiscal choice process emulating the market mechanism would fail to elicit taxpayers' true preferences. Italian and Austrian fiscal theories are based on the assumption that citizens would be willing to contribute to the financing of a public project commensurately with the benefits expected thereof. This stance disregards the fact that public goods are non-excludable and that this characteristic impels citizens to act as free riders. To circumvent this problem, the fiscal authority resorts to coercion, for otherwise it would forfeit its *raison d'être*. This results in forcing those individuals who would not contribute to the financing of a public expenditure item that they find overpriced. What is needed is to devise a collective choice process directed at producing a fiscal optimum that is not only efficient, but also just for all. Only a unanimous fiscal decision rule can deliver such equilibrium.

Expenditure side: Must be considered fully in any fiscal process. Taxpayers should be able to determine both the total public outlay and its allocation among alternative expenditure lines. The benefit principle of taxation is adequately equipped to produce this result.

Tax side: A just distribution of the tax burden cannot be had unless initial endowments were justly distributed. A just taxation policy should be applied in two steps. First, it should be so designed as to alter the existing state of distribution to make it more just. Second, after the just distribution is attained, it should be revised so that it apportions 0ther tax burden in accordance with the corrected state of distribution.[11] When a just state of endowments is attained, the tax-prices should be determined exactly the same way as those for private goods.

Subjective valuation and economic efficiency: Drawing on Marshall's discussion of joint consumption, namely, assuming that each taxpayer views the other taxpayer's demand schedule for public goods as a supply schedule, Lindahl shows that two taxpayers can attain and efficient and just fiscal equilibrium in the absence of fiscal authority. At the equilibrium, the quantity of public services supplied is determined simultaneously with the allocation of the tax shares between the two choice-makers. This solution meets the requirements of both principles of taxation, benefit as well as ability-to-pay.

Fiscal coercion: In Wicksell's original model of the public economy coercion is eliminated since fiscal decisions are subject to the rule of unanimity. But it occurred to Wicksell that perfect unanimity would be impossible to attain in a collective choice process involving a large number of participants. It is for that reason that he experimented with less-than-perfect schemes of unanimity. Lindahl did not resort to any exogenous schemes of unanimity in developing the Wicksellian ideal. However, his model comprises a community of only two people, thus actually avoids rather than addresses the problem that confronted Wicksell.

Specific issues: The formal inadequacy of Wicksell's and Lindahl's theories was recognized by Musgrave and Head.[12] Still, the Swedish fiscal theory constitutes the ultimate answer to be derived from the groundwork laid by the systems of Mazzola and Sax, and represents the ultimate consequence of the benefit principle, which determines the satisfaction of public wants on the basis of individual preferences.[13] Nevertheless, there still remains the need for the development of a political mechanism conducive to elicit the true valuations of voter-consumers with respect to public goods.

Notes

1 Introduction

1. J. Buchanan, "*La Scienza delle finanze*: The Italian Tradition in Fiscal Theory," in *Fiscal Theory and Political Economy*, Chapel Hill, North Carolina: University of North Carolina Press (1960: 22–74).
2. D. Lindenfeld, *The Practical Imagination: The German Sciences of State in the Nineteenth Century*, Chicago: University of Chicago Press (1997).
3. R. A. Musgrave and A. T. Peacock, *Classics in the Theory of Public Finance*, New York: MacMillan (1958), referred to henceforth as *Classics* (1958).
4. R. A. Musgrave and A. T. Peacock, *Classics* (1958: xix).
5. R. A. Musgrave, "A Brief History of Fiscal Doctrine," in A. J. Auerbach and M. Feldstein, *Handbook of Public Economics*, vol. 1, Elsevier, North-Holland (1985), reprinted in R. A. Musgrave, *Public Finance in a Democratic Society*, vol. 1, New York: New York University Press (1986: 338–93). The five themes are comprised of public goods, equity principles of taxation, efficiency conditions in taxation, tax shifting, and macro aspects of fiscal policy. However, Musgrave again chose to present these themes from the individual perspectives of selected pivotal authors rather than the point of view of the different national fiscal doctrines these authors actually belonged to. In an earlier essay, "Public Finance, Now and Then," *Finanzarchiv*, vol. 41, 1 (1983), reprinted in vol. 2 of his 1986 work, Musgrave does touch upon some aspects of German, Anglo-Saxon, and Swedish national fiscal doctrines, but only within the limits of an acceptance speech for an honorary doctorate conferred on him by Heidelberg University.
6. See O. Lange and F. M. Taylor, *On the Economic Theory of Socialism*, Minneapolis: University of Minnesota Press (1938). For an earlier example, refer to E. Barone, "Il ministro della produzione nello stato collettivista," *Giornale degli Economisti*, 37 (1908: 267–93), reprinted as "The Ministry of Production in the Collectivist State," in F. A. Hayek (ed.), *Collectivist Economic Planning*, London: Routledge (1935: 245–90).
7. L. von Mises, *Epistemological Problems of Economics*, Princeton, NJ: D. Van Nostrand (1960: 13).
8. A. Downs, "An Economic Theory of Political Action in a Democracy," *Journal of Political Economy*, vol. LXV, 2 (1957: 135).
9. V. Pareto, *Trattato di Sociologia Generale*, vol. 4, Florence: Barbera (1916: §2273), translated into English as *Mind and Society*, New York: Harcourt Brace & Co. (1935).
10. A. Downs (1957: 150).
11. T. Sowell, *Knowledge and Decisions*, New York: Basic Books (1980: 167).
12. For a detailed exposition of this development, refer to G. Tullock and R. B. McKenzie, *The New Worlds of Economics*, Homewood, Illinois: Irwin (1985).

13. The prototype Economic "Man," as well the third masculine singular pronoun, is used throughout this book for brevity and to comply with the historical flavor of the topic.
14. See L. Robbins, *Essay on the Nature and Significance of Economic Science*, London: Macmillan (1932).
15. Not all economists agree that the "ordinalist revolution" of the 1930s represented real progress in economic theorizing. See R. Cooter and P. Rappoport, "Were the Ordinalists Wrong About Welfare Economics?" *Journal of Economic Literature*, XXII, June (1984: 507–30).
16. G. Tullock and R. B. McKenzie (1985: 4).
17. See F. Hahn and M. Hollis (eds), *Philosophy and Economic Theory*, Oxford University Press (1979) and D. Bell and I. Kristol (eds), *The Crisis in Economic Theory*, New York: Basic Books (1981).
18. I. M. Kirzner, "The 'Austrian' Perspective on the Crisis," in D. Bell and I. Kristol (1981: 115).
19. M. Friedman, *Essays in Positive Economics*, Chicago: The University of Chicago Press (1953: 8).
20. F. Machlup, *Methodology of Economics and Other Social Sciences*, New York: Academic Press (1978). Refer to Part Four, especially ch. 11.
21. A. Lewis, *The Psychology of Taxation*, Oxford: Martin Robertson (1982: 31).
22. For many revealing examples, see T. C. Schelling, "Egonomics, or the Art of Self-management," *American Economic Review*, 2 (1978: 290–4); D. Kahneman and A. Tversky, "Prospect Theory: An Analysis of Decision under Risk," *Econometrica*, 27 (1979: 263–91); and R. Thaler, "Toward a Positive Theory of Consumer Choice," *Journal of Economic Behavior and Organization*, 1 (1980: 39–60).
23. D. Mueller, "Rational Egoism versus Adaptive Egoism as Fundamental Postulate for a Descriptive Theory of Human Behavior," *Public Choice*, 51 (1986: 3).
24. F. Hahn and M. Hollis (1979: 13).
25. F. Hahn and M. Hollis (1979: 14).
26. For early attempts to expand the behavioral foundation of economic decision-making, refer to A. W. Coats, "Economics and Psychology: The Death and Resurrection of a Research Programme," in S. Latsis (ed.), *Method and Appraisal in Economics*, Cambridge: Cambridge University Press (1976: 43–64).
27. A. K. Sen, "Rational Fools: A Critique of the Behavioral Foundations of Economic Theory," *Philosophy and Public Affairs*, 6 (1977: 317).
28. The logical blunders committed by Economic Man indeed appear grievous. To illustrate, R. Thaler (1980) shows that the utility-maximizing model, based on the principle that opportunity costs must be treated as equivalents of out-of-pocket costs, breaks down in the simplest of scenarios, such as when a homeowner who, while preferring to mow his own backyard rather than paying his neighbor's son $8 to do it, would not think of mowing his neighbor's same-sized backyard for $20. See also A. Tversky and D. Kahneman (1974); J. Elster (1977); and R. Thaler and H. M. Shefrin (1979) for many additional illustrations regarding the inadequacy of rationality and self-interest in explaining everyday economic behavior.
29. See R. A. Posner, *The Economic Analysis of Law*, Boston: Little Brown (1977) and A. Sen (1977: 317–44).

30. See J. C. Harsanyi, "Cardinal Welfare, Individualistic Ethics, and Interpersonal Comparisons of Utility," *Journal of Political Economy*, 63 (1955: 309–21); H. M. Hochman and J. D. Rodgers, "Pareto Optimal Approach to Income Redistribution," *American Economic Review*, 55 (1969: 542–57); and D. Collard, *Altruism and Economy*, New York: Oxford Press (1978).
31. See T. B. Veblen, "Why Is Economics Not an Evolutionary Science?" *Quarterly Journal of Economics*, July (1898: 373–9).
32. See G. Myrdal (1930), *Vetenskap och politik i nationalekonomien* (1930), available in English as *The Political Element in the Development of Economic Theory*, London: Routledge and Paul (1953).
33. See G. Katona's "Rational Behavior and Economic Behavior," *Psychological Review*, 5 (1953: 307–18) and his *Psychological Analysis of Economic Behavior*, Westport: Greenwood Press (1977).
34. H. Margolis, *Selfishness, Altruism, and Rationality: A Theory of Social Choice*, London: Cambridge University Press (1982: 17).
35. A. Schotter, *Free Market Economics: A Critical Appraisal*, New York: St. Martin's Press (1985).
36. R. Hardin, "Collective Action as an Agreeable n-Prisoner's Dilemma," *Behavioral Science*, 16 (1971: 472–81).
37. J. Hirshleifer, "The Expanding Domain of Economics," *American Economic Review*, 6 (1985: 53).
38. K. J. Arrow, *Social Choice and Individual Values*, New York: Wiley and Sons (1963 [1951]: 2).
39. G. Tullock and R. B. McKenzie (1985: 9).
40. K. Popper, *The Poverty of Historicism*, London: Routledge and Kegan Paul (1957: 132).
41. F. Hahn and M. Hollis (1979: 15).
42. T. Parsons, *The Structure of Social Action: A Study in Social Theory with Special Reference to a Group of Recent European Writers*, New York: McGraw-Hill (1937) as well as T. Parsons and E. A. Shils (eds), *Toward a General Theory of Action*, Cambridge, MA: Harvard University Press (1951).
43. V. Pareto's 1916 work demonstrates an exemplary attempt to apply the sociological method to public economics. For a glimpse of early efforts to graft juridical and historical approaches onto the fiscal process, refer, respectively, to B. Griziotti, *Principii di politica, diritto, e scienza delle finanze*, Padova: Cedam (1929) and H. Ritschl, *Gemeinwirtschaft und kapitalistische Marktwirtschaft*, Tübingen (1931), a key portion of which is in *Classics* (1958: 233–42).
44. G. Myrdal (1930) and A. Sen (1987) forcefully illustrate the effect of politics upon the theory of the public economy. G. Schmölders (1959) and A. Lewis (1979, 1982), in turn, provide a useful platform on which to rest the fiscal psychology of the economic agent. For a discussion of ethical consequences of state economic activity, refer to A. C. Pigou (1954). For full citations of these works, see References.
45. G. Schmölders, "Fiscal Psychology: A New Branch of Public Finance," *National Tax Journal*, 12 (1959: 340–5).
46. H. A. Simon and A. C. Stedry, "Psychology and Economics," in G. Lindsey and E. Aronson, (eds), *Handbook of Social Psychology*, vol. V, Reading, MA: Addison-Wesley (1968–70).

47. K. J. Arrow (1963 [1951]); R. A. Musgrave, *The Theory of Public Finance: A Study in Public Economy*, New York: McGraw-Hill (1959); and J. Buchanan, *The Demand and Supply of Public Goods*, Chicago: Rand McNally (1968).
48. J. Buchanan, "Public Finance and Public Choice," *National Tax Journal*, XXVIII, 8 (1975: 383). The idea that "public finance ... lie[s] on the borderline between economics and politics" was expressed much earlier by H. Dalton (1922: 3); however, neither Dalton nor his followers envisaged a collective choice mechanism in the attainment of fiscal equilibrium.
49. Hence, the constitutional framework envisaged by modern fiscal scientists is normally the "representative-democratic" rather than the "direct-democratic" political construct. The terms "parliamentary democracy" and "parliamentary government" are also used in this text as synonyms for "representative democracy."
50. As expounded by K. Wicksell in *Finanztheoretische Untersuchungen*, Jena: Gustav Fisher (1896), reprinted as "A New Principle of Just Taxation" in *Classics* (1958: 89).
51. The classic discussion of the inevitable influence of political convictions on positive economics in general and public economics in particular is in G. Myrdal (1953 [1930]).
52. A. Downs (1957:135–6).
53. E. Mueller, "Public Attitudes toward Fiscal Programs," *Quarterly Journal of Economics*, 77, 2 (1963: 210–35); B. Strumpel, "The Contribution of Survey Research to Public Finance," in A. T. Peacock (ed.), *Quantitative Methods in Public Finance*, New York: Praeger (1969); G. Schmölders, "Attitudes to Taxation and their Effects on Work Effort," *Fiscal Policy and Labour Supply*, Conference Series, No. 4, London: Institute for Fiscal Studies (1977); N. L. Enrick, "A Pilot Study of Income Tax Consciousness," *National Tax Journal*, 16 (1963: 169–73); B. Beicheit *et al.*, *Steuernorm und Steuerwirklichkeit*, Köln und Opladen: Westdeutscher Verlag (1969); and J. Vogel, "Taxation and Public Opinion in Sweden: An Interpretation of Recent Survey Data," *National Tax Journal*, 28, 4 (1974: 499–513).
54. See R. Curtin and C. D. Cowan, "Public Attitudes toward Fiscal Programs," ch. 3 in B. Strumpel, C. D. Cowan, F. T. Juster, and J. Schmideskamp (eds), *Survey of Consumers 1972–73*, Ann Arbor: University of Michigan (1975) and, especially, A. Lewis, "Attitudes to Public Expenditure and their Relationship to Voting Preferences," *Political Studies*, 28, 2 (1980: 284–92).
55. A. Lewis (1982: 222).
56. A. C. Pigou, *A Study in Public Finance*, London: Macmillan (1928: 1).
57. R. A. Musgrave, *Public Finance in a Democratic Society*, vol. 1, New York: New York University Press (1986: 94).
58. L. Johansen, *Public Economics*, Amsterdam: North-Holland Publishing Company (1968: 6–7).
59. A. Wagner, *Finanzwissenschaft*, Leipzig: Carl Winter (1883), a portion of which is reprinted in Musgrave's and Peacock's *Classics* (1958: 1 and 5).
60. H. S. Rosen, *Public Finance*, Homewood, Illinois: Irwin (1988: 6).
61. E. Lindahl, "Einige strittige Fragen der Steuertheorie," in H. Mayer (ed.), *Die Wirtschaftstheorie der Gegenwart*, vol. IV, Vienna (1928: 282–304), reprinted in *Classics* (1958: 215).

62. A. C. Pigou (1928: 33).
63. H. S. Rosen (1988: 7).
64. E. Lindahl, *Classics* (1958 [1919]: 214).

2 A National Taxonomy of Fiscal Doctrines

1. *La città del sole*, 1602.
2. *Summa teologiae*, 1273.
3. F. Ferrara, *Trattato speciale delle imposte* (1849–50), contained in *Lezioni di economia politica*, Bologna: Zanichelli (1934–35).
4. See K. Wicksell, *Finanztheoretische Untersuchungen*, Jena: Gustav Fischer (1896), a portion of which work is reprinted as "A New Principle of Just Taxation" in *Classics* (1958: 77–118).
5. E. Sax, *Grundlegung der theoretischen Staatswirtschaft*, Vienna: A. Hölder (1883).
6. F. von Wieser, *Der Natürliche Wert*, Vienna: A. Hölder (1889).
7. A. C. Pigou, *A Study in Public Finance*, London: Macmillan (1928).
8. J. Buchanan, "*La Scienza delle finanze*: The Italian Tradition in Fiscal Theory," in *Fiscal Theory and Political Economy*, Chapel Hill, North Carolina: University of North Carolina Press (1960: 71–2).
9. J. Buchanan (1960: 71–2).
10. R. A. and P. B. Musgrave, *Public Finance in Theory and Practice*, New York: McGraw-Hill (1984: 228).
11. Pp. 1–15.
12. A. Wagner, *Classics* (1958 [1883]: 5).
13. R. B. Ekelund and R. F. Hébert, *A History of Economic Theory and Method*, New York: McGraw-Hill (1983: 500). Emphases in the original.
14. K. Wicksell (1958 [1896]: 82). Emphasis in the original.
15. For a classic exposition of this topic, refer to F. Y. Edgeworth, "The Pure Theory of Taxation," *Economic Journal*, VIII (1897), reprinted in *Papers Relating to Political Economy*, London (1925) as well as *Classics* ... (1958: 119–36).
16. E. Lindahl, *Die Gerechtigkeit der Besteuerung*, Lund: Gleerupska (1919), a portion of which is in Musgrave's and Peacock's *Classics* (1958: 168–76).
17. E. Lindahl (1958 [1919]: 168).
18. R. A. and P. B. Musgrave (1984: 53) and H. S. Rosen, *Public Finance*, Homewood, Illinois: Irwin (1988: 87). Ekelund and Hébert, meanwhile, correctly recognized that the outwardly "economic exchange" theory of Lindahl was "filtered through protagonists in a political process and that resultant tax-share distributions assigned would be influenced by their relative power" (1983: 524).
19. R. A. Musgrave and A. T. Peacock, *Classics* (1958: xv–vi).
20. F. Y. Edgeworth (1958 [1897]: 119–36).
21. G. Ricca-Salerno, *Scienza delle finanze*, Florence: Barbera (1888).
22. Refer to References for full citations of the representative works of the authors mentioned in this paragraph.

3 British Fiscal Doctrine: The Sacrifice View

1. R. A. Musgrave and P. B. Musgrave, *Public Finance in Theory and Practice*, New York: McGraw-Hill (1984: 5).
2. H. Ritschl, *Gemeinwirtschaft und kapitalistische Marktwirtschaft*, Tübingen, a portion is excerpted in *Classics* (1958 [1931]: 234).
3. J. J. Rousseau, *The Social Contract and Discourses* (1762), New York: E. P. Dutton and Company (1950: 14).
4. J. J. Rousseau (1950 [1762]: 15).
5. J. J. Rousseau (1950 [1762]: 16).
6. J. J. Rousseau (1950 [1762]: 17).
7. J. J. Rousseau (1950 [1762]: 14–15).
8. M. Levin, "Social Contract," in P. P. Wiener (ed.), *Dictionary of the History of Ideas*, New York: Charles Scribner's Sons, 4 (1973: 259).
9. In Rousseau's words, "To be general, a will need not always be unanimous; but every vote must be counted: any exclusion is a breach of generality" (1950 [1762]: 24n).
10. M. Levin (1973: 289).
11. M. Levin (1973: 289).
12. E. Burke, "Reflections on the Revolution in France" (1790), in W. Ebenstein (ed.), *Great Political Thinkers*, New York: Holt, Rinehart and Winston (1961a: 475).
13. E. Burke (1961 [1790]: 491).
14. E. Burke (1961 [1790]: 476–7).
15. J. Bentham, *A Fragment on Government and An Introduction to the Principles of Morals and Legislation*, W. Harrison (ed.), Oxford: Basil Blackwell (1948 [1789]: 126). Emphases in the original.
16. Opening sentences of Ch. 1 of *Principles of Morals and Legislation* in J. Bentham (1948 [1789]: 125). Emphases in the original.
17. J. Bentham, *A Fragment of Government*, F. C. Montague (ed.), London: Geoffrey Cumberledge-Oxford University Press (1951 [1776]: 137). Emphases and capital case letters in the original.
18. A. Smith (1776), *The Wealth of Nations*, Chicago: The University of Chicago Press (1976: Book I: 17).
19. A. Smith (1976 [1776]: Book I: 18).
20. A. Smith (1976 [1776]: Book I: 278). Emphasis added.
21. A. Smith (1976 [1776]: Book IV: 208).
22. A. Smith (1976 [1776]: Book IV: 208).
23. R. B. Ekelund and R. F. Hébert, *A History of Economic Theory and Method*, New York: McGraw-Hill (1983: 109).
24. D. G. Long, *Bentham on Liberty: Jeremy Bentham's Idea of Liberty in Relation to His Utilitarianism*, Toronto: University of Toronto Press (1977: 209).
25. Since even in Bentham's utopian state "fire will burn, frost pinch, thirst parch, hunger gripe as heretofore: toil even as now must be the prelude to subsistence: that the few may be wealthy, the many must be poor: ... and how much lighter soever coercion may sit than it does now, coercion must be felt, that all may be secure" (D. G. Long (1977: 149), referring to Bentham's *Of Laws in General*).

26. S. R. Graubard, "Democracy," in P. P. Wiener (ed.), *Dictionary of the History of Ideas*, vol. I, New York: Charles Scriber's Sons (1973: 662).
27. A. Smith (1976 [1776]: Book IV: 208–9).
28. A. Smith (1976 [1776]: Book V: 349).
29. A. Smith (1976 [1776]: Book V: 352).
30. A. Smith (1976 [1776]: Book IV: 209).
31. A. Smith (1976 [1776]: Book V: 340).
32. K. J. Arrow, "Formal Theories of Social Welfare," in P. P. Wiener (ed.), *Dictionary of the History of Ideas*, vol. 4, New York: Charles Scribner's Sons (1973: 279).
33. K. J. Arrow (1973: 278–9).
34. R. B. Ekelund and R. F. Hébert (1983: 63). Emphasis in the original.
35. J. S. Mill, "The Proposed Reform of the Poor Laws," *Monthly Repository*, 8 (1834: 361). Mill softened his stance later on. In his *Principles of Political Economy* (1848) he warned the dispensers of public relief not to act as "inquisitors" in deciding who was deserving and who did not deserve assistance: guardians and overseers should dole out "the minimum which is due even to the worst" (Book V, Ch. xi, §13).
36. R. B. Ekelund and R. F. Hébert (1983: 182).
37. R. B. Ekelund and R. F. Hébert (1983: 185).
38. For Chadwick's impressive list of achievements in applying the Bentham criterion to economics of crime and courts; criminal behavior; police effectiveness; public health; value of time; institutional reforms; water supply and delivery; transportation; and, funeral service, refer to R. B. Ekelund and R. F. Hébert (1983: 184–93).
39. D. H. Munro, "Utilitarianism," in P. P. Wiener (ed.), *Dictionary of the History of Ideas*, vol. 4, New York: Charles Scribner's Sons (1973: 445).
40. D. H. Munro (1973: 447).
41. M. Pantaleoni (1958 [1883]: 23). Pantaleoni was the first political economist anywhere to apply the marginal calculus exclusively to the expenditure side of the public budget. His contribution to fiscal theory is discussed in Chapter 4.
42. F. Y. Edgeworth, "The Pure Theory of Taxation," *Economic Journal*, VIII (1897), reprinted in *Papers Relating to Political Economy*, London: Royal Economic Society (1925), a portion of which is in *Classics* (1958 [1897]: 121).
43. F. Y. Edgeworth (1958 [1897]: 122).
44. F. Y. Edgeworth (1958 [1897]: 122).
45. R. A. Musgrave and P. B. Musgrave (1984: 87).
46. R. A. Musgrave, *Public Finance in a Democratic Society*, vol. 2, New York: New York University Press (1986: 354).
47. R. A. Musgrave (1986: 354).
48. A. C. Pigou, *A Study in Public Finance*, London: Macmillan (1928: 5).
49. R. A. Musgrave and P. B. Musgrave (1984: 232).
50. A. C. Pigou (1928: 6).
51. Georgescu-Roegen excerpts an insightful passage from the Lloyd lecture:

> The utility of corn is the same as after an abundant harvest as in time of famine ... The term value [utility] therefore does not express a quality inherent in a commodity, [but] a feeling of the mind, as is variable with the variations

of the external circumstances which can influence the feeling, without any variation of the intrinsic qualities of the commodity which is the object of it (1973: 450).

52. Quoted in G. J. Stigler, "The Development of Utility Theory," *Journal of Political Economy*, LVIII (1950), reprinted in E. J. Hamilton, A. Rees, and H. G. Johnson (eds), *Landmarks in Political Economy*, The University of Chicago Press (1962: 384).
53. G. J. Stigler (1962 [1950]: 385), excerpted from Bentham's *Theory of Legislation* (1802: 102ff).
54. G. J. Stigler (1962 [1950]: 405).
55. G. J. Stigler (1962 [1950]: 405–6).
56. N. Georgescu-Roegen (1973: 456).
57. H. S. Rosen, *Public Finance*, Homewood, Illinois: Irwin (1988: 327).
58. A. Marshall, *Principles of Economics*, London: Macmillan and Co., 8th Edition (1946: 135).
59. A. C. Pigou, *A Study in Public Finance*, London: Macmillan (1962 [1928]: 118). However, Pigou points out that a consumption tax is less practical to administer than an income tax.
60. A. Marshall (1946 [1890]: 467–8).
61. R. A. Musgrave (1986: 361).
62. R. A. Musgrave (1986: 361).
63. E. R. Rolph, *The Theory of Fiscal Economics*, Berkeley, California: University of California Press (1956: 7n).
64. B. P. Herber, *Modern Public Finance: The Study of Public Sector Economics*, Homewood, Illinois: Richard D. Irwin (1975: 25).
65. E. R. Rolph (1956: 7n).
66. W. Ebenstein, "The Welfare State," in W. Ebenstein (ed.), *Great Political Thinkers*, New York: Holt, Rinehart and Winston (1961c: 815–16).
67. A. C. Pigou, "Some Aspects of the Welfare State," *Diogenes*, 7, Summer (1954) reprinted in W. Ebenstein (ed.), *Great Political Thinkers*, New York: Holt, Rinehart and Winston (1961a: 839).
68. A. C. Pigou (1961 [1954]: 841).
69. A. C. Pigou (1961 [1954]: 842). Emphasis in the original.
70. W. Ebenstein (1961c: 816).
71. A. Marshall (1946 [1890]: 284–5).
72. A. C. Pigou (1961 [1954]: 83–9).
73. H. S. Rosen (1988: 131–2).
74. B. P. Herber (1975: 39).
75. A. C. Pigou (1961 [1954]: 839).
76. B. P. Herber (1975: 41). In this connection, Pigou states: "[P]eople's economic well-being depends on the whole system of law, including the laws of property, contract, and bequest, and not merely upon the law about taxes. To hold that the law about taxes ought to affect different people's satisfactions equally, while allowing that the rest of the legal system may properly affect them very unequally, seems not a little arbitrary" (1962 [1928]: 44).
77. A. C. Pigou (1961 [1954]: 841–2).
78. A. C. Pigou (1961 [1954]: 840).

79. A. C. Pigou (1961 [1954]: 840–1).
80. R. A. Musgrave (1986: 347).
81. R. A. Musgrave (1986: 347).
82. A. C. Pigou (1962 [1928]: 44–5). Emphasis in the original.
83. R. A. Musgrave (1986: 348).
84. A. C. Pigou (1962 [1928]: 94 and 99).
85. A. C. Pigou (1962 [1928]: 99 n2).

4 Italian Fiscal Doctrine: The Benefit View

* Sections of this chapter, including the Appendix, were presented at the Fourteenth Annual Conference of the History of Economics Society at Harvard University (1987) and subsequently published in O. Kayaalp, "Early Italian Contributions to the Theory of Public Finance: Pantaleoni, De Viti, and Mazzola," in D. A. Walker (ed.), *Perspectives on the History of Economic Thought*, vol. I, London: Edward Elgar Publishing Ltd (1989: 155–66). Used with permission from the History of Economics Society and Edward Elgar.

1. Refer to Otto Weinberger, "The Importance of Francesco Ferrara in the History of Economic Thought," *Journal of Political Economy*, 48 (1940) for the contribution of Ferrara to the development of Political Economy and Public Finance in Italy. Ferrara's *Lezioni di economia politica*, Bologna: Zanichelli (1934–35) covers his lectures given between 1849 and 1873. Pages 551–765 of that work are devoted to public finance.
2. J. Buchanan, "*La Scienza delle finanze*: The Italian Tradition in Fiscal Theory," in *Fiscal Theory and Political Economy*, Chapel Hill, North Carolina: University of North Carolina Press (1960: 27), citing Ferrara (1849–50). Emphasis added.
3. Buchanan expresses surprise that, until the publication of Ferrara's *Lezioni* in 1934–35, Italian scholars of public sector economics made little reference to his works (1960: 30).
4. For a recent treatment of this topic, see Marco Bianchini, "Some Fundamental Aspects of Italian Eighteenth-Century Economic Thought," in Donald Walker (ed.), *Perspectives on the History of Economic Thought*, vol. I, London: Edward Elgar (1989: 53–67). In the opening paragraph, Bianchini states:

   > [T]he Italians can boast of some firsts: they provided the first algebraic treatment of an economic problem (1711); one of the most complete theories of value ... (1751, 1769); the most exhaustive studies on money, hypothesizing the commodity standard (1751); the first chairs of Political Economy (1754, 1769); the first indifference variety analysis (1764); and the first constant-outlay demand curve (1771).

5. Ferrara's instructive prefaces in the *Biblioteca* (1850–70) were published separately as *Esame storico-critico di economisti e dottrine economiche* (Torino, 1889–92).
6. O. Weiberger (1940: 91–2).
7. A. von Schwarzkopf, *Beitrage zur Studien in Italien im 17. Und 18. Jahrhundert* Strassburg (1872), cited in O. Weinberger (1940: 91). (Serra was an adamant critic of mercantilism, especially of the application of restrictions to economic processes by the rulers of the Kingdom of Naples. This resulted in

his incarceration around 1602 (along with Tommaso Campanella) where Serra died around 1610.)

8. Refer to References for full citations of the works of the authors listed in the paragraph.
9. For such an assessment, refer to Schumpeter's *History of Economic Analysis*, London: Allen and Unwin, in which he expresses a clear opinion of eighteenth century Italian economic thought: "In intent, scope and plan, ... eighteenth-century Italian ... works ... were not inferior to the Germans, they were superior to most of their Spanish, English, and French contemporaries in analytic power and achievement" (1954: 176–7).
10. O. Weinberger (1940: 92–3).
11. In *La città del sole* (1602), Campanella envisions the State as an organization ruled by sovereigns of pure reason in order to lead the God's rational creature to worldly beatitude. In such an environment, Campanella considers it a gross injustice for the sovereign to abuse this creature with arbitrary taxation.
12. The intellectual environment had changed enormously following Italy's unification. As remarked by Marco Bianchini (1989: 64), before 1861, when Northern Italy was under Austrian control, the political authorities were hostile to pure theory and obliged Italian economists to concern themselves mainly with matters juridical and administrative in nature and to stay away from such writers as Rousseau, Diderot, or Steuart who advocated the inalienable rights of the individual with respect to social order.
13. The same vision of the political market was revived in the English-language economic literature some 55 years later by H. R. Bowen in "The Interpretation of Voting in the Allocation of Economic Resources," *Quarterly Journal of Economics*, November (1943: 27–48).
14. An important difference still remains between the two comprehensive fiscal doctrines in that *Staatswirtschaft*, while not rejecting the interrelationship between individual utility and collective utility, maintains that the latter concept of utility subsumes the former.
15. Vol. XV: 388. My translation.
16. Buchanan (1960: 27).
17. For a masterful exposition of the "Italian-ness" of fiscal science, as well as an affirmation of De Viti's primary place in that discipline, refer to Bellanca (1993b). Da Empoli, too, finds De Viti *primus inter pares* among classical Italian fiscal theorists, including Mazzola, whose relative popularity in the international community of public economists is owed to Mazzola's *formal* derivation of fiscal equilibrium (1995: 53).
18. See Griziotti (1917, 1929) and Conigliani (1903). Antonio Cardini, pointing out the close collaboration between De Viti and Mosca, which spanned a period of forty years (1994: 191), considers Mosca's *Elementi di scienza politica* [Elements of Political Science] (1896) and De Viti's *Principii di economia finanziaria* [Principles of Financial Economics] (1928) to be two parallel texts (1985: 366). De Viti's affinity with Croce is also documented by Cardini, who reports that the two colleagues came very close to launching a "grand journal of liberal thought" together (1994: 194).
19. After more than a century following the appearance of De Viti's main work, public finance continues to be offered in Italy as a separate curriculum at departments of economics as well as law.

20. Luigi Einaudi's *Introduction* to De Viti's *First Principles of Public Finance*, London: Jonathan Cape (1934: 23).
21. Note the titles De Viti (1928) and Mazzola (1890) gave to their respective work: the first called his "The First Principles" and the second "The Scientific Elements" of Fiscal Economics.
22. Holistic, because it examined the fiscal act, not in abstract, but together with all its manifestations and consequences – economic, political, and legal; and pure, because it relied on positive methodology exclusively in the determination of the equilibrium between the demand and supply of public goods.
23. Which is exactly the conclusion reached by Samuelson (1954: 387–9) and elaborated by Buchanan (1968: 18–22). Refer to the Appendix at the end of this chapter for comparison.
24. M. Pantaleoni (1957 [1889]: 201). Pantaleoni notes that his views regarding the tribal egoist were owed to Spencer's *Social Statics*, which appeared in 1851 (1957 [1889]: 22).
25. This view, which Pantaleoni inherited from Ferrara, became a staple in Italian-language economics textbooks for a long time and continued to list the State as the fifth factor of production.
26. M. Pantaleoni (1957 [1889]: 22).
27. M. Pantaleoni (1938 [1883]: 15n and 16n).
28. R. A. Musgrave, *Theory of Public Finance*, New York: McGraw-Hill (1959: 70).
29. Pp. 16–27.
30. This essay was reprinted in the second volume of Pantaleoni's *Erotemi di economia*, Bari: Laterza e figli (1925: 1–14).
31. M. Pantaleoni (1925 [1913]: 43).
32. M. Pantaleoni (1925 [1907]: 205–6).
33. For De Viti and Mazzola, meanwhile, the archetypal marginalist was Jevons.
34. Parts of this section appeared in O. Kayaalp, "Antonio De Viti De Marco," in F. Meacci (ed.), *Italian Economists of the 20th Century*, London: Edward Elgar Publishing Ltd (1998: 95–113). Used with publisher's permission.
35. Buchanan (1960: 25).
36. *Il carattere teorico* (1888) underwent many revisions and expansions until it appeared in 1928 as *I primi principii di economia finanziaria* [First Principles of Fiscal Economics] and in 1934 as *Principî di economia finanziaria* [Principles of Fiscal Economics]. It is the latter edition that constituted the basis of the well-known English translation, *First Principles of Public Finance* (1936). The definitive edition of the *Principii* was published in 1939.
37. L. Einaudi (1936: 23).
38. This is not to say that Pareto had no reservations about applying the Walrasian calculus to *private* choice. For a detailed discussion of Pareto's apprehension in this matter, refer to his 1896–97 work listed in References.
39. De Viti and Pareto, two ardent liberals, met for the first time in 1889 at a conference for the attainment of world peace organized by Teodoro Moneta (Cardini [1994: 191]). The following year, De Viti, immediately after assuming the general editorship of the *Giornale degli economisti*, appointed Pareto as editor of the political section of the *Giornale*, the *Cronaca*. Unfortunately, bickering soon started between the two colleagues and went on for almost a decade until Pareto left the *Giornale* in 1899 (Fusco [1994: xxx–xxxi]). Whether the source of the friction was the two

economists' divergent views of the public economy would make an interesting topic of investigation.

40. Pareto termed his decision rule "sociologically-valid" because, contrary to those of coeval fiscal "scientists," it required only that a citizen express his preference for one social alternative over another without invoking any cardinal measure of utility.
41. L. Einaudi (1936: 25–7).
42. De Viti (1928: 12). All translations from this work are mine.
43. De Viti (1928: 36).
44. De Viti (1936: 37–8). Emphases in the original.
45. De Viti (1936: 39).
46. See N. Bellanca, "Intorno all teoria italiana della finanza pubblica: 1883–1946," *Rivista di diritto finanziario e scienza delle finanze*, 52 (1993a: 21–39).
47. L. Einaudi (1936: 26–7).
48. J. Buchanan (1960: 68).
49. J. Buchanan (1960: 68).
50. For a full discussion of fiscal illusion, and the place of Puviani and Fasiani in this context, refer to Buchanan's *Public Finance in Democratic Process*, Chapel Hill, North Carolina: The University of North Carolina Press (1967: 126–43).
51. This distinguishes the taxpayer envisaged by Puviani and Fasiani from the irrational taxpayer envisioned by Pareto (1916). In Pareto's view, human nature is made up of a part which is constant and another that is variable. The fixed part, which Pareto calls *il residuo*, consists of instincts, appetites, and selfishness. The variable part, termed *la derivazione*, consists of reasoning supported by deductive logic. The former prevails in the public economy while the latter governs private markets. However, on a closer analysis, a strong similarity is noted between Pareto and Puviani/Fasiani in that Pareto, too, sees politics as a struggle where certain logical-sounding schemes are packaged as *derivazioni* and fed to the populace by the ruling group to establish their own selfish *residui*.
52. J. Buchanan (1967: 127).
53. J. Buchanan (1960: 43).
54. A cursory glance at *Un trentennio di lotte politiche: 1894–1922* [Three Decades of Political Struggle: 1894–1922] (1930) will provide ample proof of De Viti's heartfelt adherence to liberal causes and the protection of the rights of the minority.
55. De Viti (1936: 51).
56. Considering that no individual taxpayer can reach such a conclusion without evoking at least a modicum of sympathy for fellow citizens, a common ground thus opens up between De Viti and Sax. Refer to Chapter 6 for Sax's view in this connection.
57. De Viti (1934a: 128). My translation.
58. De Viti (1936: 118).
59. De Viti (1936: 122).
60. See *Classics* (1958: 72n and 75–82) for evidence of Wicksell's thorough familiarity with Mazzola. As for Lindahl, it is inconceivable that he did not read Section II of Wicksell's book, which incorporates a critical review of the works of Sax *and* Mazzola.

61. P. A. Samuelson, "The Pure Theory of Public Expenditures," *Review of Economics and Statistics*, 4 (1954: 387–9).
62. R. A. Musgrave, *The Theory of Public Finance: A Study in Public Economy*, New York: McGraw-Hill (1959).
63. J. Buchanan (1960: 43).
64. For a detailed discussion of F. Benham's and Simons's critiques of De Viti's *Principii*, refer to Fausto (1995). Cardini points out that De Viti's ideas, notwithstanding Simons's harsh criticism, ultimately found a respectable niche in Britain, thanks to Duncan Black, who, in his *The Incidence of Income Taxes* (1939), affirmed that the *Principii* was an "essential and definitive contribution to the theory of income and taxation" (1985: 373).
65. Parenthetically, it was Morgenstern who contributed the entry "Antonio De Viti de Marco" in the *International Encyclopedia of the Social Sciences*, D. Sills (ed.), New York: Macmillan (1968).
66. For a discussion of what factors seem to account for the continuing failure of non-Italian students of the public economy to acclaim De Viti as a founder of the modern theory of public finance refer to O. Kayaalp, "The Public Choice Element of the Italian Theory of Public Goods," *Public Finance/Finances Publiques*, 3 (1985: 395–410).
67. Domenico da Empoli, "Beni pubblici e democrazia," in B. Jossa (ed.), *Teoria dei sistemi economici*, Torino: Utet (1989: 53). For another discussion of the public choice element in Italian fiscal doctrine in general and in De Viti's theory of public goods in particular, refer to O. Kayaalp (1985) cited in the previous note.
68. While Pantaleoni and De Viti were hailed as the founders of the pure theory of public finance by F. Benham as early as in 1934, that honor was extended to Ugo Mazzola much later by Musgrave (1959) and Musgrave and Peacock (1958). Also, while De Viti's and Pantaleoni's main works were translated into English in 1936 and 1957, respectively, Mazzola's 1890 work, *I dati scientifici della finanza pubblica*, remains untranslated, except for a single chapter, which is included in *Classics*. So far as I am aware, Mazzola's *Il fondamento scientifico dell'economia dello Stato* (1888) has never been referred to in the English-language economics literature.
69. Large sections appeared in O. Kayaalp, "Ugo Mazzola and the Italian Theory of Public Goods," in *History of Political Economy*, 20, 1 (1988: 183–93). Used with publisher's permission.
70. *I dati scientifici della finanza publica*, Rome: Ermanno Loescher (1890: vii).
71. U. Mazzola (1890: viii–ix). All excerpts from this work of Mazzola are my translation, unless otherwise noted.
72. As a historical note, Pantaleoni, De Viti, and Mazzola all started their academic careers at the University of Camerino in their early twenties. They also shared the editorship of the *Giornale degli economisti*, the foremost economic journal in Italy those days. They each moved to the University of Pavia, where Mazzola eventually took over the chair of public finance, which was vacated when Luigi Cossa died in 1896. Mazzola remained in that position until his death in 1899. De Viti and Pantaleoni, meanwhile, returned to their alma mater, the University of Rome, as chair professors in 1887 and 1901, respectively.
73. Mazzola (1890: 23).

74. U. Mazzola (1890: 171–2).
75. U. Mazzola (1890: 178).
76. U. Mazzola (1890: 180).
77. F. von Wieser, *Der Natürliche Wert*, Vienna: A. Hölder (1889), reprinted as *Natural Value*, New York: Kelley and Millman (1956: 239).
78. F. von Wieser (1956 [1889]: 242).
79. F. von Wieser (1956 [1889]: 242).
80. U. Mazzola (1890: 165).
81. U. Mazzola (1958 [1890]: 44).
82. De Viti (1936: 118).
83. U. Mazzola (1890: 175).
84. K. Wicksell, *Classics* (1958 [1896]: 89).
85. E. Whittaker, *Schools and Streams of Economic Thought*, Chicago: Rand McNally (1962: 311).
86. J. G. Head, *Public Goods and Public Welfare*, Durham, North Carolina: Duke University Press (1974: 165).
87. J. Buchanan (1960: 24). At any rate, it would be erroneous to say that Italian contributions to public finance went totally unnoticed in the Anglo-Saxon world until 1958. It was mentioned earlier that Frederick Benham (1934a) recognized Pantaleoni and De Viti as the two founders of the modern theory of public finance. Similarly, Lionel Robbins arranged for the translation of De Viti's 1929 edition of the *Principii*. But, by and large, English-speaking authors were concerned only with certain aspects of the Italian fiscal science. For example, Benham (1934b) was interested mainly in Luigi Einaudi's proposal for a tax based on "consumed" income (1929) and Hugh Dalton (1920) in Eugenio Rignano's proposal (1920) for an inheritance tax reform.
88. R. B. Ekelund and R. F. Hébert, *A History of Economic Theory and Method*, New York: McGraw-Hill (1983:517).
89. I am grateful to Professor Herbert Geyer of CUNY for raising this point.
90. Conclusions of this nature were not endemic to the Italians. Bowen's highly acclaimed suggestion of median-voter process (1943) is also based on this central concept.
91. Buchanan (1960: 43–5).
92. See, for example, Gunnar Myrdal's 1930 work, *Vetenskap och politik i nationalekonomien* translated in English as *The Political Element in the Development of Economic Theory* (1953) and Leif Johansen's "Some Notes on the Lindahl Theory of Determination of Public Expenditures," *International Economic Review*, September (1963: 346–58) and *Public Economics*, Amsterdam: North-Holland (1968).
93. See References.

5 German Fiscal Doctrine: The Organic View

1. D. A. Lindenfeld, *The Practical Imagination: The German Sciences of State in the Nineteenth Century*, Chicago: University of Chicago Press (1997: 15).
2. D. A. Lindenfeld (1997: 27–8).
3. Expounded in Montesquieu's *L'esprit des lois* (1748) as well as earlier in *Considérations sur le causes de la grandeur des Romains et le leur décadence* (1734).

4. Discussed in Voltaire's *Dictionnaire philosophique* (1764).
5. Elaborated in Rousseau's *Du contrat social* (1762).
6. C. L. Montesquieu, *The Spirit of Laws* (1748), edited by D. W. Carrithers, Berkeley, California: University of California Press (1977: 243).
7. The allusion, of course, is to the general spirit of France.
8. C. L. Montesquieu (1977 [1748]: 289).
9. C. L. Montesquieu, *Considerations on the Causes of the Greatness of the Romans and their Decline* (1734), translated by D. Lowenthal, New York: Cornell University Press (1965: 210). Similarly, according to Montesquieu, the Sultan of the Ottomans may impose a new tax on his subjects singlehandedly; but a general outcry would immediately remind him of the limits he has transgressed (1965 [1734]: 210).
10. C. L. Montesquieu (1965 [1734]: 87–8).
11. *Poème sur le désastre de Lisbonne* (1755), translated and reprinted in *A Treatise on Toleration and Other Essays*, Amherst, New York: Prometheus Books (1994).
12. W. Ebenstein, "Rousseau," in W. Ebenstein (ed.), *Great Political Thinkers*, New York: Holt, Rinehart, and Winston (1961b: 431).
13. F-M. A. Voltaire, Philosophical Dictionary (1764), translated by T. Besterman, London: Penguin (1972: 288).
14. W. Ebenstein (1961b: 431–2).
15. F-M. A. Voltaire, *Letters on England* (1726–), translated by T. Tancock, London: Penguin Books (1980: 45).
16. J. J. Rousseau, *The Social Contract and Discourses* (1762), translated by G. D. H. Cole, New York: Dutton & Co., Inc. (1950: 13–14).
17. W. Ebenstein (1961b: 437).
18. N. Rotenstreich, "*Volksgeist*," in P. P. Wiener (ed.), *Dictionary of the History of Ideas*, New York: Charles Scribner's Sons, 4 (1973: 491).
19. Though the full treatment of this concept is in Hegel's 1820 work, *Philosophy of Rights* (*Naturrecht und Staatswissenschaft im Grundrisse*), he was explicating it in his lectures at Jena as early as in the winter of 1801–02. Some of these lectures were printed posthumously in *The Philosophy of History* (1991).
20. G. W. F. Hegel, *The Philosophy of History*, Amherst, New York: Prometheus Books (1991 [1801–02]: 38).
21. A. W. Wood, *Hegel's Ethical Thought*, Cambridge/New York: Cambridge University Press (1990: 221–2), referring to Hegel's *Die Vernunt in der Geschichle* (1955 edition: 67–8; 58).
22. N. Rotenstreich (1973: 493), referring to Savigny's *Vom Beruf unserer Zeit für Gesetzgebung und Rechtswissenschaft* (1814).
23. D. G. Rohr, *The Origins of Social Liberalism in Germany*, Chicago: The University of Chicago Press (1963: 49).
24. H. K. Betz, "How Does the German Historical School Fit?" *History of Political Economy*, 20, 3 (1988: 416).
25. K. Knies, *Die Politische Oekonomie vom geschichtlichen Standpunkte*, Braunschweig: Schwetschke (1883 [1853]).
26. H. K. Betz (1988: 414), referring to G. Schmoller (1904: 384).
27. D. A. Lindenfeld (1997: 238), referring G. Schmoller (1881: 2 (465–6)).
28. R. A. Musgrave, *Public Finance in a Democratic Society*, vol. 2, New York: New York University Press (1986: 243).

29. L. von Stein, *Lehrbuchder Finanzwissenschaft*, 4 volumes, Leipzig: Brockhaus (1885), a portion of which is in *Classics* (1958: 29).
30. H. Ritschl, *Gemeinwirtschaft und kapitalistische Marktwirtschaft*, Tübingen (1931), reprinted in *Classics* (1958: 234–5).
31. H. Ritschl (1958 [1931]: 235).
32. R. A. Musgrave (1986: 244).
33. R. Goldscheid, "Staat, offentlicher Haushalt und Gesellschaft, Wesen und Aufbagen der Finanzwissenschaften vom Standpunkte der Soziologie," in W. Gerloff and F. Meisel (eds), *Handbuch der Finazwissenschaft*, vol. I, Tübingen (1925), included *Classics* (1958: 206–7).
34. R. A. Musgrave (1986: 244–5).
35. R. A. Musgrave and A. T. Peacock, *Classics* (1958: xix).
36. The following section is culled from the portion of Wagner's *Finanzwissenschaft*, Leipzig: Carl Winter (1883) that is excerpted in *Classics* (1958: 2–5).
37. J. Buchanan, "The Pure Theory of Government Finance: A Suggested Approach," in *Fiscal Theory and Political Economy*, Chapel Hill, North Carolina: University of North Carolina Press (1960a: 10).
38. J. Buchanan (1960a: 10–11).

6 Austrian Fiscal Doctrine: The Subjective Valuation Approach

1. P. Silverman, "The Cameralist Roots of Menger's Achievement," in B. J. Caldwell (ed.), *Carl Menger and His Legacy in Economics*, Durham and London: Duke University Press (1990: 70–1).
2. David Lindenfeld (1997: 247) has discovered among Menger's private papers (Box 1, Notebook 9) the evidence that Menger registered this particular view of the public economy as early as 1867, when he wrote: "In each people we see numerous individual economics, which are tied to each other ... through commerce, but which no more lose their individuality than does the physical individual by being part of a people."
3. K. Milford, "Menger's Methodology," in B. J. Caldwell (ed.) (1990: 218).
4. E. W. Streissler, "Carl Menger on Economic Policy: The Lectures to Crown Prince Rudolf," in B. J. Caldwell (ed.) (1990: 107).
5. Author of the monumental *System der Statswissenschaften* (1852–56) and *Lehrbuch der Finazwissenschaft* (1878).
6. E. W. Streissler (1990: 108).
7. R. B. Ekelund and R. F. Hébert (1983: 294–5). Emphases in the original.
8. F. von Wieser, *Der Natürliche Wert*, Vienna: A. Hölder, reprinted as *Natural Value*, New York: Kelley and Millman (1956 [1889]: 219).
9. F. von Wieser (1956 [1889]: 228–9 and 232).
10. F. von Wieser (1956 [1889]: 236).
11. F. von Wieser (1956 [1889]: 239).
12. F. von Wieser (1956 [1889]: 240–41).
13. F. von Wieser (1956 [1889]: 241).
14. F. von Wieser (1956 [1889]: 241).

15. F. von Wieser (1956 [1889]: 241).
16. K. Milford (1990: 236).
17. R. B. Ekelund and R. F. Hébert (1983: 295).
18. R. B. Ekelund and R. F. Hébert (1983: 296).
19. F. von Wieser, *Grundriß der Sozialökonomik*, from his *Theorie der Staatswitschaft*, Tübingen (1924), reprinted in *Classics* (1958: 201).
20. F. von Wieser (1958 [1924]: 193).
21. F. von Wieser (1958 [1924]: 193).
22. F. von Wieser (1958 [1924]: 198).
23. Thus, there is a striking parallel between Sax's construct of social egoism and Pantaleoni's model of tribal egoism presented in Chapter 4.
24. E. Sax, "Die Wertungstheorie der Steuer [1924]," a restatement of Sax's earlier work, *Grundlegung der theoretischen Staatswirtschaft*, Vienna: A. Hölder (1883), is reprinted in *Classics* (1958: 178–9).
25. E. Sax (1958 [1924]: 180).
26. E. Sax (1958 [1924]: 181). Thus, at this point Sax comes close to Wieser's conception of communal economy as a club or association.
27. E. Sax (1958 [1924]: 181).
28. Sax's reliance on the old Physiocratic dichotomy between material and immaterial goods (services) was criticized by U. Mazzola (1890) for constituting an irrelevant diversion.
29. Actually, the State is not a necessary fixture in Sax's vision of the public economy; however, Sax sees the State as a productive entity in the provision of a continuous flow of public services.
30. E. Sax (1958 [1924]: 186–7).
31. R. A. Musgrave and A. T. Peacock, *Classics* (1958: 189).
32. E. Sax (1958 [1924]: 188–9).

7 Swedish Fiscal Doctrine: The Collective Choice Approach

1. E. Sax, *Grundlegung der theoretischen Staatswirtschaft*, Vienna: A. Hölder (1883: 307–8).
2. F. von Wieser, *Der Natürliche Wert*, Vienna: A. Hölder (1889) reprinted as *Natural Value*, New York: Kelley and Millman (1958: 236). Emphasis in the original.
3. F. von Wieser (1956 [1889]: 237–8).
4. K. Wicksell, "Ein neues Prinzip des gerechten Besteurung," in *Finanztheoretische Untersuchungen*, Jena: Gustav Fisher (1896), reprinted in *Classics* ... (1958: 74–5).
5. T. Gårdlund, "The Life of Knut Wicksell and Some Characteristics of His Work," in S. Strøm, and B. Thalberg, *The Theoretical Contributions of Knit Wicksell*, London: The Macmillan Press, Ltd. (1979: 3).
6. K. Wicksell (1958 [1896]: 78–9).
7. K. Wicksell (1958 [1896]: 79).
8. K. Wicksell (1958 [1896]: 81).
9. K. Wicksell (1958 [1896]: 76).
10. K. Wicksell (1958 [1896]: 88).

11. K. Wicksell (1958 [1896]: 90).
12. K. Wicksell (1958 [1896]: 94).
13. K. Wicksell, *Lectures on Political Economy*, vol. 1, London: Routledge and Kegan Paul, Ltd. (1951 [1934]: 9).
14. K. Wicksell (1951 [1934]: 10).
15. K. Wicksell (1958 [1896]: 97).
16. K. Wicksell (1958 [1896]: 97–9).
17. K. Wicksell (1958 [1896]: 105).
18. K. Wicksell (1958 [1896]: 116).
19. K. Wicksell (1958 [1896]: 116).
20. B. P. Herber, *Modern Public Finance: The Study of Public Sector Economics*, Homewood, Illinois: Richard D. Irwin (1975: 86).
21. B. P. Herber (1975: 86).
22. B. P. Herber (1975: 87).
23. R. A. Musgrave, *Public Finance in a Democratic Society*, New York: New York University Press, vol. 1 (1986: 94–5).
24. J. Buchanan, "Public Finance and Public Choice," *National Tax Journal*, XXVIII, 8 (1975: 385).
25. R. B. Ekelund and R. F. Hébert, *A History of Economic Theory and Method*, New York: McGraw-Hill (1983: 523–4).
26. E. Lindahl (ed.), *Knut Wicksell: Selected Papers on Economic Theory*, Cambridge, MA: Harvard University Press (1958: 18).
27. K. Wicksell (1958 [1896]: 81).
28. E. Lindahl, "Just Taxation – A Positive Solution," *Classics* (1958 [1919]: 168).
29. E. Lindahl (1958 [1919]: 169).
30. Altered here somewhat to present it in a more familiar manner, with the quantities of units of collective good shown on the x axis, following Musgrave and Musgrave (1958: 53n).
31. E. Lindahl (1958 [1919]: 169–70).
32. E. Lindahl (1958 [1919]: 171).
33. The diagram and the explanation are taken from R. G. Holcombe, *Public Sector Economics*, Belmont, California: Wadsworth Publishing Company (1988: 61). Used with the permission of the author.
34. R. G. Holcombe (1988: 61).
35. E. Lindahl (1958 [1919]: 175).
36. E. Lindahl (1958 [1919]: 175).
37. E. Lindahl (1958 [1919]: 175–6).
38. E. Lindahl, "Einige strittige Fragen der Steuertheorie," in H. Mayer (ed.), *Die Wirtschaftstheorie der Gegenwart*, vol. IV, Vienna (1928), reprinted in *Classics* (1958: 231n).
39. E. Lindahl (1958 [1928]: 215).
40. E. Lindahl (1958 [1928]: 215), referring to E. Sax's "Die Wertungstheorie der Steuer," *Zeitschrift für Volkswirtschaft und Sozialpolitik*, Vienna (1924: 230).
41. E. Lindahl (1958 [1928]: 216).
42. E. Lindahl (1958 [1928]: 216). This observation should not be confounded with that of Sax, who envisioned the public economy as a decisional environment in which every taxpayer could discern the *cardinal* measure of utility each item of collective activity would have for him. Lindahl indicates his awareness of this distinction (1958 [1928]: 216n).

43. E. Lindahl (1958 [1928]: 217).
44. E. Lindahl (1958 [1928]: 219–20).
45. E. Lindahl (1958 [1928]: 228).
46. E. Lindahl (1958 [1928]: 231).
47. E. Lindahl (1958 [1928]: 231).

8 Epilogue

1. So described by its proponent, Herbert Simon, in *Administrative Behavior: A Study of Decision Making Process in Administrative Organization*, New York: Macmillan (1947).
2. Refer to notes 22 and 28 in Chapter 1 for the representative authors in this field and their works.
3. R. B. Ekelund and R. F. Hébert, *A History of Economic Theory and Method*, New York: McGraw-Hill (1983: 525).
4. D. Da Empoli, "A proposito del *Carattere teorico dell'economia finanziaria*," in A. Pedone (ed.), *Antonio De Viti de Marco: Tra liberismo economico e democrazia liberale*, Bari: Laterza (1995: 53).
5. G. Katona, *Psychological Economics*, Amsterdam: Elsevier (1975).
6. Refer to N. L. Enrick, "A Pilot Study of Income Tax Consciousness," *National Tax Journal*, 16 (1963: 169–73); G. Schmölders, "Survey Research in Public Finance: A Behavioural Approach to Fiscal Policy," *Public Finance*, 2 (1970: 300–6); G. Katona, *Psychological Analysis of Economic Behavior*, Westport: Greenwood Press (1977); A. Lewis, "An Empirical Assessment of Tax Mentality," *Public Finance*, 2 (1979: 245–57) and *The Psychology of Taxation*, Oxford: Martin Robertson (1982); in addition to others mentioned earlier, and many more).
7. Lewis (1982: 222 and 225).
8. As expounded by J. Hirshleifer, "The Expanding Domain of Economics," *American Economic Review*, 6 (1985: 53–68); G. Radnitzky and P. Berholz (eds.), *Economic Imperialism: The Economic Approach Applied Outside the Traditional Areas of Economics*, New York: Paragon (1985); and Tullock and McKenzie (1985).

A Synopsis of General Characteristics of National Fiscal Doctrines

1. M. Pantaleoni, "Contributo alla teoria del riparto delle spese pubbliche," *Rassegna italiana*, October 15 (1938 [1883]: 11).
2. A. De Viti De Marco, *First Principles of Public Finance*, London: Jonathan Cape (1936: 118).
3. U. Mazzola, *I dati scientifici della finanza pubblica*, Rome: Ermanno Loescher (1890: 178).
4. J. Buchanan, "*La Scienza delle finanze*: The Italian Tradition in Fiscal Theory," in *Fiscal Theory and Political Economy*, Chapel Hill, North Carolina: University of North Carolina Press (1960: 38).
5. J. Buchanan, "The Pure Theory of Government Finance: A Suggested Approach," in *Fiscal Theory and Political Economy*, Chapel Hill, North Carolina: University of Carolina Press (1960b: 10–11).

6. J. Buchanan (1960b: 10–11).
7. Sax's and Wieser's unfortunate reliance on this outdated dichotomy was effectively criticized by Mazzola (1890).
8. Refer to E. Böhm-Bawerk (1891), *Positive Theory of Capital*, translated by W. Smart, London: Macmillan.
9. Unnecessary, because the theory would hold even if this dichotomy is thrown out.
10. Sax's and Wieser's confusion on this point seems to have stemmed from their identifying the concept of group with that of total and the concept of share with that of marginal (R. A, Musgrave and A. T. Peacock, *Classics* [1958: 189n]).
11. R. A. Musgrave and A. T. Peacock, *Classics* (1958: xv).
12. R. A. Musgrave, *The Theory of Public Finance: A Study in Public Economy*, New York: McGraw-Hill (1959) and J. J. Head, *Public Goods and Public Welfare*, Duke University Press (1974).
13. R. A. Musgrave and A. T. Peacock, *Classics* (1958: xvi).

References

Arrow, K. J. (1963[1951]), *Social Choice and Individual Values*, New York: Wiley and Sons.

Arrow, K. J. (1973), "Formal Theories of Social Welfare." In P. P. Wiener (ed.), *Dictionary of the History of Ideas*, vol. 4, New York: Charles Scribner's Sons, pp. 276–84.

Barone, E. (1908), "Il ministro della produzione nello stato collettivista," *Giornale degli Economisti*, 37, pp. 267–93. Reprinted as "The Ministry of Production in the Collectivist State." In F. A. Hayek (ed.), *Collectivist Economic Planning*, London: Routledge (1935), pp. 245–90.

Barone, E. (1912), "Studi di economia finanziaria," *Giornale degli economisti*, in three parts. First part: vol 44 (April/May): 309–53; second part (June): 469–505; third part, vol. 45 (July/December), pp. 1–75.

Beccaria, C. (1763), *Dei delitti e delle pene*, Firenze.

Beccaria, C. (1771), *Elementi di economia pubblica*, Milano.

Beicheit, B. *et al.* (1969), *Steuernorm und Steuerwirklichkeit*, Köln und Opladen: Westdeutscher Verlag.

Bell D. and Kristol, I. (eds) (1981), *The Crisis in Economic Theory*, New York: Basic Books.

Bellanca, N. (1993a), "Intorno all teoria italiana della finanza pubblica: 1883–1946," *Rivista di diritto finanziario e scienza delle finanze*, 52, pp. 21–39.

Bellanca, N. (1993b), *La teoria della finanza pubblica in Italia 1883–1946*, Florence: Leo Olschki.

Benham, F. (1934a), "Book review: De Viti de Marco's *Principii di Economia Finanziaria*," *Economica*, 3, pp. 365–7.

Benham, F. (1934b), "Notes on the Pure Theory of Public Finance (Suggested by the 'Ottima Imposta' of Professor Einaudi)," *Economica*, 4, pp. 436–58.

Bentham, J. (1776), *A Fragment of Government*, F. C. Montague (ed.), London: Geoffrey Cumberledge-Oxford University Press (1951).

Bentham, J. (1789), *A Fragment on Government and An Introduction to the Principles of Morals and Legislation*, W. Harrison (ed.), Oxford: Basil Blackwell (1948).

Bergson, A. (1938), "A Reformulation of Certain Aspects of Welfare Economics," *Quarterly Journal of Economics*, LII, 2, pp. 310–34.

Betz, H. K. (1988), "How Does the German Historical School Fit?" *History of Political Economy*, XX, 3, pp. 408–30.

Bianchini, M. (1989), "Some Fundamental Aspects of Italian Eighteenth-Century Economic Thought." In Donald Walker (ed.), *Perspectives on the History of Economic Thought*, vol. 1, London: Edward Elgar, pp. 53–67.

Böhm-Bawerk, E. (1891), *Positive Theory of Capital*, translated by W. Smart, London: Macmillan.

Borgatta, G. (1920), "Lo studio scientifico dei fenomeni finanziari," *Giornale degli economisti*, 1, pp. 1–24.

Borgatta, G. (1935), *Appunti di scienza delle finanze e diritto finanziario: Raccolti alle lezioni del Prf. Gino Borgatta nell'anno academico 1932–33*. Milano: A. Giuffre.

Bowen, H. R. (1943), "The Interpretation of Voting in the Allocation of Resources," *Quarterly Journal of Economics*, 55, pp. 496–505.

Briganti, F. (1780), *L'esame economico del sistema civile*. Reprinted in *Economici classici italiani*, Milano: Destefani, 1804.

Buchanan, J. (1960a), "*La Scienza delle finanze*: The Italian Tradition in Fiscal Theory." In *Fiscal Theory and Political Economy*, Chapel Hill, North Carolina: University of North Carolina Press, pp. 22–74.

Buchanan, J. (1960b), "The Pure Theory of Government Finance: A Suggested Approach." In *Fiscal Theory and Political Economy*, Chapel Hill, North Carolina: University of North Carolina Press, pp. 8–23.

Buchanan, J. (1967), *Public Finance in Democratic Process*, Chapel Hill, North Carolina: University of North Carolina Press.

Buchanan, J. (1968), *The Demand and Supply of Public Goods*, Chicago: Rand McNally.

Buchanan, J. (1975), "Public Finance and Public Choice," *National Tax Journal* XXVIII, 8, pp. 383–94.

Burke, E. (1790), "Reflections on the Revolution in France." In W. Ebenstein (ed.), *Great Political Thinkers*, New York: Holt, Rinehart, and Winston (1961), pp. 474–95.

Cardini, A.(1985), *La democrazia incompiuta 1858–1943*, Rome-Bari: Laterza.

Cardini, A. (1994), "Antonio De Viti De Marco, economista e politico," *Rivista di diritto finanziario e scienza delle finanze*, 2, pp. 198–205.

Coats, A. W. (1976), "Economics and Psychology: The Death and Resurrection of a Research Programme." In S. Latsis (ed.), *Method and Appraisal in Economics*, Cambridge: Cambridge University Press, pp. 43–64.

Cohen Stuart, A. J. (1889), *Bijdrage tot de theorie der progressive inkomstenbelasting*, The Hague. Two sections of the original work, pp. 91–115 and 124–33, are excerpted in R. A. Musgrave and A. T. Peacock (eds), *Classics…* (1958), pp. 48–71.

Collard, D. (1978), *Altruism and Economy*, New York: Oxford Press.

Conigliani, C. (1894), "L'indirizzo teorico nella scienza finanziaria," *Giornale degli economisti*, 2, pp. 105–29.

Conigliani, C. (1903), *Saggi di economia politica e di scienze delle finanze*, Torino: Fratelli Bocca.

Cooter, R. and Rappoport, P. (1984), "Were the Ordinalists Wrong about Welfare Economics?" *Journal of Economic Literature*, XXII (June), pp. 507–30.

Cosciani, C. (1953), *Principii di scienza delle finanze*, Torino: Tipografico Editrice Torinese.

Cosciani, C. (1961), *Istituzioni di scienza delle finanze*, Torino: Unione Tipografico Editrice Torinese.

Curtin, R. and Cowan, C. D. (1975), "Public Attitudes toward Fiscal Programs." Ch. 3 in B. Strumpel, C. D. Cowan, F. T. Juster and J. Schmideskamp (eds), *Survey of Consumers 1972–73*, Ann Arbor: University of Michigan.

Cusumano, V. (1875), *Le scuole economiche della Germania in rapporto alla quistione sociale*, Napoli: G. Marghieri (1929).

Da Empoli, D. (1995), "A proposito del *Carattere teorico dell'economia finanziaria*." In A. Pedone (ed.), *Antonio De Viti de Marco: Tra liberismo economico e democrazia liberale*, Bari: Laterza, pp. 51–4.

Dalton, H. (1920), *Some Aspects of the Inequality of Incomes in Modern Communities*, London: G. Routledge & Sons.

Dalton, H. (1922), *Principles of Public Finance,* New York: Augustus M. Kelley Publishers (1967).

De Viti de Marco, A. (1879), "Qualche considerazione sulle vicende della diplomazia," *La rivista europea internazionale,* 10, pp. 268–81.

De Viti de Marco, A. (1888), *Il carattere teorico dell'economia finanziaria,* Roma: Pasqualicci.

De Viti de Marco, A. (1885), *Moneta e prezzi, ossia il principio quantitativo in rapporto alla questione monetaria,* Città di Castello: Lapi.

De Viti de Marco, A. (1898), "Contributo alla teoria del prestito pubblico," *Giornale degli economisti,* XI, pp. 61–123.

De Viti de Marco, A. (1928), *I primi principii dell'economia finanziaria,* Roma: Sampaolesi.

De Viti de Marco, A. (1930), *Un trentennio di lotte politiche (1894–1922),* Rome: Collezione Meridionale Editrice.

De Viti de Marco, A. (1934a), *Principi di economia finanziaria,* Turin: Einaudi.

De Viti de Marco, A. (1934b), *La funzione della banca: Introduzione allo studio dei problemi monetari e bancari contemporanei,* Torino: Einaudi. [First draft published in 1898 in *Rendiconti della R. Accademia dei Lincei,* VIII, pp. 7–38, reprinted by UTET, Turin (1990) with an "Introduction" by G. Parravicini.]

De Viti de Marco, A. (1936), *First Principles of Public Finance,* translated by E. P. Marget, London: Jonathan Cape. [An American edition also appeared in the same year by Harcourt-Brace & Co., Inc. (New York).]

De Viti de Marco, A .(1939), *Principî di economia finanziaria,* Turin: Einaudi.

Downs, A. (1957), "An Economic Theory of Political Action in a Democracy," *Journal of Political Economy,* LXV, 2 (April), pp. 135–50.

Ebenstein, W. (ed.) (1961a), *Great Political Thinkers,* New York: Holt, Rinehart and Winston.

Ebenstein, W. (1961b), "Rousseau." In W. Ebenstein (ed.), *Great Political Thinkers,* New York: Holt, Rinehart, and Winston (1961), pp. 431–41.

Ebenstein, W. (1961c), "The Welfare State." In W. Ebenstein (ed.), *Great Political Thinkers,* New York: Holt, Rinehart, and Winston (1961), pp. 808–19.

Edgeworth, F. Y. (1881), *Mathematical Psychics: An Essay of the Application of Mathematics to the Moral Sciences,* London: C. Kegan Paul & Co. (1932).

Edgeworth, F. Y. (1897), "The Pure Theory of Taxation," *Economic Journal,* VIII. Reprinted in *Papers Relating to Political Economy,* London: Royal Economic Society (1925), a portion of which is in R. A. Musgrave and A. T. Peacock (eds), *Classics* (1958), pp. 119–36.

Einaudi, L. (1912), "Intorno al concetto di reddito imponibile e di un sistema di imposte sul reddito consumato." In Einauidi's *Saggi sul risparmio e l'imposta,* Torino: Einaudi, pp. 1–159.

Einaudi, L. (1936), "Introduction." In De Viti de Marco A. (1936), *First Principles of Public Finance,* translated by E. P. Marget, London: Jonathan Cape.

Einaudi, L. (1948), *Principii di scienza delle finanze,* Torino: La Riforma Sociale.

Ekelund, Jr., R. B. and Hébert, R. F. (1983), *A History of Economic Theory and Method,* New York: McGraw-Hill.

Elster, J. (1977), "Ulysses and the Sirens: A Theory of Imperfect Rationality," *Social Science Information,* 5, pp. 496–526.

Enciclopedia italiana di scienze, lettere ed arti (1929–36), Rome: Istituto Treccani.

Enrick, N. L. (1963), "A Pilot Study of Income Tax Consciousness," *National Tax Journal*, 16, pp. 169–73.
Enrick, N. L. (1964), "A Further Study of Income Tax Consciousness," *National Tax Journal*, 17, pp. 319–21.
Fasiani, M. (1951–52), *Principii delle scienze delle finanze*, 2 vols, Torino: Giappichelli Editrice.
Fausto, D. (1995), "I *Principii di economia finanziaria*." In A. Pedone (ed.), *Antonio De Viti de Marco: Tra liberismo economico e democrazia liberale*, Bari: Laterza, pp. 80–102.
Ferrara, F. (1849/1850), *Trattato speciale delle imposte*. In Ferrara's *Lezioni di economia politica*, Bologna: Zanichelli (1934/1935).
Ferrara, F. (1934), *Lezioni di economia politica*, Bologna: Nicola Zanichelli. Lectures delivered by Ferrara between 1856 and 1873, pp. 551–765 of which is devoted to his lectures in public finance.
Friedman, M. (1953), *Essays in Positive Economics*, Chicago: The University of Chicago Press.
Gårdlund, T. (1979), "The Life of Knut Wicksell and Some Characteristics of His Work." In S. Strøm and B. Thalberg (eds), *The Theoretical Contributions of Knut Wicksell*, London: The Macmillan Press, Ltd., pp. 1–6.
Genovesi, A. (1769), *Lezioni di economia civile*. Reprinted in 1803, Milano.
Georgescu-Roegen, N. (1973), "Utility and Value in Economic Thought." In P. P Wiener (ed.), *Dictionary of the History of Ideas*, vol. 4, New York: Charles Scribner's Sons, pp. 450–8.
Goldscheid R. (1917), *Staatssozialismus oder Staatskapitalismus*, Vienna: Anzengruber-Verl.
Goldscheid R. (1925), "Staat, offentlicher Haushalt und Gesellschaft, Wesen und Aufbagen der Finanzwissenschaften vom Standpunkte der Soziologie." In W. Gerloff and F. Meisel, (eds), *Handbuch der Finazwissenschaft*, vol. 1, Tübingen, pp. 146–85, included in R. A. Musgrave and A. T. Peacock (eds), *Classics* (1958), pp. 202–13.
Graubard, S. R. (1973), "Democracy." In P. P. Wiener (ed.), *Dictionary of the History of Ideas*, vol. 1, New York: Charles Scribner's Sons, pp. 652–67.
Graziani, A. (1897), *Istituti di scienza delle finanze*, Florence: Fratelli Bocca.
Griziotti, B. (1917), "La diversa pressione tributaria del prestito e dell'imposta," *Giornale degli economisti*, pp. 129–64, 313–34. Translated into English and reprinted in L. Pasinetti (ed.), *Italian Economic Papers*, vol. 1, Bologna: Il Mulino-Oxford University Press (1992), pp. 81–97.
Griziotti, B. (1929), *Principii di politica, diritto, e scienza delle finanze*, Padova: Cedam.
Hahn, F. and Hollis, M. (1979), "Introduction." In F. Hahn and M. Hollis, *Philosophy and Economic Theory*, Oxford University Press, pp. 1–17.
Hardin, R. (1971), "Collective Action as an Agreeable n-Prisoner's Dilemma," *Behavioral Science*, 16, pp. 472–81.
Harsanyi, J. C. (1955), "Cardinal Welfare, Individualistic Ethics, and Interpersonal Comparisons of Utility," *Journal of Political Economy*, 63, pp. 309–21.
Head, J. J. (1974), *Public Goods and Public Welfare*, Durham, NC: Duke University Press.
Hegel, G. W. F. (1991), *The Philosophy of History*, Amherst, New York: Prometheus Books.
Herber, B. P. (1975), *Modern Public Finance: The Study of Public Sector Economics*, Homewood, Illinois: Richard D. Irwin.

Hicks, J. R. (1939), "The Foundations of Welfare Economics," *Economic Journal*, XLIX, 96, pp. 696–712.
Hirshleifer, J. (1985), "The Expanding Domain of Economics," *American Economic Review*, 6, pp. 53–68.
Hochman, H. M. and Rodgers, J. D. (1969), "Pareto Optimal Approach to Income Redistribution," *American Economic Review*, 55, pp. 542–57.
Holcombe, R. G. (1988), *Public Sector Economics*, Belmont, California: Wadsworth Publishing Company.
Hollis, M. (1977), *Models of Man*, Cambridge: Cambridge University Press.
Hyman, D.N. (1996), *Public Finance: A Contemporary Application of Theory to Policy*, New York: Dryden Press.
Jevons, W. S. (1879), *The Theory of Political Economy*, London: Macmillan and Co. Reprinted in New York by Kelley and Millman (1957). First edition, London: Macmillan, 1871.
Johansen, L. (1963), "Some Notes on the Lindahl Theory of Determination of Public Expenditures," *International Economic Review* (September), pp. 346–58.
Johansen, L. (1968), *Public Economics*, Amsterdam: North-Holland Publishing Company.
Kahneman, D. and Tversky, A. (1979), "Prospect Theory: An Analysis of Decision under Risk," *Econometrica*, 27, pp. 263–91.
Kaldor, N. (1939), "Welfare Propositions of Economics and Interpersonal Comparisons of Utility," *Economic Journal*, XLIX, 95, pp. 549–52.
Katona, G. (1953), "Rational Behavior and Economic Behavior," *Psychological Review*, LX, 5, pp. 307–18.
Katona, G. (1975), *Psychological Economics*, Amsterdam: Elsevier.
Katona, G. (1977), *Psychological Analysis of Economic Behavior*, Westport: Greenwood Press.
Kayaalp, O. (1985), "Public-Choice Elements of the Italian Theory of Public Goods," *Public Finance*, 3, pp. 395–410.
Kayaalp, O. (1988), "Ugo Mazzola and the Italian Theory of Public Goods." *History of Political Economy*, 20, 1, pp. 15–25. Abstract of the article appeared in *Journal of Economic Literature*, 26, 4 (December) (1988), p. 2075. Reprinted in Mark Blaug (ed.), *Pioneers in Economics – Section IV*, London: Elgar Publishing Ltd (1992), pp. 183–93.
Kayaalp, O. (1989), "Early Italian Contributions to the Theory of Public Finance: Pantaleoni, De Viti, and Mazzola." In Donald A. Walker (ed.), *Perspectives on the History of Economic Thought: Classical and Neoclassical Economic Thought*, History of Economics Society. vol. 1, pp. 155–66.
Kayaalp, O. (1998), "Antonio De Viti de Marco." In Ferdinando Meacci (ed.), *Italian Economists of the 20th Century*. London: Elgar Publishing Ltd, pp. 95–113.
Kirzner, I. M. (1981), "The 'Austrian' Perspective on the Crisis." In D. Bell and I. Kristol (eds), *The Crisis in Economic Theory*, New York: Basis Books, pp. 111–22.
Knies, K. (1883), *Die politische Oekonomie vom geschichtlichen Standpunkte*, Aufl.-Braunschweig, Schwetschke, which is the revised edition of Knies's original work *Politische Oekonomie vom Standpunkte der geschichtlichen Methode*, Leipzig (1853).

Lange, O. and Taylor, F. M. (1938), *On the Economic Theory of Socialism*, Minneapolis: University of Minnesota Press.

Leroy-Beaulieu, P. (1906), *Traite de la sciences des finances*, Paris. The first chapter is included in R. A. Musgrave and AS. T. Peacock (eds), *Classics* (1958), pp. 152–64.

Levin, M. (1973), "Social Contract" In P. P. Wiener (ed.), *Dictionary of the History of Ideas*, vol. 4, New York: Charles Scribner's Son, pp. 251–63.

Lewis, A. (1979), "An Empirical Assessment of Tax Mentality," *Public Finance*, 2, pp. 245–57.

Lewis, A. (1982), *The Psychology of Taxation*, Oxford: Martin Robertson.

Lindahl, E. (1919), *Die Gerechtigkeit der Besteuerung*, Lund: Gleerupska. A portion is included in R. A. Musgrave and A. T. Peacock (eds), *Classics* (1958), pp. 168–76.

Lindahl, E. (1928), "Einige strittige Fragen der Steuertheorie." In H. Mayer, (ed.), *Die Wirtschaftstheorie der Gegenwart*, vol. 4, pp. 282–304, Vienna: Springer. Included in R. A. Musgrave and A. T. Peacock (eds), *Classics* (1958), pp. 214–32.

Lindahl. E. (ed.) (1958), *Knut Wicksell: Selected Papers on Economic Theory*, Cambridge, Massachusetts: Harvard University Press.

Lindenfeld, D. F. (1997), *The Practical Imagination: The German Sciences of State in the Nineteenth Century*, Chicago: University of Chicago Press.

Long, D. G. (1977), *Bentham on Liberty: Jeremy Bentham's Idea of Liberty in Relation to His Utilitarianism*, Toronto: University of Toronto Press.

Loria, A. (1886), *La teoria economica della costituzione politica*, Rome: Fratelli Bocca.

Loria, A. (1889), *La teoria economica della costituzione politica*, Torino: Bocca.

Loria, A. (1913), *Le basi economiche della costituzione sociale*, Torino: Bocca.

Machlup, F. (1978), *Methodology of Economics and Other Social Sciences*, New York: Academic Press.

Margolis, H. (1982), *Selfishness, Altruism, and Rationality: A Theory of Social Choice*, London: Cambridge University Press.

Marshall, A. (1890), *Principles of Economics*, London: Macmillan (1946).

Mazzola, U. (1888), *Il fondamento scientifico dell'economia dello Stato*, Naples: Stabilimento Tipografico dell'Unione.

Mazzola, U. (1890), *I dati scientifici della finanza pubblica*, Rome: Ermanno Loescher. Chapter 9 of this book, translated as "The Formation of the Prices of Public Goods," is in R. A. Musgrave and A. T. Peacock (eds), *Classics* (1958), pp. 37–47.

M'Culloch, J. R. (1825), *Literature of Political Economy*, London: Longmans.

Menger, C. (1871), *Grundsätze der Volkswirtschaftslehre*, Vienna: Wilhelm Braumuller.

Milford, K. (1990), "Menger's Methodology." In B. J. Caldwell (ed.), *Carl Menger and His Legacy in Economics*, Durham and London: Duke University Press, pp. 215–39.

Mill, J. S. (1834), "The Proposed Reform of the Poor Laws," *Monthly Repository*, 8.

Mises, von L. (1960), *Epistemological Problems of Economics*, Princeton, NJ: D. Van Nostrand.

Montemartini, G. (1900), "Le basi fondamentali di una scienza finanziaria pura," *Giornale degli economisti*, 2, pp. 556–76.

Montesquieu, C. L. (1734), *Considerations on the Causes of the Greatness of the Romans and their Decline*, translated by D. Lowenthal, New York: Cornell University Press (1965).

Montesquieu, C. L. (1748), *The Spirit of Laws*, edited by D. W. Carrithers, Berkeley, CA: University of California Press (1977).

Mosca, G. (1896), *Elementi di scienza politica*. Rome: Bocca.

Mueller, D. (1986), "Rational Egoism versus Adaptive Egoism as Fundamental Postulate for a Descriptive Theory of Human Behavior," *Public Choice*, 51, pp. 3–23.

Mueller, E. (1963), "Public Attitudes toward Fiscal Programs," *Quarterly Journal of Economics*, 77, 2, pp. 210–35.

Munro, D. H. (1973), "Utilitarianism." In P. P. Wiener (ed.), *Dictionary of the History of Ideas*, New York: Charles Scribner's Sons, vol. 4, pp. 444–9.

Muratori, L. A. (1749), *Della pubblica felicità*, Modena.

Musgrave, R. A. (1959), *The Theory of Public Finance: A Study in Public Economy*, New York: McGraw-Hill.

Musgrave, R. A. (1986), *Public Finance in a Democratic Society*, 2 vols, New York: New York University Press.

Musgrave, R. A. and Musgrave, P. B. (1984), *Public Finance in Theory and Practice*, New York: McGraw-Hill.

Musgrave, R. A. and Peacock A. T. (eds) (1958), *Classics in the Theory of Public Finance*, New York: MacMillan.

Myrdal, G. (1930), *The Political Element in the Development of Economic Theory*, London: Routledge and Paul (1953).

Nitti, F. S. (1905), *Principi di scienza delle finanze*, Napoli: Pierro.

Ortes, G. (1790a), *Calcolo sopra il valore delle opinioni e sopra i piaceri e dolori*, reprinted in *Scrittori classici italiani di economia politica*, Milano: Destefanis. (1804), 24, pp. 257–318.

Ortes, G. (1790b), *Riflessioni sulla popolazione*, Venice, reprinted in antiquarian book: *Scrittori classic italiani di economia politica*, Milano: Destefanis (1816), 49, pp. 169–254.

Pantaleoni, M. (1883), "Contributo alla teoria del riparto delle spese pubbliche," *Rassegna italiana*, October 15, pp. 25–60. Reprinted in *Studi di finanza e di statistica*, Bologna: Nicola Zannichelli (1938).

Pantaleoni, M. (1889), *Principii di economia pura*, Florence: Barbera, translated into English by T. B. Bruce as *Pure Economics*, New York: Kelly and Millman (1957) from 1931 edition.

Pantaleoni, M. (1925), *Erotemi di economia* (2 vols), Bari: Laterza e figli. Includes the three essays mentioned in the text:

"Cenni sul concetto di massimi edonistici individuali e collecttivi," vol. 2, pp. 1–44. Originally published in *Giornale degli economisti*, Series II, vol. 4, (1891).

"Una visione cinematografica del progresso della scienza economica (1890–1907)," vol. 1, pp. 189–222. Originally presented at conference of Associazione per il Progresso della Scienza, Parma (1907);

"L'Atto economico," vol. 1, pp. 67–156. Lecture notes collected by N. Trevisonno (1913).

Paoletti, F. (1772), *I veri mezzi di rendere felici le soccietà*, Firenze.

Pareto, V. (1896/1897), "The New Theories of Economics," *Journal of Political Economy*, V. Reprinted in E. Hamilton *et al.* (eds) *Landmarks in Political Economy*, Chicago: The University of Chicago Press (1962), pp. 45–60.

Pareto, V. (1916), *Trattato di Sociologia Generale*, 4 vols, Florence: Barbera. Translated into English as *Mind and Society*, New York: Harcourt Brace & Co. (1935).

Parsons, T. (1937), *The Structure of Social Action: A Study in Social Theory with Special Reference to a Group of Recent European Writers*, New York: McGraw-Hill.

Parsons, T. and Shils, E. A. (eds) (1951), *Toward a General Theory of Action*, Cambridge, MA: Harvard University Press.

Pigou, A. C. (1920), *Economics of Welfare*, London: Macmillan.

Pigou, A. C. (1928), *A Study in Public Finance*, London: Macmillan (1962).

Pigou, A. C. (1954), "Some Aspects of the Welfare State," *Diogenes*, No. 7 (Summer). Reprinted in W. Ebenstein (ed.), *Great Political Thinkers*, New York: Holt, Rinehart and Winston (1961), pp. 838–43.

Popper, K. (1957), *The Poverty of Historicism*, London: Routledge and Kegan Paul.

Posner, R. A. (1977), *The Economic Analysis of Law*, Boston: Little Brown.

Radnitzky, G. and Berholz, P. (eds) (1985), *Economic Imperialism: The Economic Approach Applied Outside the Traditional Areas of Economics*, New York: Paragon.

Ricca-Salerno, G. (1887), "Nuove dottrine sistematiche nella scienza delle finanze," *Giornale degli economisti*, 4, pp. 375–402.

Ricca-Salerno, G. (1888), *Scienza delle finanze*, Florence: Barbera Editore.

Ricca-Salerno (1896), *Storia delle dottrine finanziere in Italia: Col raffronto delle dottrine forestiere e delle istituzioni e condizioni di fatto*, Palermo: A. Reber.

Rignano, E. (1920), *Per una riforma socialista del diritto successorio*, Bologna. Available in English as *The Social Significance of the Inheritance Tax*, New York: Alfred A. Knopf, (1924).

Ritschl, H. (1931), *Gemeinwirtschaft und kapitalistische Marktwirtschaft*, Tübingen. A portion is R. A. Musgrave and A. T. Peacock (eds), *Classics* (1958), pp. 233–42.

Robbins, L. (1932), *Essay on the Nature and Significance of Economic Science*, London: Macmillan.

Robbins, L. (1938), "Interpersonal Comparisons of Utility," *Economic Journal*, XLVIII, 8, pp. 635–41.

Rohr, D. G. (1963), *The Origins of Social Liberalism in Germany*, Chicago: The University of Chicago Press.

Rolph, E. R. (1956), *The Theory of Fiscal Economics*, Berkeley, CA: University of California Press.

Rosen, H. S. (1988), *Public Finance*, Homewood, Illinois: Irwin.

Rotenstreich, N. (1973), "*Volksgeist*." In P. P. Wiener (ed.), vol. 4, *Dictionary of the History of Ideas*, New York: Charles Scribner's Sons, pp. 490–6.

Rousseau, J. J. (1762), *The Social Contract and Discourses*, translated by G. D. H. Cole, New York: Dutton & Co., Inc. (1950).

Samuelson, P. A. (1954), "The Pure Theory of Public Expenditures," *Review of Economics and Statistics*, 4, pp. 387–9.

Sax, E. (1883), *Grundlegung der theoretischen Staatswirtschaft*, Vienna: A. Hölder

Sax, E. (1924), "Die Wertungstheorie der Steuer," *Zeitschrift fur Volkwirtschaft und Sozialpolitik*, vol. 4, Vienna. Reprinted in R. A. Musgrave and A. T. Peacock *Classics*... (1958), pp. 177–89.

Schäffle, A. (1880), Die Gründsätze der Steuerpolitik und die Schwebenden finanzfragen Deutchland und Oesterreichs, Tübigen: H. Laupp.

Schäffle, A. (1895–97), *Die Steuern*, Leipzig: C. L. Hirschfeld.

Schelling, T. C. (1978), "Egonomics, or the Art of Self-management," *American Economic Review*, 2, pp. 290–4.

Schmoller, G. (1881), "Ueber Zweck und Ziele des Jahrbuchs," *Jahrbuch fürGesetzebung, Verwaltung, und Volkwirtschaft*, Leipzig-Munchen: Gesselschaften fur Wirtschafts und Socialwissenschaften.

Schmoller, G. (1900–04), *Grundriss der Allgemeinein Volkwirtschaftslehre* 2 vols, Leipzig: Duncker & Humblot.

Schmoller, G. (1904), "Wechselnde Theorien und feststehende Wahrheiten im Gebiete der Staats- und Sozialwissenschaften und die heutige deutsche Volkwirtschaftslehre." In Schmoller's *Ueber einige Grundfragen der Sozialpolitik und der Volkswirtschaftslehre*, 2nd edn. Leipzig: Duncker & Humblot.

Schmölders, G. (1955), *Finanzpolitik*, Berlin: Springer.

Schmölders, G. (1959), "Fiscal Psychology: A New Branch of Public Finance," *National Tax Journal*, 12, pp. 340–5.

Schmölders, G. (1970), "Survey Research in Public Finance: A Behavioural Approach to Fiscal Policy," *Public Finance*, 2, pp. 300–6.

Schmölders, G. (1977), "Attitudes to Taxation and their Effects on Work Effort," *Fiscal Policy and Labour Supply*, Conference Series, 4, London: Institute for Fiscal Studies.

Schotter, A. (1985), *Free Market Economics: A Critical Appraisal*, New York: St. Martin's Press.

Schumpeter, J. A. (1954), *History of Economic Analysis*, London: Allen and Unwin, pp. 176–77.

Sen, A. K. (1977), "Rational Fools: A Critique of the Behavioral Foundations of Economic Theory," *Philosophy and Public Affairs*, 6, pp. 317–44.

Sen, A. K. (1987), *On Ethics and Economics*, Oxford/New York: Blackwell.

Sidgwick, H. (1883), *The Principles of Political Economy*, London: Macmillan.

Simon, H. A. (1947), *Administrative Behavior: A Study of Decision Making Process in Administrative Organization*, New York: Macmillan.

Simon, H. A. and Stedry, A. C. (1968–70), "Psychology and Economics." In G. Lindzey and E. Aronson (eds), *Handbook of Social Psychology*, vol. 5, Reading, MA: Addison-Wesley.

Simons, H. C. (1937), "First Principles of Public Finance by Antonio De Viti De Marco (Harcourt-Brace & Co., Inc., New York, 1936) – Grundlehren der Finanzwirtschaft. A. De Viti De Marco (J. C. B. Mohr, Tübingen, 1932)," *Journal of Political Economy*, XLV, 5 (October), pp. 712–17.

Simons, H. C. (1938), *Personal Income*, Chicago: The University of Chicago Press, pp. vii and 17–19.

Smith, A. (1776), *The Wealth of Nations*, Chicago: The University of Chicago Press (1976).

Sowell, T. (1980), *Knowledge and Decisions*, New York: Basic Books.

Stein, von L. (1878), *Lehrbuchder Finanzwissenschaft*, 4 vols, Leipzig: Brockhaus. A portion from the 1885 edition is reprinted in R. A. Musgrave and A. T. Peacock (eds), *Classics* (1958), pp. 28–36.

Stigler, G. J. (1962), "The Development of Utility Theory." In E. J. Hamilton, A. Rees, and H. G. Johnson (eds), *Landmarks in Political Economy*, Chicago: The University of Chicago Press, pp. 380–452. Original article appeared in *Journal of Political Economy*, LVIII (1950), pp. 307–27, 373–96.

Streissler, E. W. (1990), "Carl Menger on Economic Policy: The Lectures to Crown Prince Rudolf." In B. J. Caldwell (ed.), *Carl Menger and His Legacy in Economics*, Durham and London: Duke University Press, pp. 107–30.

Strumpel, B. (1969), "The Contribution of Survey Research to Public Finance" In A. T. Peacock (ed.), *Quantitative Methods in Public Finance*, New York: Praeger.

Thaler, R. (1980), "Toward a Positive Theory of Consumer Choice," *Journal of Economic Behavior and Organization*, 1, pp. 39–60.

Thaler, R. and Schefrin, H. M. (1979), *An Economic Theory of Self-control*, Ithaca, NY: Cornell University Press.

Tullock, G. and McKenzie, R. B. (1985), *The New Worlds of Economics*, Homewood, IL: Irwin.

Tversky, A. and Kahneman, D. (1974), "Judgment under Uncertainty: Heuristics and Biases," *Science*, 185, pp. 1124–31.

Veblen, T. B. (1898), "Why Is Economics Not an Evolutionary Science?" *Quarterly Journal of Economics*, July, pp. 373–9.

Verri, P. (1771), *Meditazioni sull'economia politica*, Livorno: Stamperia dell'Enciclopedia.

Vogel, J. (1974), "Taxation and Public Opinion in Sweden: An Interpretation of Recent Survey Data," *National Tax Journal*, XXVIII, 4, pp. 499–513.

Voltaire, F.-M. A. (1726), *Letters on England*, translated by L. Tancock, London: Penguin Books (1980).

Voltaire, F.-M. A. (1755), *A Treatise on Toleration and Other Essays*, translated by J. McCabe, Amherst, New York: Prometheus Books, (1994).

Voltaire, F.-M. A. (1764), *Philosophical Dictionary*, translated by T. Besterman, London: Penguin Books (1972).

Wagner, A. (1876), *Allgemeine oder Theoretische Volkswirtschaftslehre*, Leipzig: Carl Winter.

Wagner, A. (1883), *Finanzwissenschaft*, Leipzig: Carl Winter. 3 vols. A portion reprinted in R. A. Musgrave and A. T. Peacock (eds), *Classics*… (1958), pp. 1–15.

Wagner, A. (1892), *Grundlegung der politischen ökonomie*, Leipzig: Carl Winter.

Walras, L. (1889), *Eléments d'économie politique pure*, Lausanne: F. Rouge [Lecture notes 1874–77].

Weinberger, O. (1940), "The Importance of Francesco Ferrara in the History of Economic Thought," *Journal of Political Economy*, 48, pp. 91–104.

Whittaker, E. (1960), *Schools and Streams of Economic Thought*, Chicago: Rand McNally.

Wicksell, K. (1896), *Finanztheoretische Untersuchungen*, Jena: Gustav Fisher. A portion is reprinted as "A New Principle of Just Taxation." In R. A. Musgrave and A. T. Peacock (eds), *Classics*… (1958), pp. 77–118.

Wicksell, K. (1951), *Lectures on Political Economy*, vol. 1, London: Routledge and Kegan Paul, Ltd. (1934).

Wicksell, K. (1958), *Selected Papers on Economic Theory*, Cambridge, MA: Harvard University Press. Edited with an Introduction by E. Lindahl.

Wicksell, K. (1997), *Selected Essays in Economics*, London: Allen & Unwin. Edited with an Introduction by E. Lindahl.

Wieser, von F. (1889), *Der Natürliche Wert*, Vienna: A. Hölder. Reprinted as *Natural Value*, New York: Kelley and Millman (1956).

Wieser, von F. (1924), *Theorie der Staatswirtschaft*, Tübingen. A portion is reprinted in R. A. Musgrave and A. T. Peacock (eds), *Classics* ... (1958), pp. 190–201.

Wood, A. W. (1990), *Hegel's Ethical Thought*, Cambridge/New York: Cambridge University Press.

Index of Authors

P

R

S

T

V

W